D1083228

THE MARKET SAVVY INVESTOR

Profit from the Techniques of the Top Traders

Howard Abell
Robert Koppel

TO OUR FAMILIES

Mara, Lily, and Niko
Roslyn and Alexander

This publication is designed to provide accurate and authoritative information in regard to the subject matter covered. It is sold with the understanding that the publisher is not engaged in rendering legal, accounting, or other professional service. If legal advice or other expert assistance is required, the services of a competent professional should be sought.

Associate Publisher: Cynthia A. Zigmund
Managing Editor: Jack Kiburz
Interior Design: Lucy Jenkins
Cover Design: Scott Rattray, Rattray Design
Typesetting: the dotted i
SuperCharts is a registered trademark of Omega Research, Inc.

© 1999 by Innergame Partners

Published by Dearborn, a Kaplan Professional Company

All rights reserved. The text of this publication, or any part thereof, may not be reproduced in any manner whatsoever without written permission from the publisher.

Printed in the United States of America

99 00 01 10 9 8 7 6 5 4 3 2 1

Library of Congress Cataloging-in-Publication Data

Abell, Howard.
The market savvy investor : profit from the techniques of the top traders / Howard Abell, Robert Koppel.
p. cm.
Includes bibliographical references and index.
ISBN 0-7931-2792-0
1. Futures—United States. 2. Speculation—United States. 3. Investment analysis. I. Koppel, Robert. II. Title.
HG6024.U6A624 1999
332.64′5—dc21 99-36071
CIP

Dearborn books are available at special quantity discounts to use as premiums and sales promotions, or for use in corporate training programs. For more information, please call the Special Sales Manager at 800-621-9621, ext. 4514, or write to Dearborn Financial Publishing, Inc., 155 North Wacker Drive, Chicago, IL 60606-1719.

332.645
A

CONTENTS

PREFACE

The Market Savvy Investor is designed to make you exactly that: a well-informed, clearly focused, highly researched market participant who can identify and benefit from gaining the "trader's edge." This book is written to serve as a practical investment guide with hands-on profitable techniques in major market sectors that are currently available and that provide high-yield opportunities into the 21st century.

The intended audience for this book is the many thousands of investors who have chosen to take their financial destinies into their own hands; that is, to chart the waters of their own fortunes, independent of the advice and explanations of brokers, advisers, and market analysts. They are seasoned independent and professional traders and investors as well as first-time market participants. What unites both groups is a willingness and commitment to learn as much as possible about market phenomena in order to gain control and independence in their investment decisions.

Unlike other books on investments, *The Market Savvy Investor* does not describe abstract investment theories or offer a list of specific investments. Rather, it includes battle-forged market insights and strategies of the best and brightest traders and shows investors how to make money by utilizing proven methods to identify opportunities in different asset classes, such as precious and industrial metals (gold, silver, copper, etc.), equities and traditional commodities (grains, livestock, "softs"), interest rates (bonds, T-notes, Eurodollars), and foreign currencies (Swiss franc, Japanese yen, European currency unit, British pound, Canadian and Australian dollars, and Mexican peso). It also provides an in-depth discussion of the recently popular market phenomenon of day trading (particularly Nasdaq Level II trading).

Based on an academic knowledge and practical application of portfolio theory, *The Market Savvy Investor* analyzes individual markets by class with charts and commentary as well as intermarket relationships in the context of diversified asset allocation. As mentioned above, specific consideration is devoted to sharpening the investor's understanding of individual market behavior through analysis and interviews with top traders in these markets—bonds, equities, foreign currencies, stock indexes, metals, energy, and agriculture. In particular, we will

- examine fundamental and technical analysis (including the electronic platform and proposed industry changes),
- establish how to develop a market strategy for profitable returns in different market conditions,
- demonstrate how to develop a diversified portfolio,
- distinguish high-risk from low-risk trading opportunities,
- explain asset allocation and profitable money management techniques, and
- analyze market sectors that present short- and long-term opportunities.

The key to success in markets is as true today as it was 50 years ago and, we assume, will be so 50 years into the future.

It involves old-fashioned, time-proven approaches of strict emotional and monetary discipline, effective strategy, thoughtful research, the ability to embrace calculated risk, and most of all patience. Many of the psychological skills of investment were once thought to be inborn; however, it is our belief they can be taught and, with practice, mastered. An old Chicago Mercantile Exchange poster read: "Was Toulouse Lautrec too short to trade commodities? No. Too temperamental." Lautrec was a highly emotional man given to impulsive changes of opinion. Such a personality is ill suited for trading. Leo Melamed also expressed a similar idea when we interviewed him for *The Innergame of Trading:*

> "There is much to being a successful trader and investor. There are many rules to be applied and many lessons to be learned. There must be a willingness and ability to learn, to comprehend fundamentals and statistics, to grasp technical application, to develop an inner trading sense, to accept defeat and live with victory, and much more. But most of all, there must be present a multitude of inborn characteristics relating to the trader's personality, psychology, emotional equilibrium, courage, and patience."

The Market Savvy Investor includes in-depth coverage of the psychological aspects of trading and investing in order to fully bolster the investor's complement of effective market behavior—from opportunity awareness and analysis through trial and evaluation right down to the point of position adoption and management. As one trader reminded us years ago in an interview about developing trading models: "The bottom line is still the bottom line!" We mention this to assure you that our particular focus is always a simple one: to identify strategies that work and are profitable to use.

In *Reminiscences of a Stock Operator* (Wiley, 1994), Edwin Lefevre spoke to this very point when talking about his own development as an investor: "It takes a man a long time to learn all the lessons of all his mistakes. They say there are two sides to everything. But there is only one side to the stock market; and it is not the bull side or the bear side, but the right side. It took longer to get that general principle fixed firmly in my mind than it did most of the more technical phases of the game of speculation."

In short, then, *The Market Savvy Investor* serves as your guide to investing in global markets using specific strategies and techniques of some of the world's best traders, with full cognizance of the extraordinary complexity of trading markets successfully. A glossary of terms and strategies also is provided to help avoid confusion and clarify investment "technologicalese."

Success in all your investments.

—Howard Abell and Bob Koppel

ACKNOWLEDGMENTS

It is with a deep sense of appreciation that we acknowledge the contributions of the financial analysts, traders, and fund managers who agreed to be interviewed for *The Market Savvy Investor.* Despite demanding schedules, each was generous with time and ideas, furnishing valuable insight into their trading tactics and strategies. In particular, we wish to acknowledge David Held, Joanne Pekin, Rick Santelli, David Silverman, Jeffrey Silverman, and Dick Stoken. The success of this book is a testament to the outstanding talents and fertile minds of its contributors. We are humbly grateful.

We also wish to thank our families, Mara, Lily, and Niko, and Roslyn and Alexander, for demonstrating understanding, patience, and good humor when we had to spend many hours away from those whom we love.

A special acknowledgment also is due Cindy Zigmund and the entire staff of Dearborn Trade for their strong support throughout this project.

Lastly, we would like to express our sincere gratitude to our many readers who have written and called, offering a wealth of ideas and suggestions. Their interest and enthusiasm make all our work worthwhile.

"The entire enterprise of trading is about communicating a particular idea or response to something investors have spied in the overwhelming flow of information that darts electronlike around the globe. It can best be understood as active communication, a 'conversation' between a buyer and a seller."

—Mara Koppel, *Women of the Pits*

PART ONE

KNOWING THE MARKETS

1

A journey of a thousand miles begins with the first step.

YOUR TRADING STRATEGY AND GAME PLAN

This ancient Chinese saying has great relevance today to a serious discussion of learning markets in order to become a successful investor. Along with this idea of modest beginnings is a lesser-known Chinese proverb that states: "Before climbing a perilous summit, one must study all possible routes of access and escape, and only then, *really* learn how to climb it from someone who has already made the journey." With this in mind, it is our goal to identify and examine how some of the world's top traders and investors came to know markets through effective strategy and planning. What specific elements of their strategies work—the ultimate test—and what distinguishes their approaches from those that are less successful?

As you think about your own previous or current experiences with markets, we would like you to consider several questions we believe will help increase your chances for successful market performance:

- How would you characterize your overall approach to markets?
- What are the unique strengths and weaknesses you bring to this arena?
- What are your motives or motivations for investing?
- What do you find most interesting (i.e., analysis, evaluation, long- or short-term investing) about participating in markets?
- How much effort, desire, and commitment are you willing to "invest"?
- Is your approach mechanical, technical, fundamental, or discretionary (intuitive)?
- What is your basic market philosophy?
- What specific beliefs or biases do you bring to investing?

Yes, it is important for you to answer each of these questions in a thoughtful and detailed way. Why? Because knowing the "right" answer—for you—will greatly increase the probability of a positive result.

Warren Buffett once said that he surely would have failed if he had tried to be a floor trader. He understood that in order to be effective he had to consider his unique strengths and weaknesses to function best in markets. As a long-term value buy-and-hold investor, he must have thorough conversance with a company's annual reports, management, quality of earnings, market dominance, and so on. It suits his market temperament and methods and, in so doing, reflects his personality.

Short-term traders, on the other hand, rely on strategies that exploit market psychology that influences sudden and dramatic shifts in price action. They can read the market based on their unique "feel" of market tone and personality. Often they have little or no concern for the underlying market fundamentals or technical analytical data. They have cultivated the ability and honed skills relying on specific information, conscious and subliminal, that is geared for just such an environment. Mr. Buffett would have difficulty succeeding in such an atmosphere.

So what's the point? It is really quite simple: As Albert Einstein remarked, "Everything should be made as simple as possible, but not simpler!" Your market approach must have a clear understanding and relationship to you; that is, to your unique personality, strengths, weaknesses, and overall market philosophy. We all have particular preconceptions and biases that intrude on an objective reading of a market opportunity. Just because you have read about a specific technique or strategy that someone has used successfully, don't assume you can merely copy it with the same result.

Many people have had the sad experience of buying systems that have an audited, positive track record, only to find they cannot benefit from it because they are psychologically unable to share the developer's tolerance for risk. Unfortunately, this is an old story. Also, one person's calculated investment (the short-term trader) compared to another's (Warren Buffett, for example, for whom anything less than ten years is short term) may be pure noise and unworthy of investment. William F. Sherrod made this point in a much more lighthearted way: "If you bet on a horse, that's gambling; if you bet you can pull three spades, that's entertainment. If you bet cotton will go up three cents, that's business. See the difference."

ELEMENTS OF A SUCCESSFUL INVESTMENT STRATEGY

So what then, in essence, are the essential elements of a successful investment strategy? The list and following discussion encompass what we believe to be the essential elements of a successful investment strategy, notwithstanding your specific investment time horizon or individual market preference.

THE ESSENTIAL ELEMENTS OF A SUCCESSFUL INVESTMENT STRATEGY

- Encourages personal responsibility for all market actions.
- Considers your motivation for trading.
- Allows you to be profitable.
- Establishes goals and formulates a definite plan of action.
- Controls your anxiety.
- Creates a specific point of focus.
- Is consistent and congruent with your personality.
- Allows you to have an investment edge.
- Is automatic, effortless, and decisive in its implementation.
- Manages risk and assumes losses.
- Allows for patience and investing in a resourceful state of mind.
- Is profit-oriented and practical instead of theoretical.
- Leaves no uncertainty.
- Allows you to produce consistent results.
- Identifies opportunities.

Encourages Personal Responsibility for All Market Actions

This is the starting point of all investment strategies: knowing without qualification that you and only you are responsible for your actions. We have a tendency to believe, supported by language, that we *make* profits and *take* losses, as if we catch them like a common cold. Successful investing requires the full integration of this idea into your investment psyche. You're the one! You get all the glory and the blame. It isn't your broker, your brother-in-law, the chairman of the board of the Fed, the fill, the computer, the unemployment report—it is *you!* It's a simple fact that must be understood in the adoption of any market strategy: *You* produce the results. The Nordstrom Corporation Policy Manual has just one sentence in it: "Use your own best judgment at all times."

Considers Your Motivation for Trading

Your trading strategy must reflect your motive for trading. If you like the excitement of being in the market, perhaps you should not invest in software that takes four trades a year! It is important that your market behavior be consistent with your motive and motivation for investing. Most investors do not fully acknowledge the importance of this point. But as we mentioned above, it is important to establish—before you invest. Do your investment style and motivation have more in common with Warren Buffett or Donald Sliter (a well-known Chicago S&P pit trader)? To the extent that you can answer this question decisively, your chances are better for a positive market performance.

Allows You to Be Profitable

To invest profitably you need to adopt well-calculated risk and, in so doing, not allow your decisions to be based on intruding anxieties or mitigating investment apprehensions. Once the investment is researched and well planned, your job is to let it mature like a fine wine!

Most investors don't trade to win, they trade not to lose. An effective strategy adopts a proactive market behavior that allows you (1) to get involved, (2) to buy aggressively in your areas based on sound analysis and a proven methodology, (3) to catch breakouts, and (4) to enter and exit at your signal. And yes, to win you have to risk loss. It is only by embracing the possibility of loss (risk) that you are assured a profitable outcome.

Establishes Goals and Formulates a Definite Plan of Action

Your strategy must have short- and long-range goals built into it. What are you trying to accomplish today? This week?

This month? This year? In addition, what specific investment plan can you adopt right now to achieve this goal in terms of outcome, performance, and motivation? There is a lot to think about! Success in investing is the dividend paid for hard work, research, and most of all patience.

Controls Your Anxiety

There are a variety of anxieties you have to deal with when you are investing in markets. A well-planned strategy minimizes anxiety by addressing the factors that inevitably produce these feelings (e.g., loss, risk control, market reentry).

Creates a Specific Point of Focus

The problem with most investment strategies is that in the final analysis there is no point of focus. You must know what you're looking for and what you're looking at. You must be able to distinguish the signal from the noise, winning from losing trades, high-probability from low-probability outcomes. Specifically, you need to know if your investment decision is based on fundamental or technical analysis or a combination of the two. In addition, what specific market indicators are leading you to place money at risk? When conditions change, so must you. In short, you must know how you will react!

Is Consistent and Congruent with Your Personality

How many times have traders who tell us their strategy (system) just doesn't feel right, look right, or sound right, consulted us! If your strategy is going to be successful, it literally *must feel good.* It must be consistent with your unique investment belief system, which includes your tolerance for risk and money management comfort levels.

SOURCES OF INVESTOR ANXIETY

What's It Called?	What You Feel	What to Do
Fear of failure	You feel intense pressure to perform and tie your self-worth to trading perfection. You are concerned about what others think.	Focus on applying your methodology. Mentally rehearse the mechanics, tactics, and strategy of your approach. Also, say to yourself that trading and investing are not about proving anything to anyone. The closer you can get to focusing on your methodology, the more you will feel in control of this anxiety.
Fear of success	You lose control; euphoric trading. You doubt yourself.	If your market approach has shown statistical reliability in its performance, rehearse feelings of confidence as you mentally run through the placement, following and closing out of the trade. Feel in a literal sense how you personally experience confidence in your investment decisions.
Loss of control	You feel the market is out to get you. (Be assured it's not!) You lose your sense of personal responsibility when involved in the market.	Teach yourself how to get into a physically and psychologically relaxed state when reaching a trading decision. Focus on your specific methodology and approach.

Allows You to Have an Investment Edge

Unfortunately, there is no "edge" sold at your local department store, ready-made, one size fits all. It is just one more paradox of investing that in order to trade successfully you need an edge, but someone else's edge will do you no good. The expression "One man's sugar is another man's salt" also applies to edge: You have to find your own, and this fact is essential to having a winning strategy! The good news is it can be done!

Is Automatic, Effortless, and Decisive in Its Implementation

He who hesitates is lost. Opportunity, as the saying goes, knocks but once. Occasionally, it may knock a second and third time, but the point is you must act decisively when you hear its sound. All too often, investors know they should react but wait for secondary sources to confirm what they already "know" is a potentially profitable situation.

Manages Risk and Assumes Losses

A good investment strategy has the inevitability of loss built into it. Risk management assumes that no single loss will ever get out of hand. As in baseball, hitting safely three out of ten times can pay off very handsomely. Your strategy must inform you with certainty when you're wrong. Using this idea in real market time helps flesh out the old Wall Street adage, "Let profits run and cut losses short!"

Allows for Patience and Investing in a Resourceful State of Mind

Once the trade is made, your strategy must allow you to remain calm, patient, and focused by presenting you with objective criteria. You must work out, in your own mind, the contingency plans for dealing with a variety of market scenarios. Anything less is gambling!

It was not surprising to us, as you will see in the interviews with market professionals in Part Three, how often patience was cited as the sine qua non of successful investment planning.

Is Profit-Oriented and Practical Instead of Theoretical

This point may seem obvious, although in reality it's not. There are many investors who develop strategies to be consistent with a particular ideological or technical bias rather than to make money. The name of the game is performance! Winston Churchill said, "It is a socialist idea that making profits is a vice; I consider the real vice is making losses." This is a point to be remembered in your investing as well!

Leaves No Uncertainty

Think in probabilities, invest in certainties. Your strategy must allow you to know! Once an opportunity is defined and positions in the marketplace adopted, you must have an operational definition of where you are wrong—so that you get out and reevaluate your approach and retool your market technique.

Allows You to Produce Consistent Results

Your strategy provides the organization necessary for you to be consistent. The rest is up to you! Your approach should be based on the expectation of a high-probability outcome based on statistical back testing, historical price action, or fundamental conditions that can reliably be seen to ensure a well-analyzed result. As we said above, when conditions change, so must you!

Identifies Opportunities

According to Anthony Robbins, "The difference between those who succeed and those who fail isn't what they have—it's what they choose to see and do with their resources and their experiences of life." This also applies to trading and investing. Your investment strategy should allow you to open your eyes and see market opportunities so you can act!

These essential elements of a successful investment plan can provide a significant advantage to the investor. By adopting an approach that addresses the individual's financial goals, risk tolerance, money management style, time frame, and point of focus, one is assured the probability of a successful result. Now let's turn to specific market strategies and techniques that work in the overall context of an investor's reaction to markets. The discussion that follows will put you on track to becoming a truly market savvy investor.

2

MARKET APPROACHES THAT WORK

Strategy: The process of determining your major investment goals and then adopting a course of action whereby you allocate the resources necessary to achieve those ends

Tactics: The process of translating broad strategic goals into specific objectives that are relevant to a single component of your trading plan

In order for an investment strategy to be successful, it must incorporate all the psychological, technical, and financial resources that are at your disposal. In metaphorical terms, your strategy is the bull's-eye; specific trading tactics are the arrows that allow you to hit the target of your overall trading goals. The difficulty with most successful trading strategies is that they don't adequately deal with the central issue of trading; namely, taking a loss.

In *The Psychology of Technical Analysis* (McGraw-Hill, 1994), Tony Plummer states this issue very succinctly: "The question for the trader is whether it really is possible to divorce the longer-term goal of profitable trading from the potentially traumatic short-term effects of incurring losses." The answer lies in the making of two specific commitments. The first is the commitment to use a technical trading system that provides automatic entry and exit criteria and that incorporates money management principles. This encourages the trader to remain disengaged from the emotional contagion of the marketplace and to limit his or her risk. The second commitment is the adoption of an attitude toward yourself that is supportive of trading. The basic need is to maintain the energy levels necessary to cope with the inevitable shock.

PSYCHOLOGICAL ISSUES

Most investors deal with the issue of loss in a variety of maladaptive ways, the most common of which are:

- Denial
- Inaction
- Confusion
- Anger

Denial

Is it any wonder most investors are not getting the results they want in the market? The reason is that they choose to trade with their eyes closed, ears shut, and nervous systems turned off. How else could they tolerate an investment that continues going against them, day after day with no defined risk, until the discomfort gets so severe that even painkillers no longer stave off the pain. Denial won't help. Snap out of it!

Inaction

There is an old American saying that goes like this: "If you sleep on the floor, you can't fall out of bed." Many investors have adopted this "position" when it comes to the question of risk. If you don't pull the trigger, they think, you can't miss the target. But the truth of the matter is you have to pick up the gun and steady your aim; that is, you have to know what you're shooting at before you can pull the trigger with confidence. Developing a strategy with a specific point of focus (i.e., underlying market fundamentals, price-earnings ratios, Elliott Wave, Fibonacci, retracement, etc.) and possessing the intellectual recognition that taking a loss (the real fear) is not only inevitable but essential, will give you the conviction to exploit market opportunities and not miss out.

It is only when missing out becomes more psychologically painful than being inactive that "triggers" get pulled and "targets" get hit.

Confusion

Confusion and uncertainty result from not working out a well-defined risk management formula prior to opening the specific trade that you're in. Reevaluating the cost of your summer vacation at the time your stock position is sinking to new lows is not an optimum trading strategy. The more emotion that can be eliminated from your trading, the greater your sense of clarity about market decisions. Jeffrey Silverman made this point very well when he said: "Doing things that avoid having an emotional content in your decision making is where all the discipline comes in. . . . Be unemotional about getting in, be unemotional about the position, and be unemotional when getting out."

Anger

Reacting to the market out of anger is like choosing to hold your breath until your neighbor turns blue. It's not going to work! Your anger will not affect the loss positively. It certainly may influence it negatively by turning a small loss into a larger one!

Taking a Loss

There is another aspect of taking a loss that is rarely addressed in books on investing: the physiological and emotional responses that inhibit the development and implementation of an effective trading strategy. Learning to take a loss is the single hardest lesson an investor has to learn. It is not an intellectual lesson; taking a loss involves every aspect of the human being.

PSYCHOLOGICAL SKILLS THAT ENSURE SUCCESS

In describing the psychology of a successful trader, Leo Melamed said:

> "Living as a trader day after day teaches you many things about the people who inhabit this arena. You learn to distinguish the good traders from the bad, the successful techniques from the unsuccessful, and the good habits from the faulty. You also learn to distinguish the lover from the fighter, the winner from the losers, the serious from the frivolous, the cerebral from the superficial, and the friend from the foe. But above all, you learn that the psychological makeup of the trader is the single most critical element of success."

The following summarizes the syntax of successful trading.

THE SYNTAX OF SUCCESSFUL TRADING

Well-analyzed trade → System of empowering personal beliefs and attitudes → Proper execution based on positive focus → Decisive, resourceful state of mind → Successful trading performance

There are a number of psychological skills that we have identified as being critical for success in investing. They are:

- Compelling motivation
- Goal setting
- Confidence
- Focus
- State management
- Positive imagery
- Mental conditioning

Compelling Motivation

Compelling motivation is possessing the intensity to do whatever it takes to have a successful result; to overcome a bad day or setback in order to achieve your investment goals. Think of the intensity of a world-class athlete: fully engaged and not afraid to play the game, not afraid of "being there," totally involved in the moment.

Goal Setting

Goal setting is imperative to the investor, not only in terms of setting realistic and measurable goals within the context of a specific time frame, but also in terms of enhancing motivation and performance. Setting goals, in fact, will condition you on an ongoing basis to boost your trading and investing strategies to the next level. It is excellence, not perfection, that is the point here—excellence produces results, perfection produces ulcers.

Confidence

Confidence based on competence is purely a result of motivation, belief (in oneself and the market), and state of mind.

Confidence in psychological terms is no more than consistently expecting a positive outcome. Think of anything you have ever done in your life with that feeling of confidence (positive expectation). Did not that feeling ultimately predict a successful result? It is the same with trading and investing.

Focus

The tighter your focus, and the finer the distinctions that you bring to your investing focus, the better the results. Focus is one of those terms that sounds like a cliché unless you understand how to utilize it in your trading. It is through focus that one stays consistent and is able to maintain a high level of confidence. Focus derives from developing a specific strategy that allows you to feel certain and act accordingly.

State Management

How you feel at any given moment in time will determine your state of mind, including what you feel physically, represent visually, and process emotionally about your investing. Learning how to manage your state will determine whether you hesitate or act and whether you are emotionally drained or physically and psychologically energized.

Positive Imagery

You have the power and ability to choose what imagery you process in your mind and body. You can literally choose the character and intensity of the images (feeling on a physical level) that are of a visual, auditory, and kinesthetic (physical) nature. You can see failure or success, trading loss or market information, paralyzing circumstances or trading opportunities. It is your mind—you run it!

SUCCESSFUL INVESTMENT PERFORMANCE

Physical Response	The Visualization	Auditory Input
Your body feels light. Your shoulders are erect; your torso is straight. Your facial muscles are taut. Your breathing is deep and relaxed. Your eyes are looking up and straight ahead. You are feeling strong, energized, and enthusiastic.	You see yourself succeed. You watch yourself in control and relaxed. You look competent, confident, and positive.	You hear the voice of confidence and control. You hear the sound of relaxed, effortless trading.

The winning state of mind → Strategy → Positive trading and investing responses

These are the qualities that characterize a winning state of mind:

- Anxiety-free
- Self-trusting
- Confident
- High self-esteem

Psychological Characteristics of the Winning State

- Expect the best of yourself.
- Establish a personal standard of excellence.
- Create an internal atmosphere for success based on compelling motivation and focus.
- Communicate effectively with yourself; see yourself as positive, resourceful, and self-empowering.

Visual Imagery That Enhances Performance

- Picture success.
- See yourself in control.
- Look competent, relaxed, confident, and positive.
- View a positive visual image that improves your performance.

Auditory Imagery That Enhances Performance

- Hear the voice of confidence in yourself.
- Say to yourself: "I know I am right."
- Listen to the voice of positive expectation.

Kinesthetic Imagery That Enhances Performance

- Your body feels light and confident.
- Your body is energized and strong.
- Your focus is direct and alert.
- Your breathing is relaxed, effortless, long, and deep.

Positive Beliefs That Enhance State

- I believe I will be successful.
- I believe I can achieve excellent results.
- I believe I can identify and execute winning trades.
- I believe I can act with confidence.
- I believe I can trade effortlessly and automatically.
- I believe each day's performance is fresh.
- I believe I am personally responsible for all my investment results.
- I believe I can be successful without being perfect.
- I believe my investment performance does not reflect on my self-worth.
- I believe one bad trade is just that.
- I believe investing is a process.

- I believe that by believing in myself and in my proven methodology, and by approaching the market each day with a fresh, positive state of mind, I possess the ultimate edge.

Mental Conditioning

The psychological skills necessary to trade or invest successfully require ongoing conditioning. They must be practiced every day. They are certainly as important as your daily chart work or market analysis.

THE RECIPE FOR TRADING SUCCESS

In *The Innergame of Trading* we discussed the recipe of the top traders that allows for consistent positive results. We offer it again, this time for all investors. But first, let's take a look at the innergame of most investors.

The Innergame of Most Investors

- They identify market signals (i.e., point, line, etc.).
- They react in a confused, anxious, or inconsistent manner.
- Investors feel "bad" (angry, guilty, nervous, hesitant, unsure, etc.) about their investments.

The Innergame of Top Traders

- They identify market signals.
- They react automatically with confidence.
- They feel "good" (confident, high self-esteem, etc.) about their investment decisions.

THE FORMULA FOR INVESTING SUCCESS

"Take the obvious, add a cupful of brains, a generous pinch of imagination, a bucketful of courage and daring, stir well and bring to a boil."

—Bernard Baruch

Now that we have addressed the psychological aspects of trading we are ready to talk about some of the technical analytical considerations of investing in markets.

TECHNICAL CONSIDERATIONS

The specific technical system or approach that is utilized by you as an investor must take into account these three conditions:

1. *Market position and/or trend identification.* Is the market in an uptrend, downtrend, or trading range? (A trading range indicates the market trades within a range rather than establishing an up or down trend.)
2. *Automatic entry and exit.* Where do I get in? Where do I get out? What is the specific area or price level?
3. *Defined money management.* How much do I invest when the market doesn't share my enthusiasm for my position or appreciate my point of view?

Once these three factors have been adequately addressed, it should become obvious that a 360-degree universe exists for the investor to exploit market opportunities. We are now going to look at some basic market strategies.

The Basic Strategies

In essence, there are only a few "basic" strategies for trading and investing in markets, although they are used interchangeably by investors in an endless number of exotic combinations. They are:

- Scalping or short-term trading
- Day trading
- Position (with varying time horizons) or long-term trading
- Spreading
- Options trading

Scalping

On the trading floor of world exchanges, scalpers are the equivalent of market makers in the securities world, although unlike securities traders they are under no obligation to make markets. Their main focus, plain and simple, is to make small profits by carefully calculated surgical attacks in order to capture small price changes on each transaction. They buy and sell for eighths and quarters. The scalper limits his or her exposure by moving quickly with a closely defined risk, which, given the short-term perspective, also limits profit potential (see Figure 2.1). Ideally, the scalper buys close to point *x* and sells close to point *y*. Whether conducted on or off the floor, this method of trading is based primarily on volume rather than on a large profit potential on any given trade. It is a form of investing that is now open to everyone as a result of the introduction of the electronic trading platform (i.e., Nasdaq Level II). Read more about this in Chapter 13.

Day Trading

The day trader's focus is more long term than the scalper's. He or she seeks to identify pivotal points in the market's daily action. The day trader searches for entry points based on perceived buy-

FIGURE 2.1 Short-Term Perspective

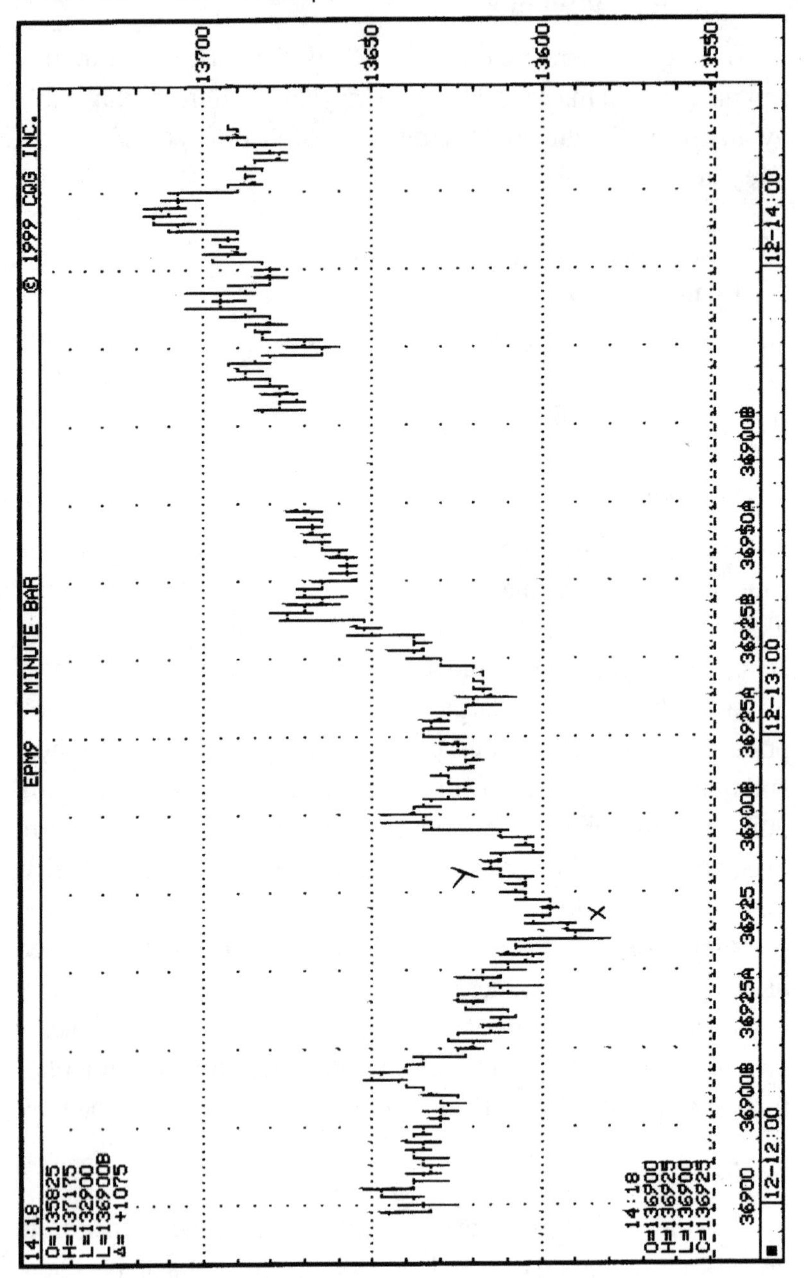

TRADING TERMS

selling climax A selling climax occurs when the recent selling that has entered the market exhausts itself and may provide for a change of trend and a buying opportunity. A buying climax is the reverse.

retracement A retracement is a price movement opposite of the most recent trend; sometimes called a correction.

trendline A trendline is a line drawn on a price chart that connects a series of highs or lows in an attempt to define a trend. A trendline can indicate support (a buy area) in a rising market or resistance (a sell area) in a declining market.

trendline pullback A trendline pullback can be seen when a rising market corrects to an area of support or resistance based on a previously established trendline.

ing and selling climaxes, retracements, and trendline pullbacks. The day trader's time frame is illustrated in Figures 2.2 and 2.3.

The day trader's risks are also close and well defined but with increased upside potential, because he or she is looking for critical daily turns that may materialize into larger market moves. Typically, the position is liquidated at the end of the trading session. This strategy does not allow for the exposure of an open position overnight.

Position Trading

The position trader's time horizon may extend anywhere from a week to many years. His or her trading/investing is based on a well-formulated calculation based on price level or market economics that may be arrived at by either a fundamental or technical bias, or more usually a combination of the two. The position trader is invested for the long term (e.g., he or she believes gold prices will rise from $280 an ounce to $500 an ounce as fundamental economic changes occur). Figure 2.4 is an example of a position trader's perspective.

FIGURE 2.2 Day Trader Time Frame

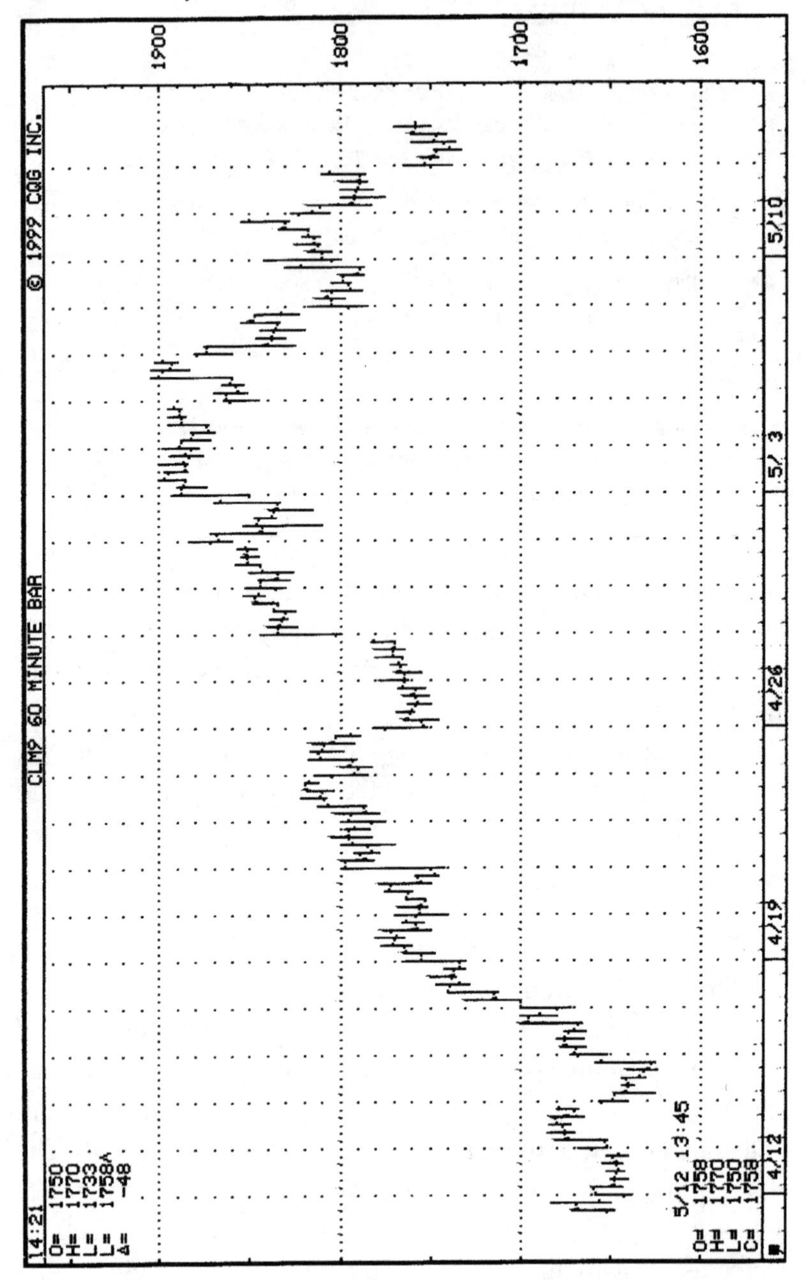

FIGURE 2.3 Day Trader Time Frame

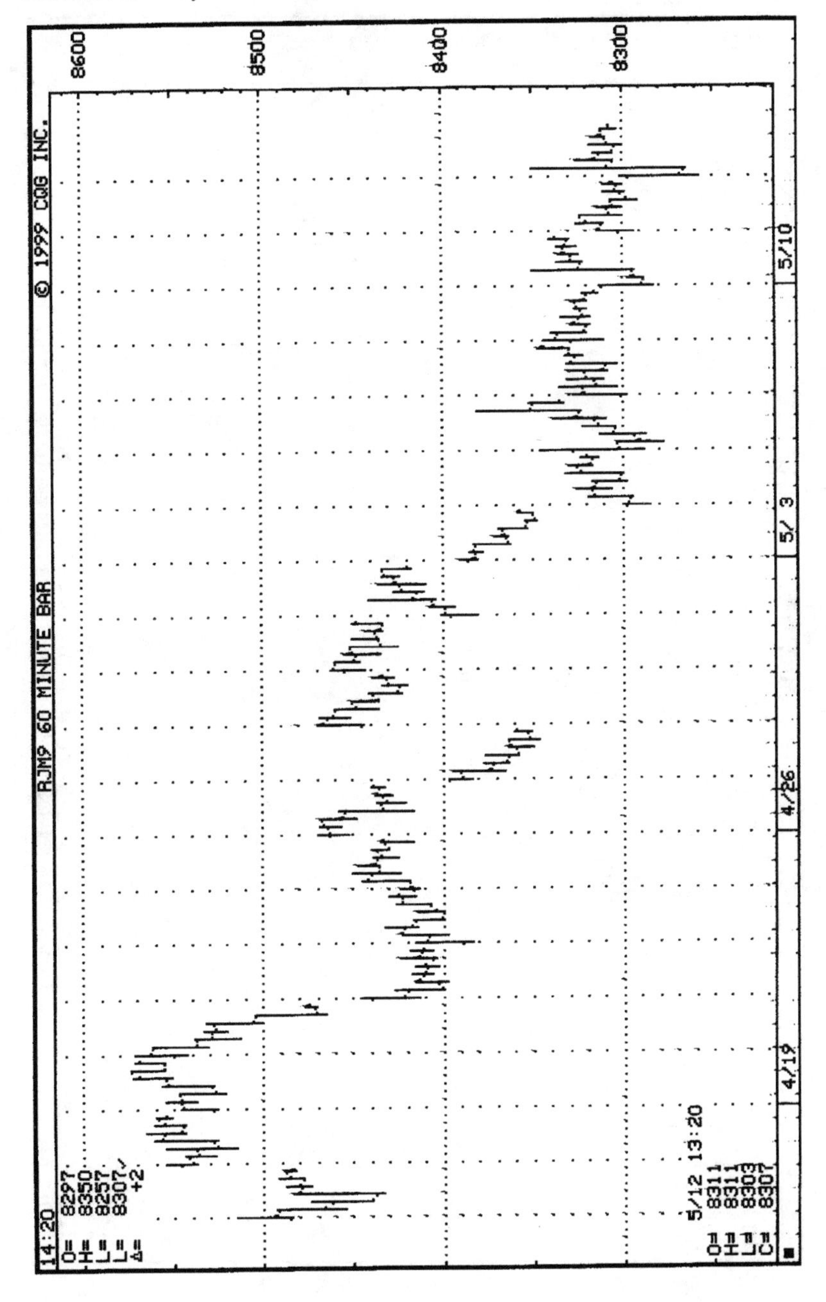

FIGURE 2.4 Position Trader's Perspective

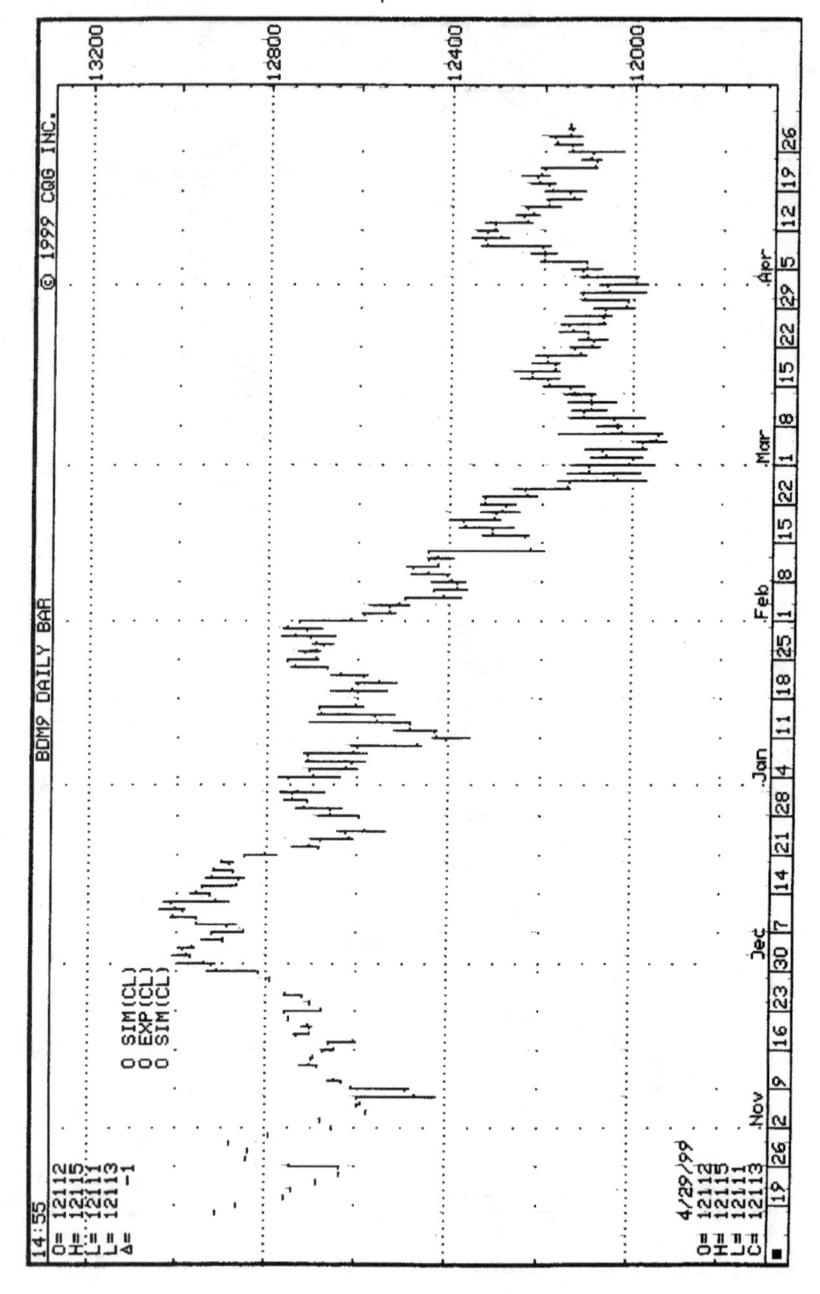

Hedgers and commercials as well as conventional investors are predominantly position traders. Position traders will stay with their opinion until market dynamics have aligned measurably, targeted price levels have been reached, or fundamental economic conditions have changed. There is of necessity greater risk in position trading, although it is still well calculated. Profit potential is also greatly increased given the expansion of risk and perspective.

Spreading

Spreaders can be scalpers, day traders, or position traders. However, the techniques they utilize are fundamentally different from those of outright traders. The spreader focuses on the differential, that is, the difference in price between one futures contract month and another contract month, or the difference in prices between related markets (e.g., corn and wheat, gold and silver, Eurodollars and bonds). Although successful spreading strategies always involve good risk management, the unlimited spreading possibilities create widely varying risk/reward ratios. Leo Melamed said this about the successful spreader:

> "The professional spreader is an artist. His aptitude, agility, and ability to detect the slightest market shift is extraordinary. He is constantly active, moving as a buyer of one month to a seller of another, and immediately back again. In fact, many spreaders perform this activity among three or four contract months at the same time. The object is to pick up even the smallest increment of profit in the shift of the differentials(s). The spreader is always alert to a new offer or bid on one given month that could be spread profitably into another month. He is quick to react to any sudden downdraft or up-draft in the market so that he can unwind one side of his spread for that small moment of market movement and hook it up again as soon as the price movement has stopped." (*Melamed on the Markets,* Wiley, 1993)

In *The Futures Game* (McGraw-Hill, 1974), Teweles and Jones defined the strategy of spreading:

Most Common Types of Spread Positions

Strategy	Example Trade
Intracommodity spread	Long March, 98 Eurodollars Short June, 99 Eurodollars
Intercommodity spread	Long gold, short silver
Intermarket spread	Long S&P 500, short FTSE

Spread position strategies are always based on the concept of differential. Each strategy is based on the trader's bias to market direction, seasonality, volatility, and individual performance within or outside of particular market groups, providing the following market opportunities:

- Many spreads within specific asset classes follow seasonal patterns.
- Spreads often can be defined in money management terms very specifically in terms of risk and objective in a way outright positions cannot (e.g., carrying charge spreads).
- Spreads offer a means to trade directionally in volatile markets.
- Spreads provide market opportunities in seemingly dull markets.
- Spreads can be utilized for both long- and short-term strategies as well as long and short positions.
- Spreads are routinely utilized by professionals, hedgers, and commercial traders.
- Spreads provide greater risk management and opportunity within an overall portfolio (e.g., butterflies, ratios, tandems, etc.) with specific benefits in terms of margin requirements.

Reasons for adopting a spread strategy include:

- To capture the price differential between intracommodity, intercommodity, or intermarket spreads
- To capture the price differential based on market bias
- To capture the price differential based on time and volatility

Note that *differential* is the operative word here. If you are not spreading for differential, don't do it!

Reasons for *not* adopting a spread strategy include:

- Because it's easier than taking an outright buy or sell position
- Because taking a net long and net short position always defines your risk more clearly
- Because in spreading you can't lose a lot and it's easier to get out
- To spread off a loss (prevent an open loss from becoming a realized one)
- To reduce margin requirements
- To spread a market because there's nothing outright to do

Spreading can be costly when not considered in terms of the internal logic of the differential. Spreading can in fact be many times more costly than outright positions. Anyone who has ever been the "wrong way" on old and new crop spreads or currency spreads understands this point very well!

Strategy selection. Specific strategy selection is based on considerations of price, timing, volatility, and direction. In addition, the trader must also consider risk/reward characteristics of the trade, expected returns, and percent of equity to invest. Figures 2.5 to 2.8 illustrate graphically spread relationships in different time frames.

FIGURE 2.5 Daily Spread Time Frame

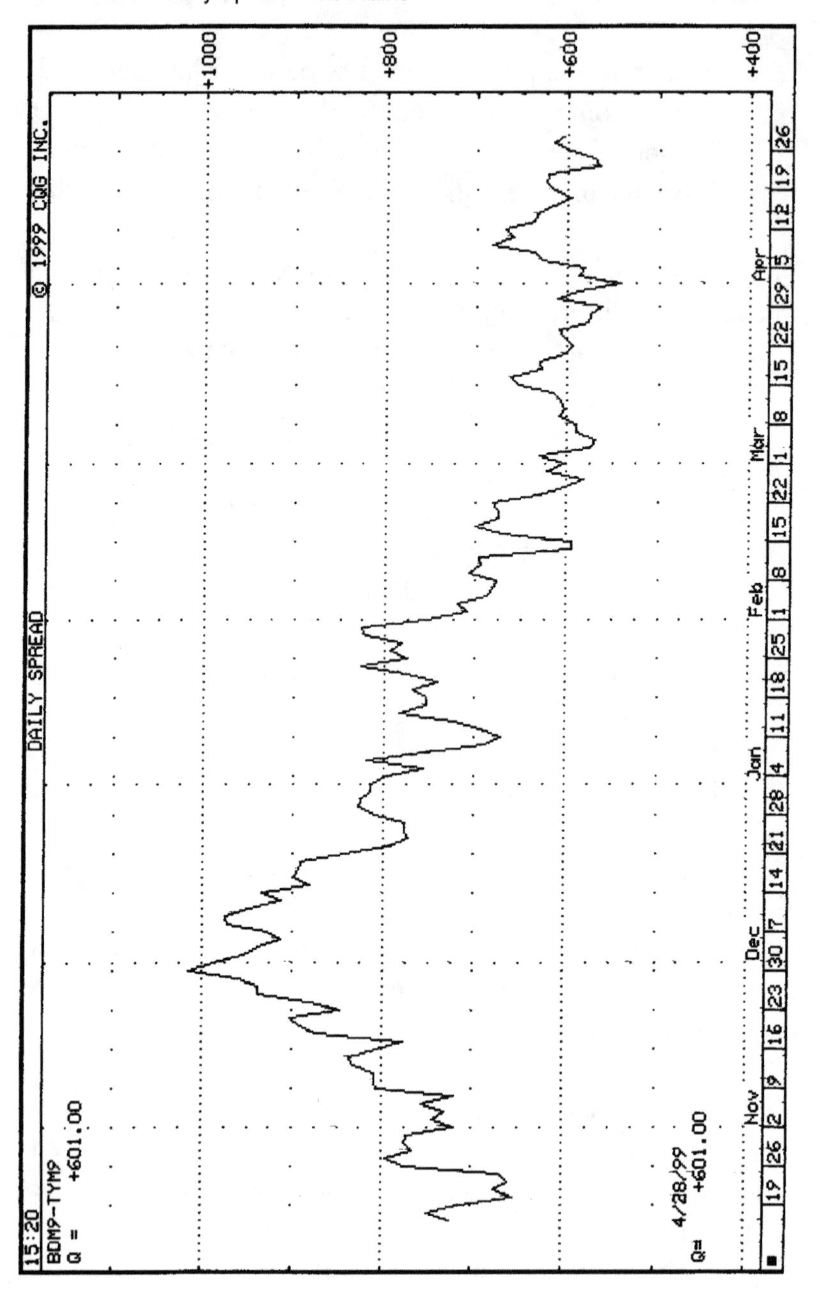

FIGURE 2.6 Daily Spread Time Frame

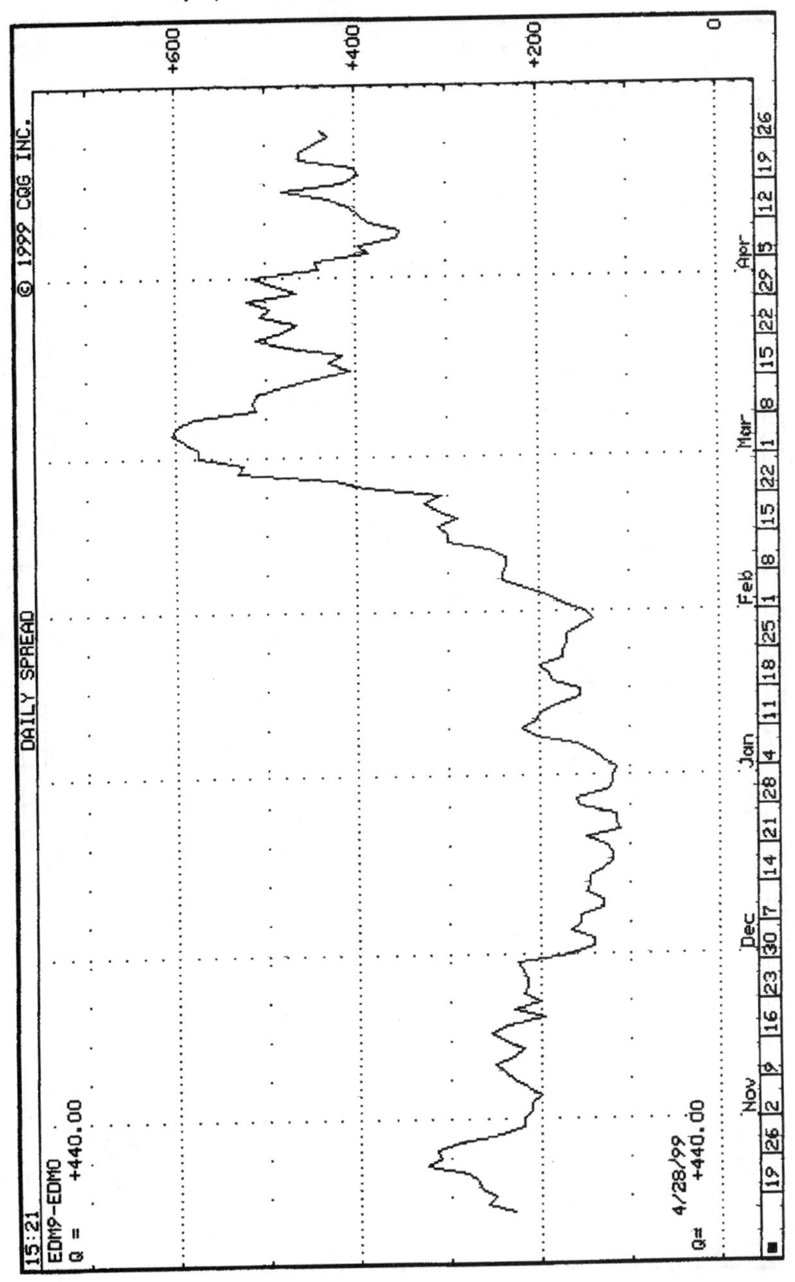

FIGURE 2.7 Weekly Spread Time Frame

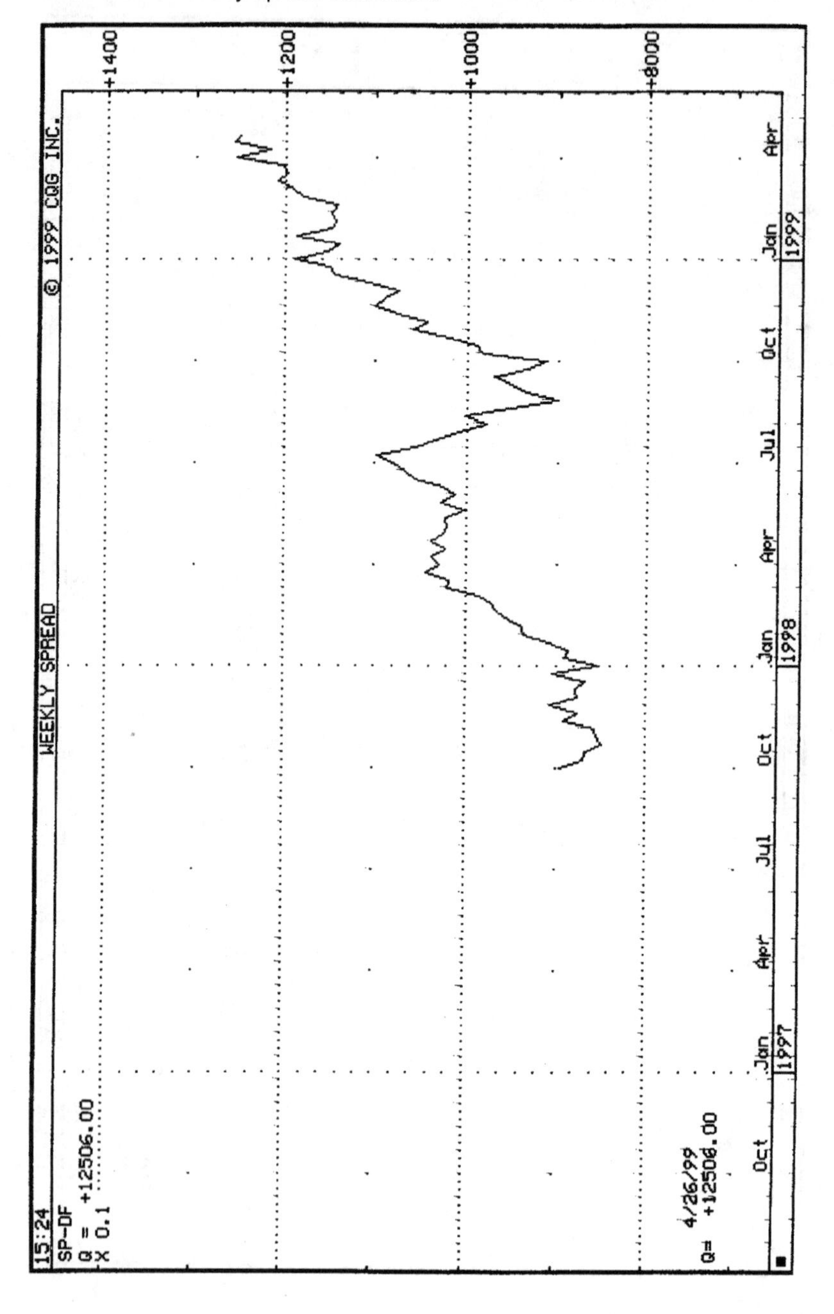

FIGURE 2.8 Weekly Spread Time Frame

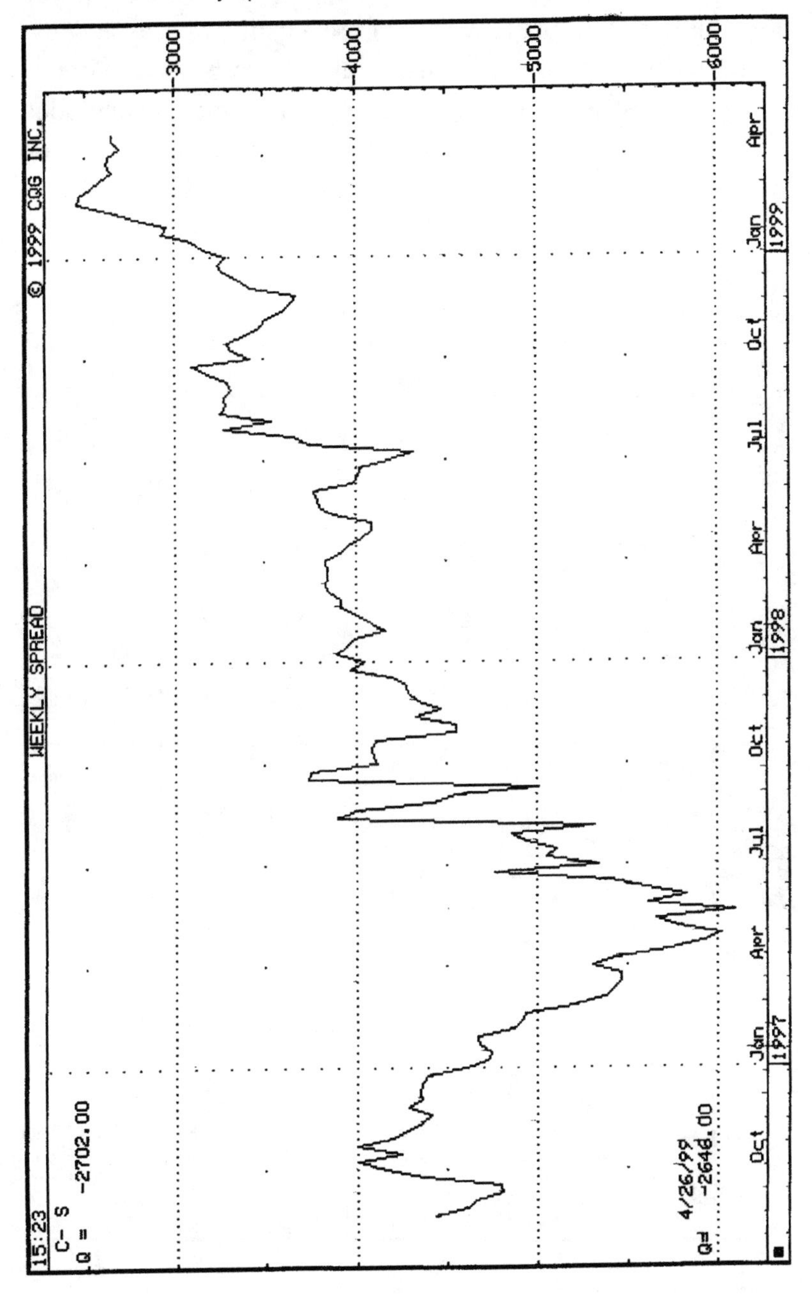

Seasonal, cyclical, and historical spread relationships. The tables shown in Figures 2.9 to 2.11 are a listing of seasonal, cyclical, and historical spread trades that have been researched by Moore Research Center, Inc. The spread strategies included here do not constitute buy or sell recommendations but are

FIGURE 2.9 Spread Strategies

Moore Research Center, Inc. — *January Spread Strategies*

	Futures Trade	Entry Date	Exit Date	Win Pct	Win Years	Loss Years	Total Years	Average Profit	Avg Pft Per Day
1335	Buy Mar Japanese Yen(IMM)- JYH^9 Sell Mar Deutsche Mark(IMM)- DMH^9	1/6	1/17	87	13	2	15	877	79.70
1336	Buy Jul Wheat(CBOT)- WN^9 Sell Jul Soybeans(CBOT)- SN^9	1/7	2/11	93	14	1	15	883	25.24
1337	Buy Jul Cotton(CTN)- CTN^9 Sell Dec Cotton(CTN)- CTZ^9	1/9	3/16	87	13	2	15	1157	17.53
1338	Buy Jul Wheat(CBOT)- WN^9 Sell Mar Wheat(CBOT)- WH^9	1/10	2/7	100	15	0	15	460	16.43
1339	Buy Mar Coffee "C"(CSCE)- KCH^9 Sell Jul Coffee "C"(CSCE)- KCN^9	1/11	2/7	87	13	2	15	1309	48.48
1340	Buy May Silver(CMX)- SIK^9 Sell Apr Gold(CMX)- GCJ^9	1/11	2/15	100	15	0	15	1491	42.60
1341	Buy Nov Soybeans(CBOT)- SX^9 Sell Jul Soybeans(CBOT)- SN^9	1/11	2/27	93	14	1	15	480	10.21
1342	Buy May Heating Oil(NYM)- HOK^9 Sell Mar Heating Oil(NYM)- HOH^9	1/12	1/23	87	13	2	15	424	38.56
1343	Buy Mar Unleaded Gas(NYM)- HUH^9 Sell Mar Heating Oil(NYM)- HOH^9	1/12	1/29	92	12	1	13	420	24.72
1344	Buy Jul Lean Hogs(CME)- LEN^9 Sell Jul Pork Bellies(CME)- PBN^9	1/13	2/9	93	14	1	15	918	33.99
1345	Buy May Sugar #11(CSCE)- SBK^9 Sell "Red" May Sugar #11(CSCE)- SBK^0	1/16	3/31	87	13	2	15	486	6.57
1346	Buy Jun 5-Year T-Notes(CBOT)- FVM^9 Sell Jun 30-Year T-Bonds(CBOT)- USM^9	1/18	3/6	90	9	1	10	997	21.21
1347	Buy Mar Deutsche Mark(IMM)- DMH^9 Sell Mar Swiss Franc(IMM)- SFH^9	1/24	2/13	87	13	2	15	678	33.92
1348	Buy Jun Lean Hogs(CME)- LEM^9 Sell Apr Lean Hogs(CME)- LEJ^9	1/26	2/17	100	15	0	15	331	15.07
1349	Buy Apr Live Cattle(CME)- LCJ^9 Sell Mar Feeder Cattle(CME)- FCH^9	1/30	3/17	100	15	0	15	928	20.18

quantified historical fact. Ideally, these trading ideas should be entered only with the assistance of fundamental and/or technical analysis; for instance, with indicators that confirm seasonal movement or timing signals that trigger entry.

FIGURE 2.9 Continued

Note: One column in the above table equates each trade by its *impact* or daily return. Ave Pft Per Day quantifies the average historical profit (including losses) per day of trade maintenance, i.e., historical daily return.

Note: These trade strategies have worked with historical consistency. No representation is being made that they will work this year or in the future. Please check current market fundamentals and technical conditions before considering these trades. This information is not a recommendation to buy or sell at this time, but merely a historical presentation of trade strategies. Past results are not necessarily indicative of future results. No representation is being made that an account will or is likely to achieve profits or incur losses similar to those shown.

HYPOTHETICAL PERFORMANCE RESULTS HAVE MANY INHERENT LIMITATIONS, SOME OF WHICH ARE DESCRIBED BELOW. NO REPRESENTATION IS BEING MADE THAT ANY ACCOUNT WILL OR IS LIKELY TO ACHIEVE PROFITS OR LOSSES SIMILAR TO THOSE SHOWN. IN FACT, THERE ARE FREQUENTLY SHARP DIFFERENCES BETWEEN HYPOTHETICAL PERFORMANCE RESULTS AND THE ACTUAL RESULTS SUBSEQUENTLY ACHIEVED BY ANY PARTICULAR TRADING PROGRAM. ONE OF THE LIMITATIONS OF HYPOTHETICAL PERFORMANCE RESULTS IS THAT THEY ARE GENERALLY PREPARED WITH THE BENEFIT OF HINDSIGHT. IN ADDITION, HYPOTHETICAL TRADING DOES NOT INVOLVE FINANCIAL RISK, AND NO HYPOTHETICAL TRADING RECORD CAN COMPLETELY ACCOUNT FOR THE IMPACT OF FINANCIAL RISK IN ACTUAL TRADING. FOR EXAMPLE, THE ABILITY TO WITHSTAND LOSSES OR ADHERE TO A PARTICULAR TRADING PROGRAM IN SPITE OF TRADING LOSSES ARE MATERIAL POINTS WHICH CAN ALSO ADVERSELY AFFECT ACTUAL TRADING RESULTS. THERE ARE NUMEROUS OTHER FACTORS RELATED TO THE MARKETS IN GENERAL OR TO THE IMPLEMENTATION OF ANY SPECIFIC TRADING PROGRAM WHICH CANNOT BE FULLY ACCOUNTED FOR IN THE PREPARATION OF HYPOTHETICAL PERFORMANCE RESULTS AND ALL OF WHICH CAN ADVERSELY AFFECT ACTUAL TRADING RESULTS. RESULTS NOT ADJUSTED FOR COMMISSION AND SLIPPAGE.

Copyright ©1989-98 Moore Research Center, Inc.

Spread Summary

FIGURE 2.10 Spread Strategies

Moore Research Center, Inc. — February Spread Strategies

	Futures Trade	Entry Date	Exit Date	Win Pct	Win Years	Loss Years	Total Years	Average Profit	Avg Pft Per Day
1350	Buy Mar Japanese Yen(IMM)- JYH^9 Sell Mar Swiss Franc(IMM)- SFH^9	2/2	2/15	93	14	1	15	1173	90.26
1351	Buy Jun 5-Year T-Notes(CBOT)- FVM^9 Sell Jun 30-Year T-Bonds(CBOT)- USM^9	2/4	3/5	90	9	1	10	836	28.83
1352	Buy Jul Unleaded Gas(NYM)- HUN^9 Sell Apr Unleaded Gas(NYM)- HUJ^9	2/6	3/9	85	11	2	13	483	15.58
1353	Buy Sep Soybeans(CBOT)- SU^9 Sell Sep Corn(CBOT)- CU^9	2/11	4/27	93	14	1	15	787	10.49
1354	Buy Jun Unleaded Gas(NYM)- HUM^9 Sell Jun Heating Oil(NYM)- HOM^9	2/12	4/1	100	13	0	13	618	12.87
1355	Buy Jun Live Cattle(CME)- LCM^9 Sell Mar Feeder Cattle(CME)- FCH^9	2/13	3/8	100	15	0	15	583	25.35
1356	Buy Jul Soybeans(CBOT)- SN^9 Sell Jul Wheat(CBOT)- WN^9	2/13	4/1	87	13	2	15	1014	21.58
1357	Buy Jun Lean Hogs(CME)- LEM^9 Sell Oct Lean Hogs(CME)- LEV^9	2/17	3/9	93	14	1	15	445	22.27
1358	Buy Jul Unleaded Gas(NYM)- HUN^9 Sell Jul Crude Oil(NYM)- CLN^9	2/23	3/29	100	13	0	13	535	15.73
1359	Buy 2 Jul Platinum(NYM)- PLN^9 Sell Jun Gold(CMX)- GCM^9	2/24	4/15	100	15	0	15	1963	39.25
1360	Buy May Sugar #11(CSCE)- SBK^9 Sell "Red" Mar Sugar #11(CSCE)- SBH^0	2/25	3/20	93	14	1	15	323	14.06
1361	Buy Aug Pork Bellies(CME)- PBQ^9 Sell Aug Lean Hogs(CME)- LEQ^9	2/25	3/22	93	14	1	15	671	26.85
1362	Buy May Corn(CBOT)- CK^9 Sell Dec Corn(CBOT)- CZ^9	2/25	3/29	93	14	1	15	236	7.37

Some listings may be similar to others but illustrate a longer or shorter trade window. Others may be coincident with first delivery and should be approached accordingly. Sound money management principles should always prevail in any spread strategy.

FIGURE 2.10 Continued

Note: One column in the above table equates each trade by its *impact* or daily return. Ave Pft Per Day quantifies the average historical profit (including losses) per day of trade maintenance, i.e., historical daily return.

Note: These trade strategies have worked with historical consistency. No representation is being made that they will work this year or in the future. Please check current market fundamentals and technical conditions before considering these trades. This information is not a recommendation to buy or sell at this time, but merely a historical presentation of trade strategies. Past results are not necessarily indicative of future results. No representation is being made that an account will or is likely to achieve profits or incur losses similar to those shown.

HYPOTHETICAL PERFORMANCE RESULTS HAVE MANY INHERENT LIMITATIONS, SOME OF WHICH ARE DESCRIBED BELOW. NO REPRESENTATION IS BEING MADE THAT ANY ACCOUNT WILL OR IS LIKELY TO ACHIEVE PROFITS OR LOSSES SIMILAR TO THOSE SHOWN. IN FACT, THERE ARE FREQUENTLY SHARP DIFFERENCES BETWEEN HYPOTHETICAL PERFORMANCE RESULTS AND THE ACTUAL RESULTS SUBSEQUENTLY ACHIEVED BY ANY PARTICULAR TRADING PROGRAM. ONE OF THE LIMITATIONS OF HYPOTHETICAL PERFORMANCE RESULTS IS THAT THEY ARE GENERALLY PREPARED WITH THE BENEFIT OF HINDSIGHT. IN ADDITION, HYPOTHETICAL TRADING DOES NOT INVOLVE FINANCIAL RISK, AND NO HYPOTHETICAL TRADING RECORD CAN COMPLETELY ACCOUNT FOR THE IMPACT OF FINANCIAL RISK IN ACTUAL TRADING. FOR EXAMPLE, THE ABILITY TO WITHSTAND LOSSES OR ADHERE TO A PARTICULAR TRADING PROGRAM IN SPITE OF TRADING LOSSES ARE MATERIAL POINTS WHICH CAN ALSO ADVERSELY AFFECT ACTUAL TRADING RESULTS. THERE ARE NUMEROUS OTHER FACTORS RELATED TO THE MARKETS IN GENERAL OR TO THE IMPLEMENTATION OF ANY SPECIFIC TRADING PROGRAM WHICH CANNOT BE FULLY ACCOUNTED FOR IN THE PREPARATION OF HYPOTHETICAL PERFORMANCE RESULTS AND ALL OF WHICH CAN ADVERSELY AFFECT ACTUAL TRADING RESULTS. RESULTS NOT ADJUSTED FOR COMMISSION AND SLIPPAGE.

Copyright ©1989-98 Moore Research Center, Inc.

Spread Summary

The spread tables presented are spread strategies for the months of January through March 1999. Current tables are available from Moore Research Center, Inc. (541-484-0243, or at www.mrci.com).

FIGURE 2.11 Spread Strategies

Moore Research Center, Inc.

March Spread Strategies

	Futures Trade	Entry Date	Exit Date	Win Pct	Win Years	Loss Years	Total Years	Average Profit	Avg Pft Per Day
1363	Buy Jul Soybeans(CBOT)- SN^9 Sell Jul Wheat(CBOT)- WN^9	3/2	3/23	93	14	1	15	408	19.44
1364	Buy Jul Unleaded Gas(NYM)- HUN^9 Sell Jul Crude Oil(NYM)- CLN^9	3/2	4/7	100	13	0	13	421	11.70
1365	Buy May Silver(CMX)- SIK^9 Sell Apr Gold(CMX)- GCJ^{9*}	3/6	3/31	87	13	2	15	859	34.37
1366	Buy Jun Crude Oil(NYM)- CLM^9 Sell Oct Crude Oil(NYM)- CLV^9	3/12	4/21	87	13	2	15	435	10.87
1367	Buy Jun Unleaded Gas(NYM)- HUM^9 Sell Sep Unleaded Gas(NYM)- HUU^9	3/12	5/1	85	11	2	13	878	17.57
1368	Buy Aug Unleaded Gas(NYM)- HUQ^9 Sell Aug Heating Oil(NYM)- HOQ^9	3/13	5/21	92	12	1	13	710	10.29
1369	Buy Jun British Pound(IMM)- BPM^9 Sell Jun Deutsche Mark(IMM)- DMM^9	3/17	4/12	87	13	2	15	1536	59.09
1370	Buy Jun British Pound(IMM)- BPM^9 Sell Jun Swiss Franc(IMM)- SFM^9	3/19	4/10	93	14	1	15	1268	57.61
1371	Buy Jun Japanese Yen(IMM)- JYM^9 Sell Jun Swiss Franc(IMM)- SFM^9	3/27	4/15	80	12	3	15	1078	56.75
1372	Buy Dec Live Cattle(CME)- LCZ^9 Sell Jun Live Cattle(CME)- LCM^9	3/27	5/20	93	14	1	15	637	11.80
1373	Buy Jul Wheat(KCBT)- KWN^9 Sell Jul Corn(CBOT)- CN^9	3/28	5/12	87	13	2	15	742	16.48
1374	Buy 2 Jul Platinum(NYM)- PLN^9 Sell Jun Gold(CMX)- GCM^9	3/29	4/14	87	13	2	15	1118	69.88
1375	Buy Jul Wheat(CBOT)- WN^9 Sell Jul Soybeans(CBOT)- SN^9	3/29	4/15	87	13	2	15	555	32.65
1376	Buy Aug Lean Hogs(CME)- LEQ^9 Sell Aug Live Cattle(CME)- LCQ^9	3/29	5/21	100	15	0	15	1306	24.64
1377	Buy Jul Cotton(CTN)- CTN^9 Sell Dec Cotton(CTN)- CTZ^9	3/29	6/2	80	12	3	15	862	13.27

Options Trading

Options offer a very attractive avenue of investment because they present so many strategic possibilities. In addition, strike prices—the specified price at which an option contract

FIGURE 2.11 Continued

Note: One column in the above table equates each trade by its *impact* or daily return. Ave Pft Per Day quantifies the average historical profit (including losses) per day of trade maintenance, i.e., historical daily return.

Note: These trade strategies have worked with historical consistency. No representation is being made that they will work this year or in the future. Please check current market fundamentals and technical conditions before considering these trades. This information is not a recommendation to buy or sell at this time, but merely a historical presentation of trade strategies. Past results are not necessarily indicative of future results. No representation is being made that an account will or is likely to achieve profits or incur losses similar to those shown.

HYPOTHETICAL PERFORMANCE RESULTS HAVE MANY INHERENT LIMITATIONS, SOME OF WHICH ARE DESCRIBED BELOW. NO REPRESENTATION IS BEING MADE THAT ANY ACCOUNT WILL OR IS LIKELY TO ACHIEVE PROFITS OR LOSSES SIMILAR TO THOSE SHOWN. IN FACT, THERE ARE FREQUENTLY SHARP DIFFERENCES BETWEEN HYPOTHETICAL PERFORMANCE RESULTS AND THE ACTUAL RESULTS SUBSEQUENTLY ACHIEVED BY ANY PARTICULAR TRADING PROGRAM. ONE OF THE LIMITATIONS OF HYPOTHETICAL PERFORMANCE RESULTS IS THAT THEY ARE GENERALLY PREPARED WITH THE BENEFIT OF HINDSIGHT. IN ADDITION, HYPOTHETICAL TRADING DOES NOT INVOLVE FINANCIAL RISK, AND NO HYPOTHETICAL TRADING RECORD CAN COMPLETELY ACCOUNT FOR THE IMPACT OF FINANCIAL RISK IN ACTUAL TRADING. FOR EXAMPLE, THE ABILITY TO WITHSTAND LOSSES OR ADHERE TO A PARTICULAR TRADING PROGRAM IN SPITE OF TRADING LOSSES ARE MATERIAL POINTS WHICH CAN ALSO ADVERSELY AFFECT ACTUAL TRADING RESULTS. THERE ARE NUMEROUS OTHER FACTORS RELATED TO THE MARKETS IN GENERAL OR TO THE IMPLEMENTATION OF ANY SPECIFIC TRADING PROGRAM WHICH CANNOT BE FULLY ACCOUNTED FOR IN THE PREPARATION OF HYPOTHETICAL PERFORMANCE RESULTS AND ALL OF WHICH CAN ADVERSELY AFFECT ACTUAL TRADING RESULTS. RESULTS NOT ADJUSTED FOR COMMISSION AND SLIPPAGE.

Copyright ©1989-98 Moore Research Center, Inc.

Spread Summary

may be exercised—and expiration—the last date the option is available for settlement—can be selected to create myriad interesting market opportunities. See the box for some important terms concerning options.

OPTIONS TERMS YOU SHOULD KNOW

call An options contract that gives the buyer the right but not the obligation to buy the underlying instrument (futures, stock) at a specific price on or before a specific date.

put An option contract that gives the buyer the right but not the obligation to sell the underlying instrument (futures, stock) at a specific price on or before a specific date.

straddle An options position consisting of a call and put in the same stock or futures contract, the same expiration date, and the same strike price.

strangle An options position in which one buys (or sells) both a put and a call.

ratio writing A market position using more than one option to hedge a position.

at-the-money An option with a strike price equal to or approximately equal to the current trading price of the underlying instrument (e.g., futures contract, stock).

in-the-money A term used to describe options with intrinsic value. A call option is in-the-money when the instrument is trading above the strike price. A put option is in-the-money when the instrument is trading below the strike price.

out-of-the-money A term used to describe an option with no intrinsic value.

butterfly spread An option position involving the simultaneous buying of an at-the-money option, selling two out-of-the-money options, and buying one out-of-the-money option.

What follows here is a list of options trading strategies based on various market scenarios. For example, if a trader expects stable prices in the near term, he or she could sell straddles, sell strangles, etc. (Check the glossary at the end of the book for a detailed explanation of these terms.)

Stable Prices	**Bearish Strategies**
Sell straddles	Buy puts
Sell strangles	Bear spreads
Ratio write	Sell calls
Short butterfly	Sell instrument—buy call
Ratio spreads	Covered put write
	Buy put-sell call

Volatile Prices	**Bull Strategies**
Buy straddle	Buy calls
Buy butterfly	Bull spreads

Time Decay Tactics

Time Helps	**Time Hurts**	**Time Mixed**
Short call	Long call	Bull spread
Short put	Long put	Bear spread
Short straddle	Long straddle	Long butterfly
Covered call write		Short butterfly
Covered put write		

Profit/Loss Characteristics of Option Strategies

Strategy	**Profit**	**Loss**
Buy call	Unlimited	Limited
Buy put	Unlimited	Limited
Short call	Limited	Unlimited
Short put	Limited	Unlimited
Covered call write	Limited	Unlimited
Covered put write	Limited	Unlimited
Bull spread	Limited	Unlimited
Bear spread	Limited	Unlimited
Long butterfly	Limited	Unlimited
Short butterfly	Limited	Unlimited

FUNDAMENTAL ANALYSIS

Fundamental analysis is concerned with supply and demand factors, which influence the price movement of futures contracts. Fundamental analysis also considers market trends over a relatively long period of time; for example, an investor looks at the forecasts and present economic trends of the economy to determine the course of the stock market for the next several years. Traders rarely use fundamental analysis exclusive of technical considerations.

Factors entering into fundamental analysis include:

- Supply and demand
- Degree to which each subset of supply and demand factors are important (i.e., production, imports and exports, and usage)
- Seasonal and cyclical considerations (e.g., growing and harvest seasons in grains or heating oil requirements in winter)
- Monetary and fiscal policies (watching the Federal Reserve Board actions)
- Government reports (Many reports are specific to the individual markets and issued frequently.)
- Political developments (congressional actions or election year politics)
- The relationship of market prices to volume, open interest, and hedging interest

The main problem with a fundamental analysis approach is in answering these two questions:

1. Where do I get in?
2. How do I know when I'm wrong?

Another problem with fundamental analysis is that the significance of information within the context of price action is hard to evaluate; it is the rare trader who can distinguish the signal from the noise. As with all other strategies in trading, fundamental analysis is subject to individual interpretation, like deriving meaning from the old axiom: "Buy low and sell high." There are, however, successful traders who employ fundamental analysis consistently. Jeffrey Silverman and Dick Stoken stand out in this respect as we will see in their interviews in Chapters 9 and 10.

3

THE OVERALL APPROACH

The Technical View

One of our fundamental assumptions in approaching markets is that no trading system is perfect; however, the use of one is essential for trading success. And in order for a trading system to be successful, it must be profitable, consistent, and personal.

Let's begin by looking at some of the basic concepts of classical chart analysis with the intention to demonstrate how a fully integrated trading strategy can be developed that will be profitable, personal, and consistent over time. Our focus here is on the use of technical concepts for you to identify opportunities and execute trades within your overall strategy.

Let's begin with the belief that markets do not, contrary to the view of most academics, trade randomly. Any investor who has spent time studying simple price charts can easily verify the upward or downward bias of most markets. This bias within a defined time frame is referred to as a trend. Trends can be seen, as we stated in *The Innergame of Trading,* as market psychology at work.

TRENDS—CATCHING THE BIG WAVE

The classic definition of a trend: "higher highs and higher lows," has a strong psychological foundation. Emotionally and intellectually, there is great comfort for the trading public when a market makes new highs, falls off, and fails to make new lows in a particular period of time. Traders then become willing buyers at higher price levels and sellers are only attracted to the market at even higher levels. Of course, the opposite is true for downward trending markets.

Whether the markets are trending up or down, or for that matter, not at all, there is an opportunity for profit. Top traders have all devised some methodology or combination of methods and techniques to trade markets with consistency. It doesn't matter if the trader is a fundamentalist or a technician, each one has developed a unique "solution" to markets. This solution is what we call a trading system. It's important to understand that trading systems are nothing more than an attempt to put order into a chaotic world, the world of trading markets.

The trading system gives the trader the ability to control his or her emotional and mental states rather than allowing them to control him or her. A system is a disciplined method for organizing dynamic, ever-changing market phenomena.

A successful trading system is composed of a number of independent elements that are joined together to make the whole. These elements, as we described above, are discrete and mutually interactive. They are:

- Trend identification
- Entry and exit strategies
- Money management

TREND IDENTIFICATION

The three primary methods of trend identification are:

1. Linear, or trendlines
2. Moving averages
3. Channel breakouts

Trendlines are the simplest device to use to indicate a trend. By drawing a line from low to low to establish an uptrend or from high to high to establish a downtrend, we can easily and quickly define a market's trend (see Figure 3.1).

Moving averages—usually obtained by adding up a series of closes and dividing the sum by the number of days used in the series—are effective in smoothing erratic market movement and indicating trend (see Figure 3.2). Generally, a trend is said to be in effect when the market is trading above the moving average (uptrend) or below the moving average (downtrend).

The *channel breakout* is created when a market trades in a confined area of highs and lows within some specified time, and then moves out of this area, thereby establishing a new trend (see Figure 3.3). The channel also can be said to be a sideways trend, and many traders find this type of market very profitable.

ENTRY AND EXIT STRATEGIES

There is a difference in learning to identify trends and creating a successful strategy to profit from that knowledge. Many traders easily can define the trends on a chart, but few are successful in profiting from the information. How many times

FIGURE 3.1 Linear Trendline

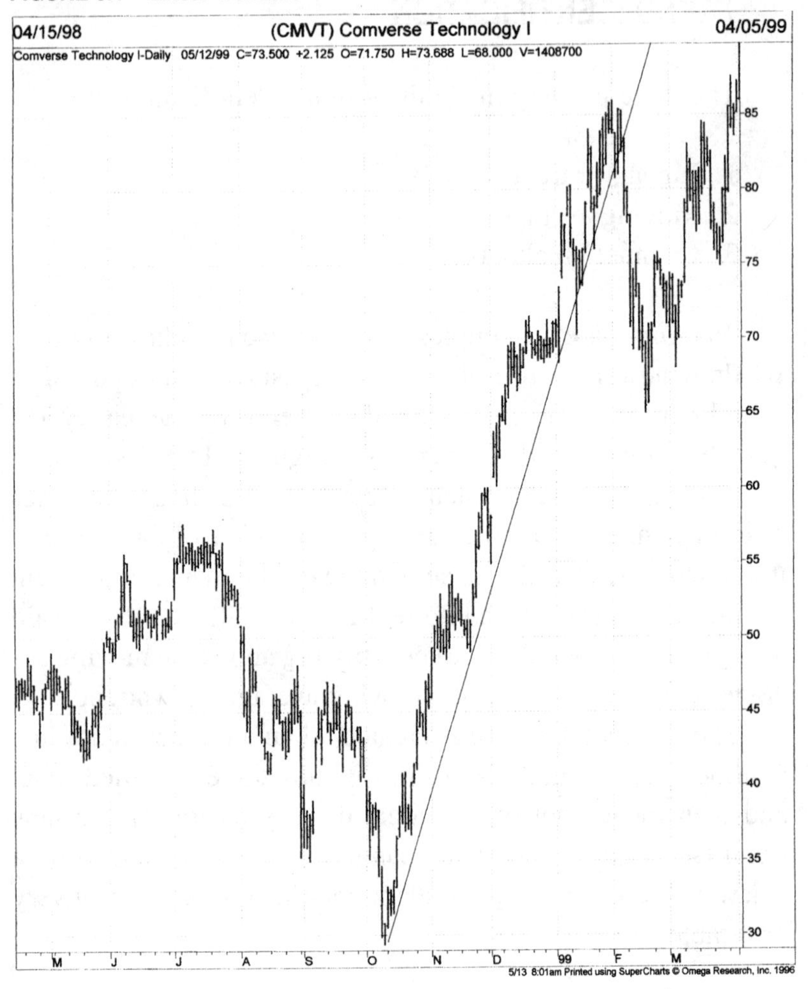

have you heard, "The market came right down to my trendline, or moving average or old low, and I couldn't pull the trigger"? Have you heard that from anyone you know personally?

A strategy that you create can overcome the many barriers that prevent a trader from taking advantage of "the moment." A simple strategy that can be used effectively is to buy the

FIGURE 3.2 Moving Average

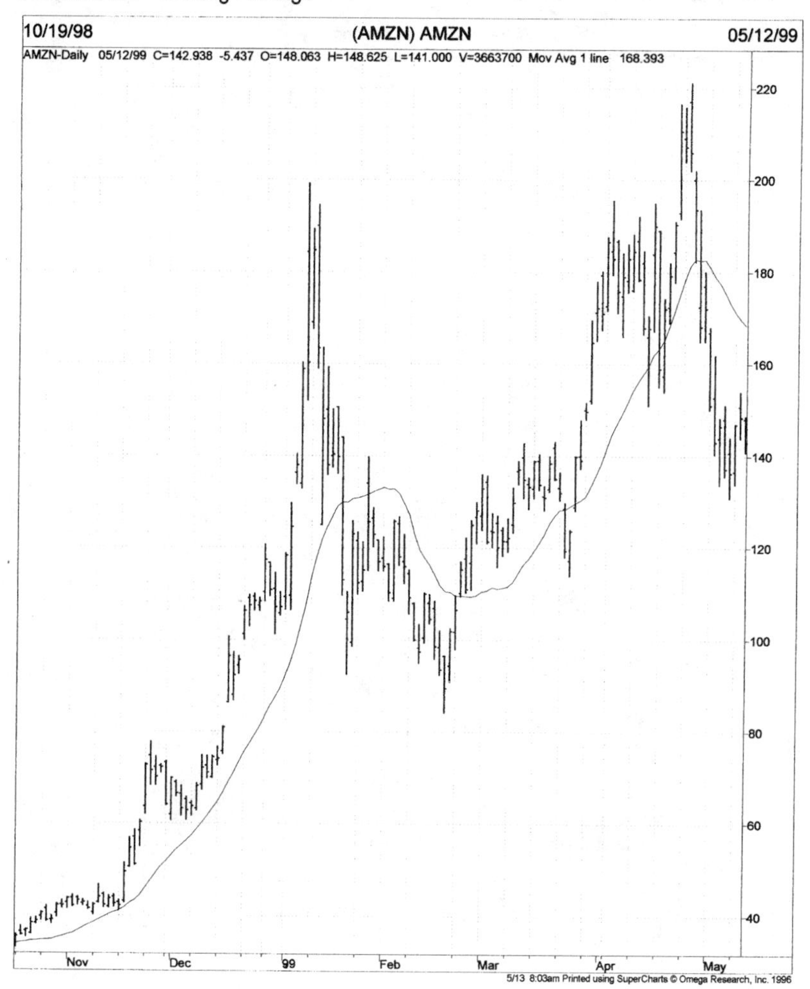

market anytime it falls to an uptrend line or sell the market anytime it rallies to a downtrend line. If the market violates the line by some number of our choosing, we automatically exit the trade. So, what happens if the market stops us out and then goes back over or under the line? Easy! Let's make a reentry signal part of our strategy and go back into the market.

FIGURE 3.3 Channel Breakout

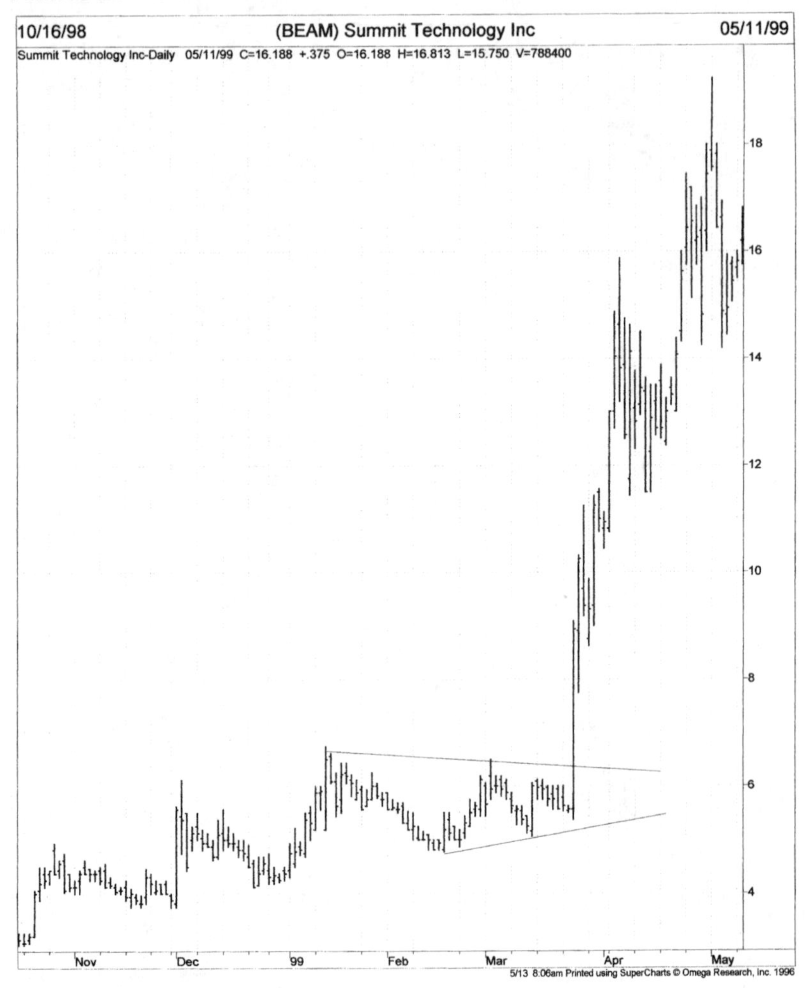

What we have created here is a simple strategy that will enable you to do what we have found all the top traders do; that is, to identify a signal or reason to enter the market. You can act automatically, and because you are in control you feel good about the trade, whether it turns out right or not.

Reversal Patterns

More often than not markets do not end an established trend easily or quickly. Bottoms are usually quieter and take a long time to develop, except for the occasional spike or double bottom that occurs in a short period of time. Tops are quicker to form, are often very volatile, and are accompanied by lots of noise and attention. These patterns include:

- Head and shoulders bottoms (Figure 3.4)
- Head and shoulders tops (Figure 3.5)
- Double bottoms and tops (Figures 3.6 and 3.7)
- Triple bottoms (Figure 3.8)
- Rounded bottoms (Figure 3.9)
- V or spike bottoms and tops (Figure 3.10)

Here again many traders will see these reversal patterns develop and watch them turn into very strong trends without ever entering the market.

Indecision, doubt, fear, lack of confidence, and confusion make for missed opportunity. Creating a strategy that automatically gets you into the market, defines your risk, and takes you out at the proper time is key to capturing profits from these easy-to-read patterns.

Many of these reversal patterns have high probabilities of success. Taking these signals when they occur, therefore, should translate into a high probability for profits. A strategy designed to enter the market each time a bottom or top appears to be completed can be highly successful. It's the strategy that instills the confidence and strong belief that will make you consistently take these trades.

FIGURE 3.4 Head and Shoulders Bottom

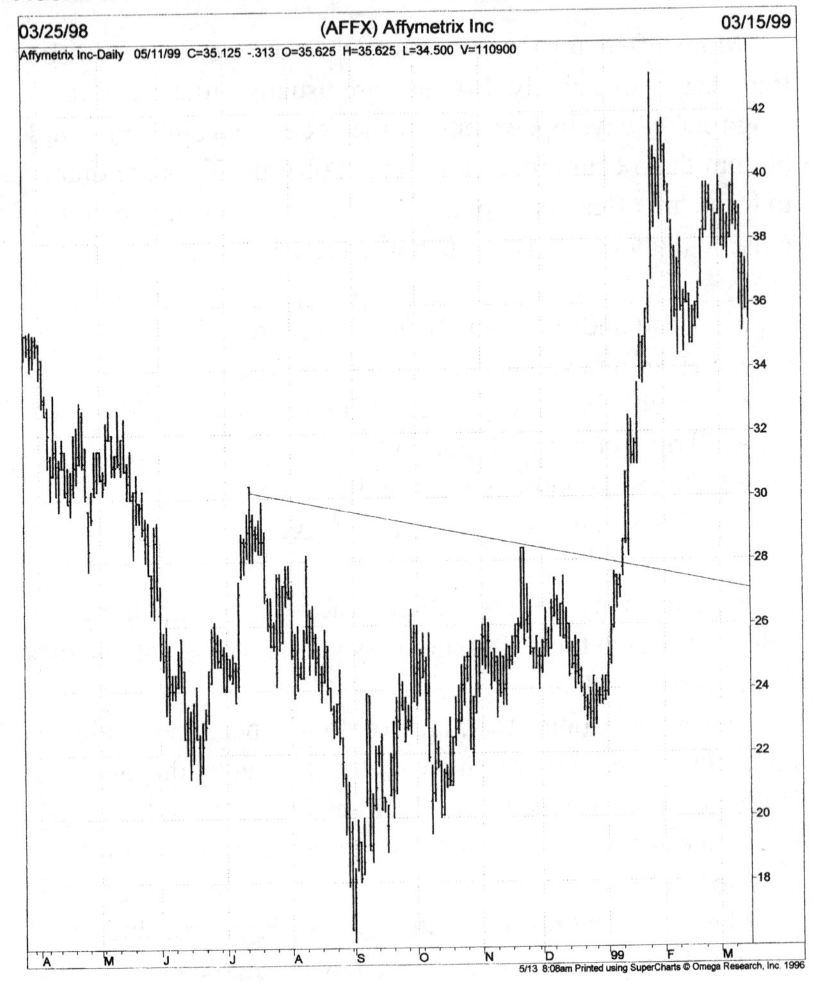

Continuation Patterns

After a trend has been established and the market has moved away from its basic trendline, a series of patterns called *continuation patterns* are formed. They are pauses in the established trend and offer excellent opportunities to enter the market with

FIGURE 3.5 Head and Shoulders Top

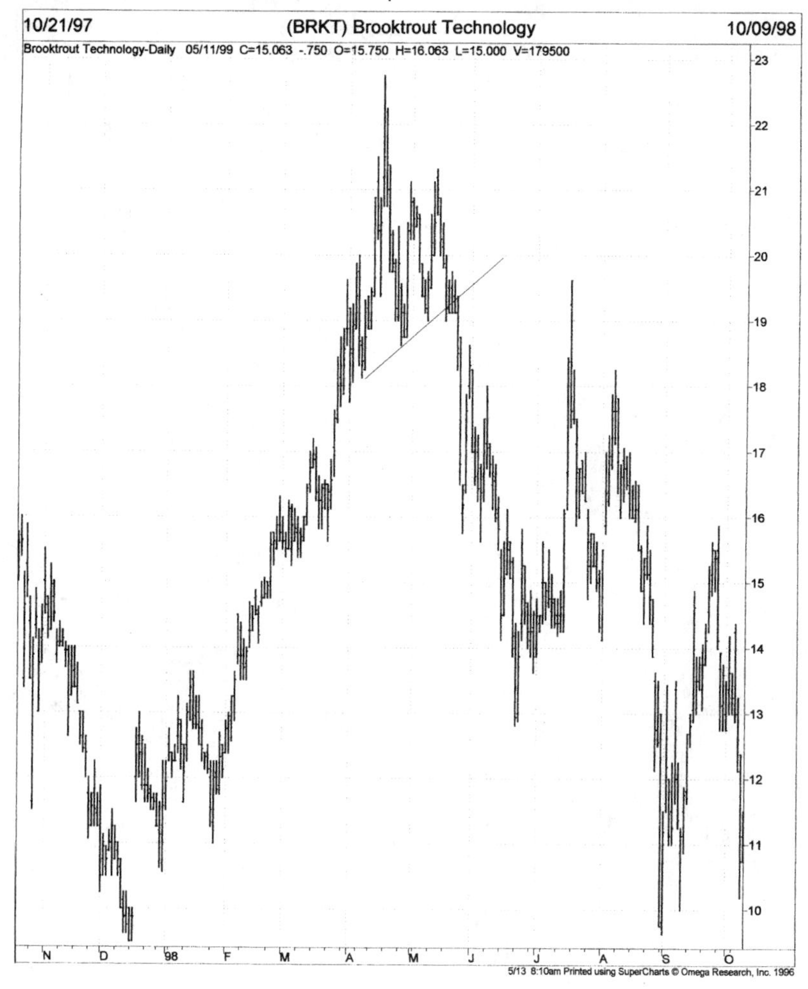

limited risk in the direction of the main trend (see Figure 3.11). Here again is an opportunity for you to design personal strategies to take advantage of reliable patterns set up by the market.

As a market moves significantly in one direction, it will very often pause over a short period of time. It could be several days or a week or two. The patterns created by the market dur-

FIGURE 3.6 Double Bottom

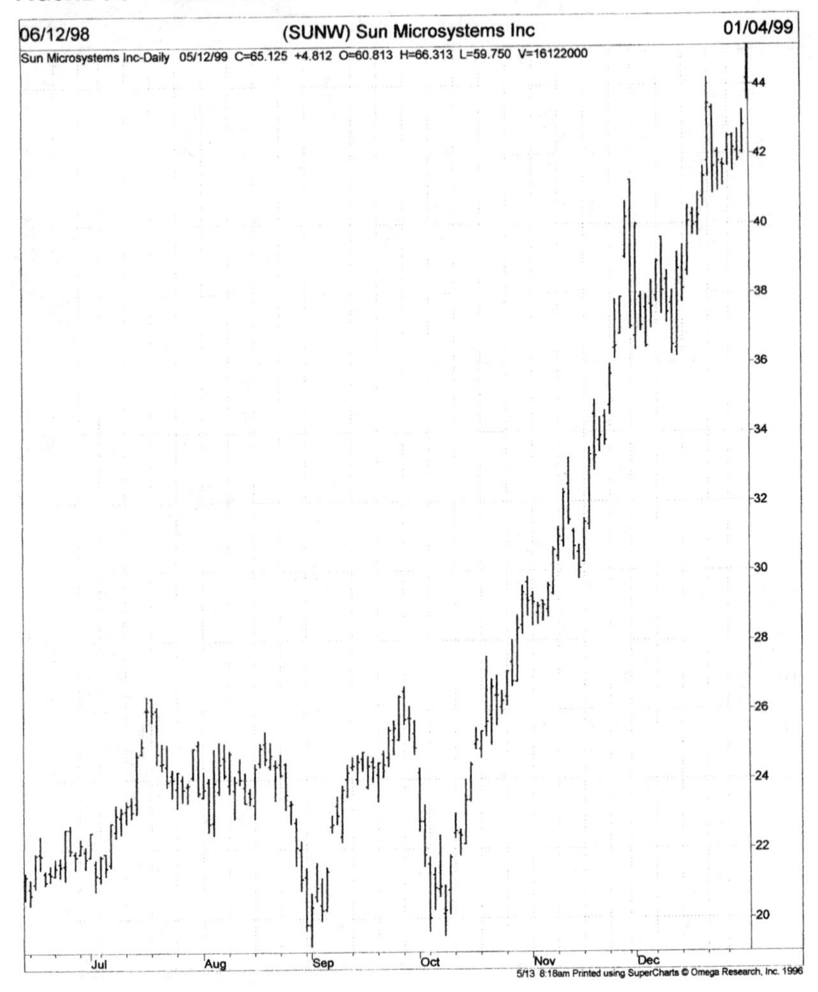

ing this period offer opportunities to profit from the price movement within those patterns or enter the market in the direction of the trend at reduced risk. Flags and triangles (Figure 3.12) are an example of common continuation patterns.

You can devise several strategies that fit your personal trading style in order to take advantage of these patterns. If you are

FIGURE 3.7 Double Top

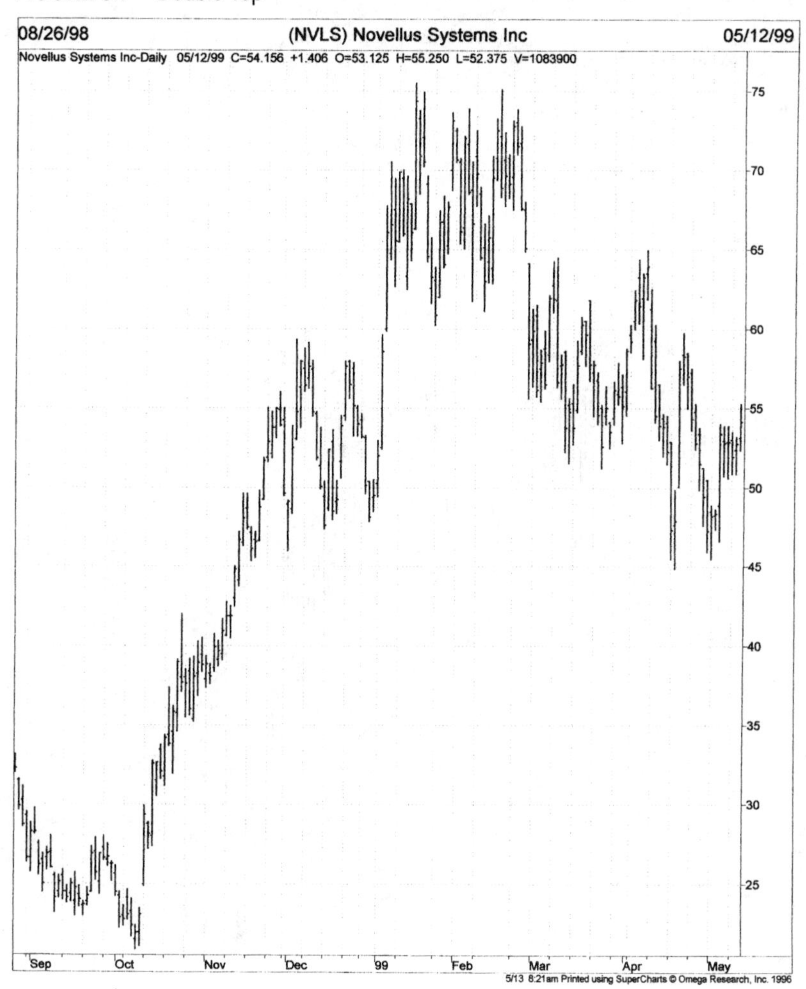

an investor who is comfortable buying breaking markets, then a strategy that waits for a market to test or even break the low end of a continuation pattern offers a low-risk area to make that trade. Defining the risk and knowing that you are buying in a high-probability area of success will allow you to have the confidence to make this trade.

FIGURE 3.8 Triple Bottom

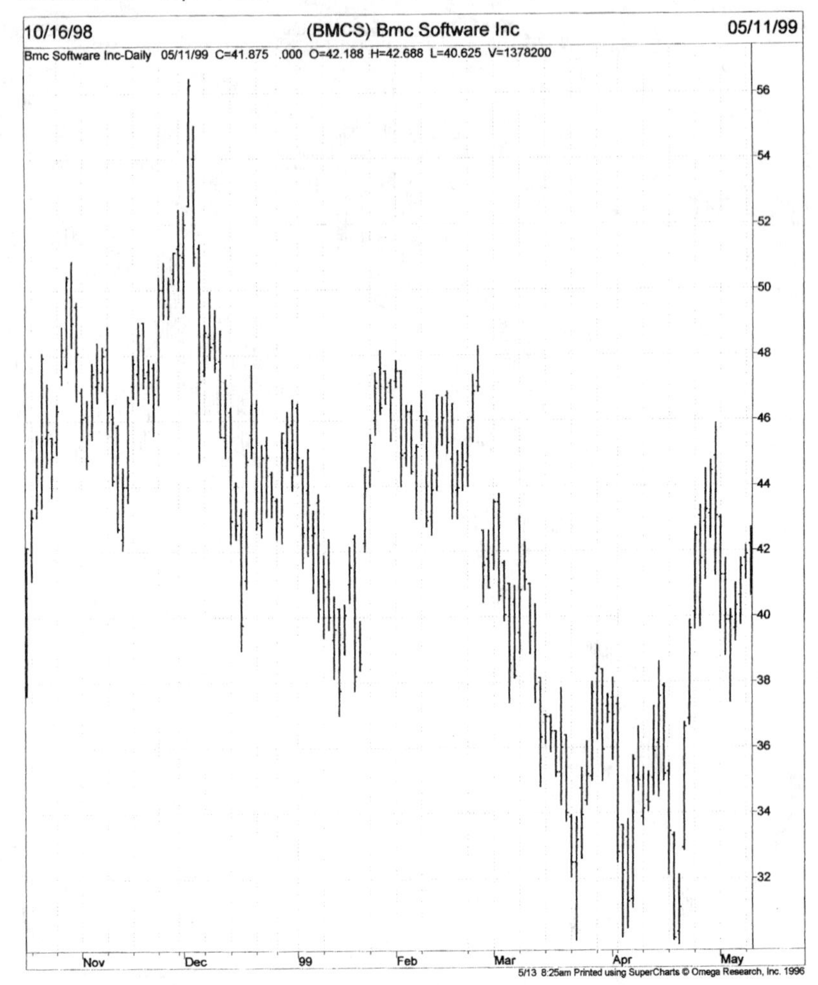

If your objectives are to play for the top end of the pattern, you will already have a profit area in mind. If your goal is to enter a trending market, then you have accomplished that and can wait for the market to resume its trend. Some traders are more comfortable buying or selling the breakout of these patterns; that is, they wait for the market to show that it is resum-

FIGURE 3.9 Rounded Bottom

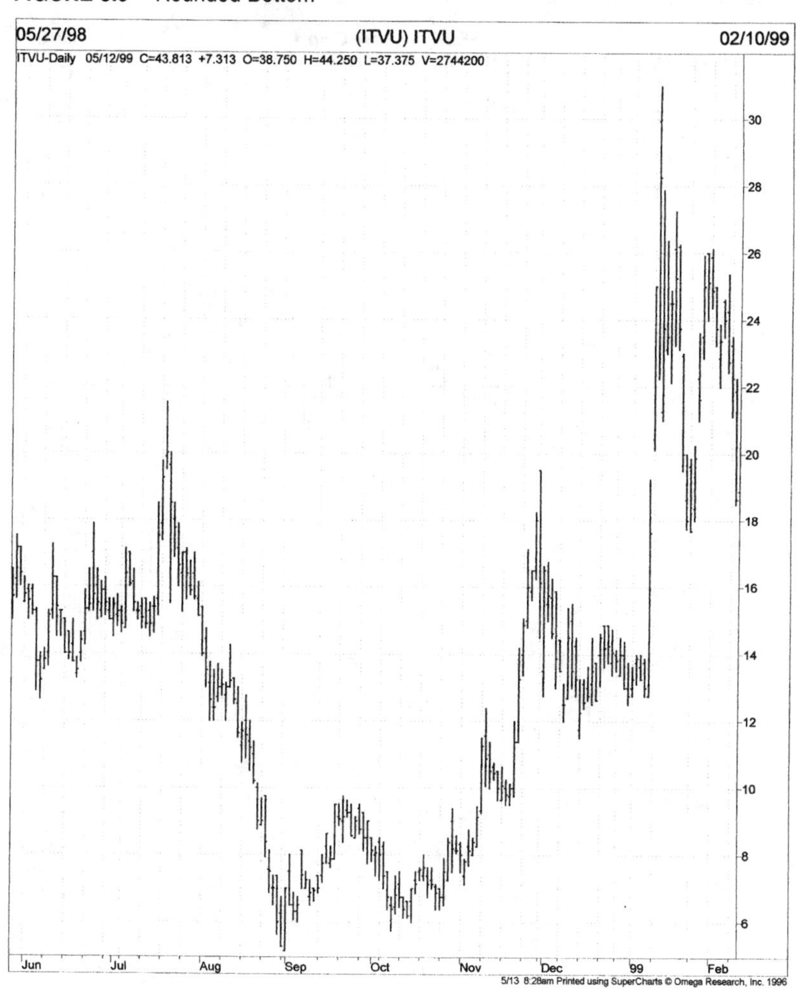

ing the trend and then buy or sell into that trend. This strategy can be very successful when the market is in a strong trend, as the probabilities are high that a breakout of a continuation pattern will be successful.

Risk can be defined with this strategy in several ways, and many traders feel most confident when a market moves out of

FIGURE 3.10 Spike Top

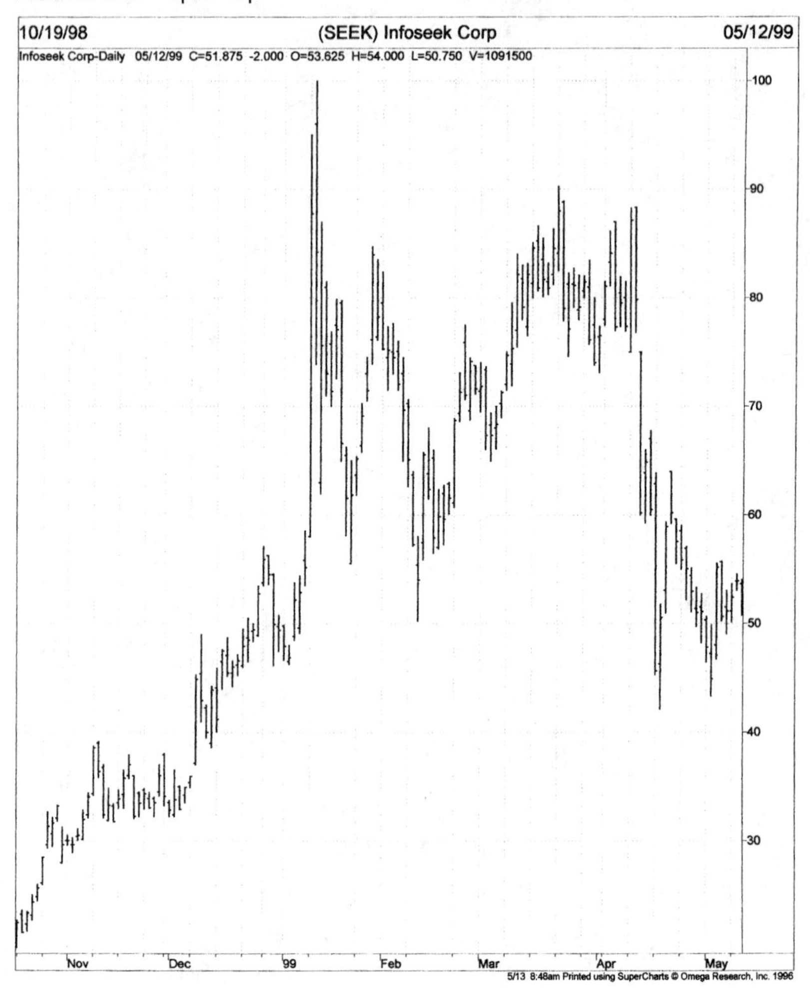

these patterns. The point to remember is your personal market strategy and psychological skills of enhanced belief and confidence are what enable personal involvement in the market at these times.

FIGURE 3.11 Triangle Continuation Patterns

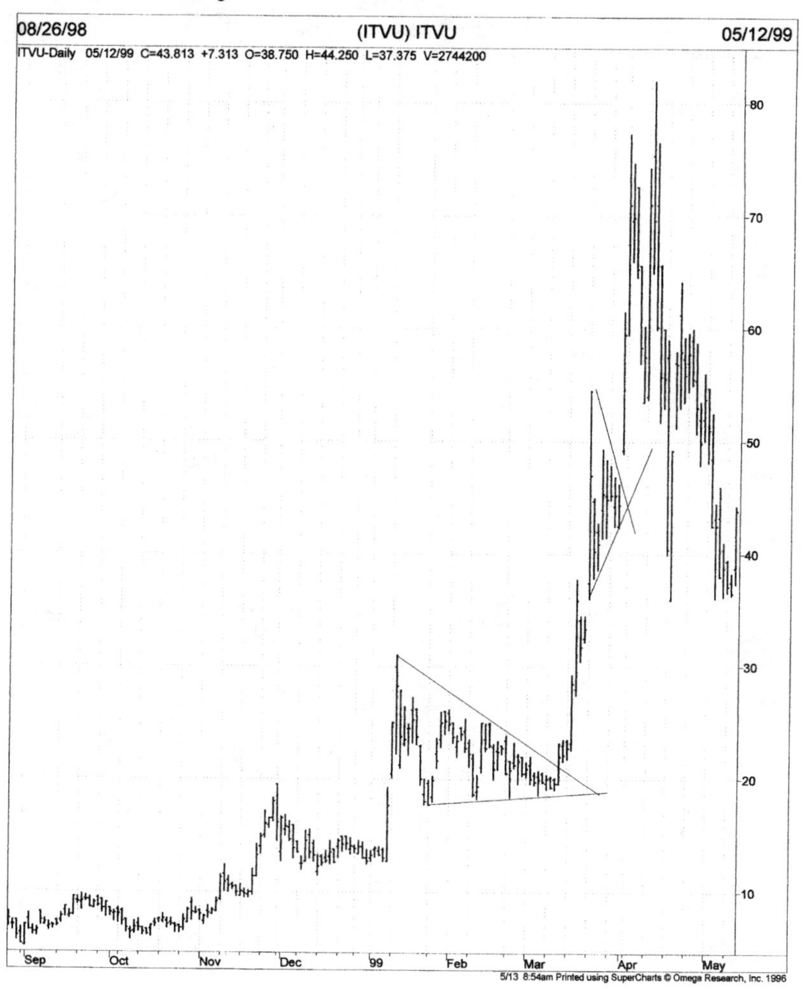

MONEY MANAGEMENT

This discussion on creating strategies for the various technical patterns would not be complete if we did not include the most important element of all: money management. No strat-

FIGURE 3.12 Flags and Triangles

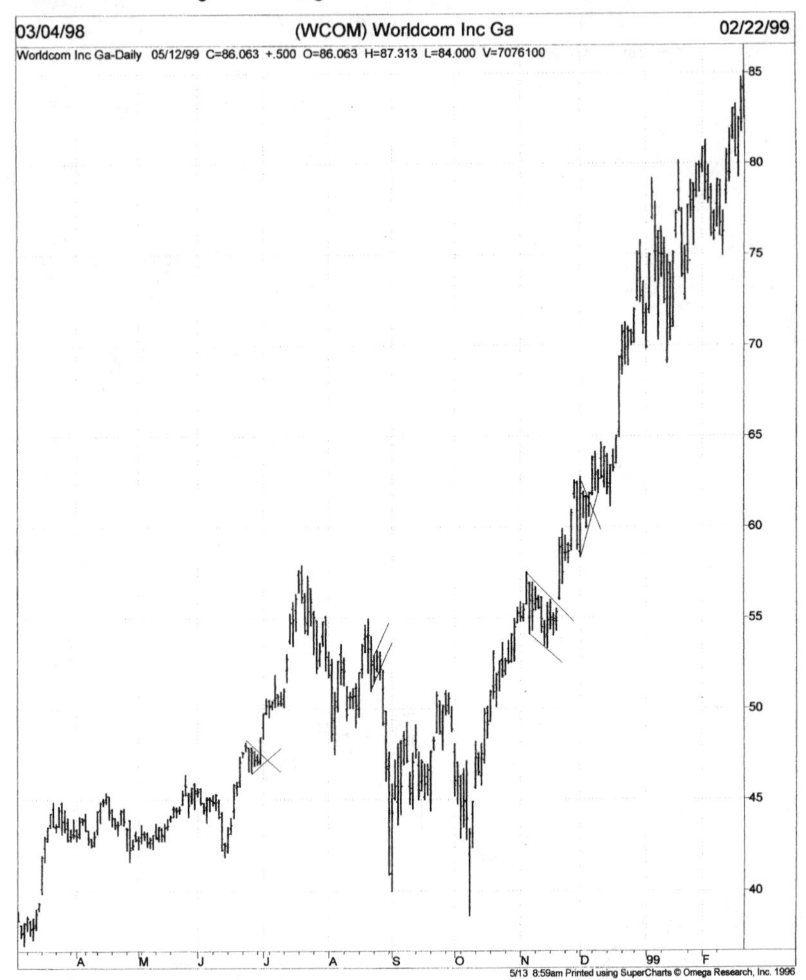

egy will be successful over time without proper money and risk management. Traders accept that they cannot be successful 100 percent of the time if they make a series of trades. The top traders know that they will be successful 40 to 50 percent of the time and include the concept of small losses and larger profits to net them significant results. If there is one common thread among the most successful traders, it is the discipline of taking small losses and managing the trading equity.

> "Two hemispheres of the brain are better—and more profitable than one."
>
> —Bennett W. Goodspeed, *The Tao Jones Averages*

In Bernard Baruch's autobiography, *Baruch: My Own Story,* the legendary entrepreneur offers ten rules for successful speculation:

1. Don't speculate unless you do it full-time.
2. Resist so-called inside information or tips.
3. Before purchasing a security, know everything you can about a company: its earnings and its capacity for growth.
4. Never attempt to buy a bottom or sell a top of a market: "This is a feat only achieved by liars."
5. Take your losses swiftly and clearly. The first loss is your easiest loss.
6. Don't buy too many securities. Focus on a few investments that can be monitored carefully.
7. Periodically reappraise all your investments to make sure they are appropriate to your particular strategy.
8. Know when you can sell to your greatest advantage (of course, this also applies to buying).
9. Never invest all your funds. Keep some liquid.
10. Don't try to be a "jack of all investments." Stick to the field you know best.

Baruch, who was a lifelong skeptic of both giving and taking advice, qualified his rules of sound speculation with the following caveat: "Being so skeptical about the usefulness of advice, I have been reluctant to lay down any rules or guidelines on how to invest or speculate wisely. Still, there are a number of things I have learned from my own experience that might be worth listing for those who are able to muster the necessary self-discipline."

Now let's look at some of the factors that may prevent you from getting the results you want in the market.

4

OVERCOMING THE PSYCHOLOGICAL BARRIERS THAT HOLD INVESTORS BACK

You might be wondering at this point why we put so much emphasis on individual psychology. Why not just get right to sector analysis? Our answer to that is that we have interviewed and trained literally hundreds of traders and investors and understand just how critical this aspect of trading and investing is. Once you have the proper attitudes and beliefs in place, strategy and technique follow naturally. Being a market savvy investor is not only knowing the market you are involved in but fully appreciating and responding to its effect on you.

PSYCHOLOGICAL BARRIERS TO SUCCESSFUL TRADING AND INVESTING

There are specific psychological barriers that need to be addressed when trading and investing. The following box list identifies the essential psychological barriers to trading and investing.

THE ESSENTIAL PSYCHOLOGICAL BARRIERS TO SUCCESSFUL TRADING AND INVESTING

- Not defining a loss
- Not taking a loss or a profit
- Getting locked into a belief
- Trading on "inside" information or taking a tip
- Kamikaze trading
- Euphoric trading
- Hesitating at your numbers
- Not catching a breakout
- Not focusing on opportunities
- Being more invested in being right than in making money
- Trying to be perfect
- Not consistently applying your trading system
- Not having a well-defined money management system
- Not being in the right state of mind

Not Defining a Loss

No one enters a trade or investment expecting to lose! No one buys thinking the market will break, and conversely, no one sells assuming the market is about to rally to new highs. But to paraphrase a famous saying: Things happen! It is essential for you to identify without qualification your loss point before, not after, entering the trade. When you get *stopped out* (a term used to describe liquidation of a position based on the execution of a stop order, an order placed to buy or sell at a specific price level), "just pick yourself up, dust yourself off, and start all over again."

"'Look both ways before you cross the street!' I've heard it a million times, but you know what? I almost got hit by a car as I was walking across the street, talking on the cellphone with a trader upstairs, and didn't notice the light had changed. A car came off the ramp, honked his horn, and missed me by about two feet. It scared the hell out of me! My four-year-old nephew said, 'Uncle Tony, stop, look, and listen. Right?' It's a cliché! How many traders follow that market truth?"

—Tony Saliba, *Market Wizard*

Not Taking a Loss or a Profit

Each investment should have its own internal logic, based on probability, consistent with your own methodology. When the market has moved to your exit point, either on the upside or downside, you must react automatically, without hesitation; that is to say, you must take the profit or loss. If the market continues to move in your direction once again, based on probability consistent with your technical bias, find a new entry point. Reentry is an essential element in any system. The point here is: When the market gives you profit, we believe it is essential that you take it. It is psychologically important that you walk away from the table with change in your pocket!

Getting Locked into a Belief

It is easy to get locked into this jail cell of personal opinion. The market does not lie, it reveals all to the keen observer. You must not confuse your subjective opinion with the objective action of the market. Remember that the market feels no obligation to gratify *your* opinion! Focus on a single rigorous method that works, all else is just another opinion. Money talks, all else walks!

Trading on "Inside" Information or Taking a Tip

For losers only! By the time you've heard it, it has circulated widely. If you don't enjoy playing the role of salami entering the slicer, don't day trade on someone else's tip. Typically, this information comes from the phone man or trading desks. They will tell you that if the market gets below a certain level, the trader will start buying or selling. If they were so smart, they would be in the ring carding trades not manning the phones! The same goes for CNBC!

Kamikaze Trading

What more can we say! Crashing airplanes is a dead end. If you feel angry, betrayed, in need of revenge, apply to law school! Do not trade, you will crash-land! There is no future in getting angry at the market.

Euphoric Trading

Euphoric trading is the opposite of kamikaze trading. You're feeling invincible, heroic, bulletproof. Your lottery ticket is a sure thing. As soon as you lose your objectivity, bullets start piercing flesh!

Hesitating at Your Numbers

You do not have the luxury to hesitate once you have identified a market opportunity. It is both financially and psychologically debilitating not to pick up the ball and run. The discipline always must be: Take the trades or investments that are consistent with your methodology no matter what! If you get stopped out, welcome to the real world of investing. Remember that you can't score touchdowns without the ball.

Not Catching a Breakout

Another form of hesitation, it is like going to the airport and watching planes take off. Wouldn't it be fun just once to get on board and arrive at an exciting destination?

Not Focusing on Opportunities

There are many constant and consistent distractions in the market. So much of investing is just having the ability to get beyond the noise, the talk, and the smoke! Consistency to your approach with a high degree of confidence and optimism will keep your focus clear. You must find a way to get beyond all the false opportunities!

Being More Invested in Being Right Than in Making Money

Is it your goal to be an analyst or an investor? You must know the answer to that question. If your technical analysis is turning you into a Ph.D. in the S&P, join a university faculty, you'll save money! Trading and investing are not about scholarship. They are about making money. That is not to say money should be the sole object of all efforts; we believe it shouldn't. But this is one game where the scorecard is denominated in hard currency. It is not enough to point to the fact that you predicted the high or low of a market!

"**I** know it may sound strange to many readers, but there is an inverse relationship between analysis and trading results. More analysis or being able to make more distinctions in the market's behavior will not produce better trading results. There are many traders who find themselves caught in this exasperating loop, thinking that more or better analysis is

> going to give them the confidence they need to do what needs to be done to achieve success. It's what I call a trading paradox that most traders find difficult if not impossible to reconcile, until they realize you can't use analysis to overcome your fear of being wrong or losing money. It just doesn't work!"
>
> —Mark Douglas, *The Disciplined Trader*

Trying to Be Perfect

You don't have to be perfect, merely excellent! Excellence produces results, perfection produces ulcers!

Not Consistently Applying Your Trading System

It is there for one purpose only: To be used so you can garner profits, letting them pile up like pleasing snowdrifts!

Not Having a Well-Defined Money Management System

There are literally hundreds of books written on this subject. You don't have to read them! For investment purposes, your position should give you a minimum 2:1 risk to reward ratio. In general, we will not take trades with less than a 3:1 return.

Not Being in the Right State of Mind

Funny, but it comes down to this. In our experience, over 90 percent of all trading and investing failure is the result of not being in the right state of mind. The right state of mind produces the right results!

CRITICAL FACTORS IN BECOMING A MARKET SAVVY INVESTOR

Investor Response	Having the Investor's Edge	Losing the Investor's Edge
Patience	You wait for opportunities to materialize based on a well-thought-out game plan.	You do little planning and react according to personal whim.
Discipline	You see the big picture and respond deliberately.	You are emotional, anxious, and often confused about what to do.
Strategy	You have a highly planned strategy that limits losses and lets profits run.	You do little planning and do not rely on a consistent methodology
Expertise	You are well prepared. You've done the necessary homework.	You have little market knowledge and are unprepared.
Motive	Your motives are long term.	Your goal is instant gratification.
Goals	You have clearly defined goals.	Your goals are ill defined.
Risk control	You have a highly controlled risk/reward ratio.	You have little or no control over the risk/reward ratio.
State of mind	You are positive, resourceful, and embrace empowering beliefs and focus. You have a high level of self-esteem and trust and are relaxed and confident.	You are nervous and anxious and believe the worst will happen. Your focus is distracted. You trade in conflict.

> "It is our belief that continually elevating your state of mind by focusing on internal and external phenomena that allow you to stay resourceful and true to your trading strategy is the answer. We have demonstrated how to do this through processing positive beliefs and thoughts and by directing your physiology. When a negative thought comes into consciousness and begins to distract your focus don't fight it. Acknowledge its existence and go forward."
>
> —Robert Koppel and Howard Abell, *The Innergame of Trading*

Successful investing, in essence, comes down to this: Formulate a trading plan that works, overcome your personal psychological barriers, and condition yourself to produce feelings of self-trust, high self-esteem, and unshakeable conviction and confidence. Doing this naturally leads to good judgment and winning market positions with a proven methodology, based on probability.

PART TWO

MARKET SECTOR ANALYSIS

5

MARKET ANALYSIS

"Some investors have trouble making decisions to buy or sell. In other words, they vacillate and can't make up their minds. They are unsure because they really don't know what they are doing. They do not have a plan, a set of principles, or rules to guide them and, therefore, are uncertain of what they should be doing."

—William J. O'Neil, *How to Make Money in Stocks*

Successful market analysis cannot be accomplished by focusing a single lens on the market. Much has been written about analyzing markets by studying the discrete fundamental factors of each market, placing those factors in the context of a macro economic view of scenarios and conditions in order to form a determination of "true" market value. At the same time, much has been written about the application of technical analysis; that is, using market data such as price, volume, time, and patterns to generate trading decisions. There are also those traders who rely on internal or subjective data of the "gut" variety or act out of a sixth market sense—namely, intuition; that is, judgments based on well-defined or ill-defined personal feelings about markets. These traders are often reacting to much of the same formal information that others are using, only they are not quantifying and labeling specific component factors as such.

After interviewing hundreds of consistently profitable traders and investors, it is clear to us that successful market analysis results from combining technical indicators and methods with knowledge of the fundamental factors that ultimately underlie all significant market behavior. Of course, included in this observation is the investor's awareness and consistent application of calculated and well-circumscribed risk management.

FUNDAMENTAL ANALYSIS

For the sake of our discussion, it might be useful to define the fundamentals of a market as those factors that influence the price at any point in time. Unfortunately, the idea that one can fully know all the fundamental factors that impart changes in market price is erroneous. There is an old joke about two gold market analysts who knew everything there was to know about the gold market. Each was fully aware of production costs, yields, and earnings, but one of them was always long and the other was always short! This anecdote is played out in real market time every day in the real world.

Even with the sophisticated information gathering ability we now possess in the form of the computer and the Internet, the amount of facts and statistics available in any one market is too difficult to analyze on its own in order to arrive at a successful analytical result by considering fundamental factors alone.

In the following sections, we will outline the general information necessary for someone to become sufficiently acquainted with the important elements of each asset class to be able to make an informed judgment based on fundamental information. That judgment about the underlying conditions of a market, along with its technical analytical characteristics, offers you the ultimate edge that makes the difference in achieving a profitable result in the market.

EQUITIES

In the United States, equities mean the stock market. There are over 9,000 listed securities on the New York Stock Exchange, the American Stock Exchange, and the Nasdaq market. You can choose one stock, put together a portfolio of stocks, or place your money with a professional money manager in the form of mutual funds. Investing in securities has never been easier or cheaper. Online trading even allows you total access on a timely basis to most of the securities traded in the United States. Online trading should not be confused with electronic day trading, which we will cover in a later section. Online trading refers to the ability to send your buy and sell orders on the Internet directly.

Long-term investing in equities has been very successful for the patient investor. The stock market has had a steady return on equity of close to an average 10 percent per year. In 1982, the U.S. stock market began a bull market that has taken the Dow Jones Industrial Average of 30 stocks from under 800 points to over 11,000 points 17 years later. A similar move is also represented by the Standard and Poor's 500 Stock Index, which consists of some of the largest capitalized companies in the United States (see Figure 5.1). This has been one of the longest bull markets in history.

Economic conditions, inflation expectation, interest rates, government policies, and the productivity of workers, in general, guide the stock market movement. Individual companies must be viewed in the general context and then individually analyzed on the basis of specific market criteria.

Fundamentals Affecting Stock Prices

William J. O'Neil, in his book *How to Make Money in Stocks* (McGraw-Hill, 1995), says this about stock selection: "You can

FIGURE 5.1 Standard and Poor's 500 Index

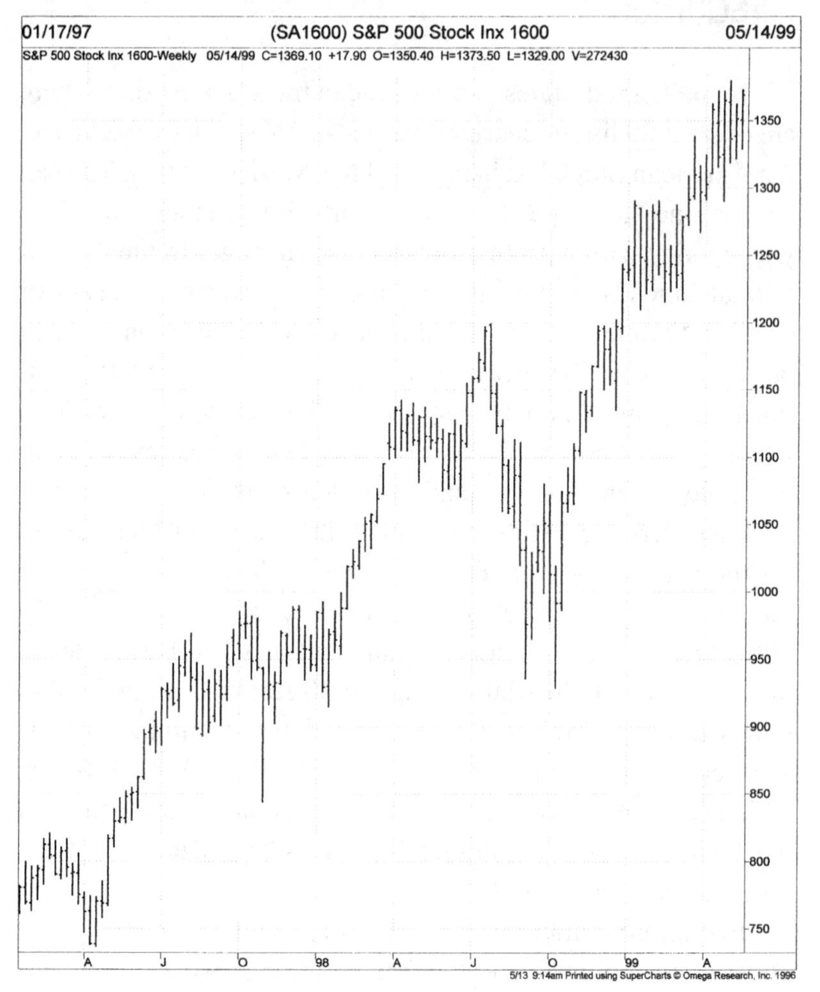

learn how to pick winners in the stock market, and you can become part owner in the best companies in the world." The formula he offers is a simple one based on the following criteria:

C = Current quarterly earnings per share: How much is enough?

A = Annual earnings increases: Look for meaningful growth.
N = New products, new management, new highs: Buying at the right time.
S = Supply and demand: Small capitalization plus volume demand.
L = Leader or laggard: Which is your stock?
I = Institutional sponsorship: A little goes a long way.
M = Market direction: How to determine it.

The message here is that successful fundamentals in stock picking are focused on earnings growth, product development, and good management. All of this information is readily available through any broker, the Internet, information services, or the library.

INTEREST RATES

The interest rate market is structured according to the maturity or length of time of the instrument traded. There is a 30-year bond (long term), a 10-year and 5-year note (intermediate term), and T-bills and Eurodollars (short term). Chart examples of the 30-year bond future and the Eurodollars are shown in Figures 5.2 and 5.3. The markets move inversely to the value of interest rates; that is, if interest rates are moving down, the bonds and notes will be rallying.

An important concept in interest rates is the yield curve. The yield curve is the relationship between the interest rate and the maturity of each of the instruments. In the normal course of events, the longer the maturity, the higher the rate of interest. However, there are times when short-term rates are higher than long-term rates; this is known as an inverted yield curve.

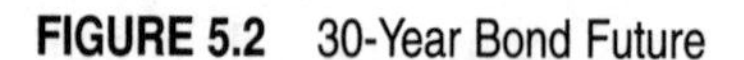

FIGURE 5.2 30-Year Bond Future

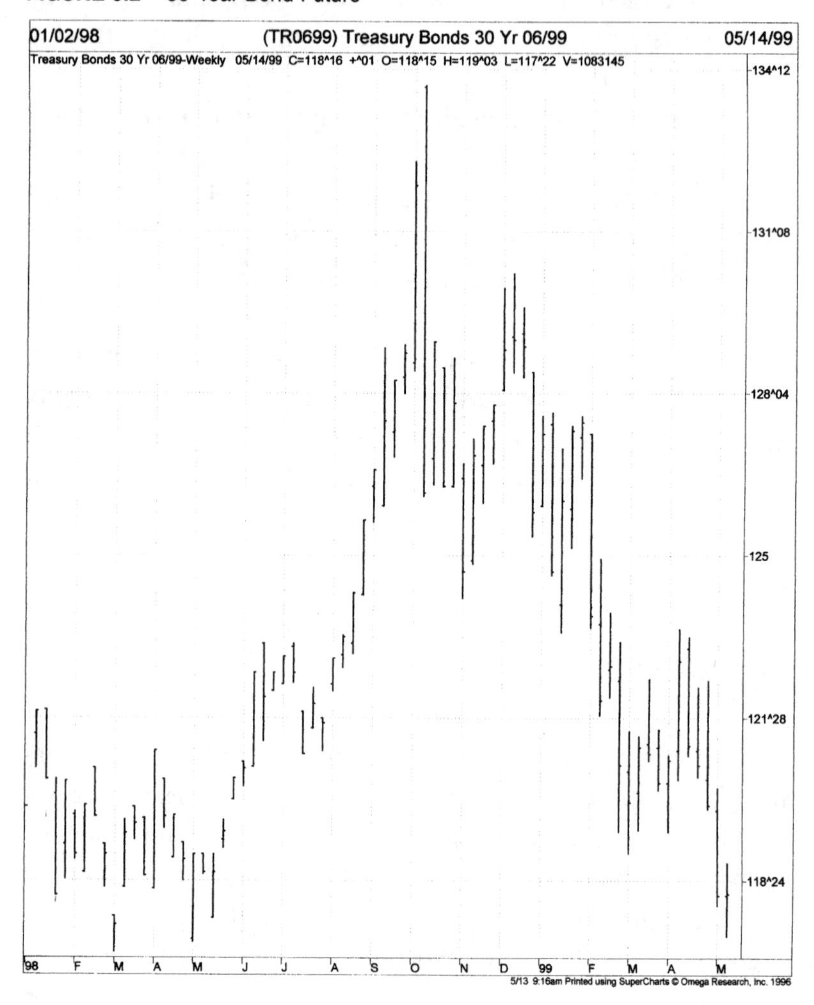

One of the most important indicators of interest rate movement is the Board of Governors of the Federal Reserve System (the Fed). The Fed is responsible for conducting monetary policy and in so doing can cause interest rates to rise or fall. In a general way, this is accomplished by tightening or loosening

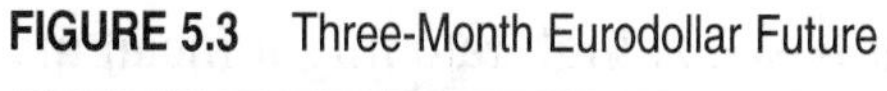

FIGURE 5.3 Three-Month Eurodollar Future

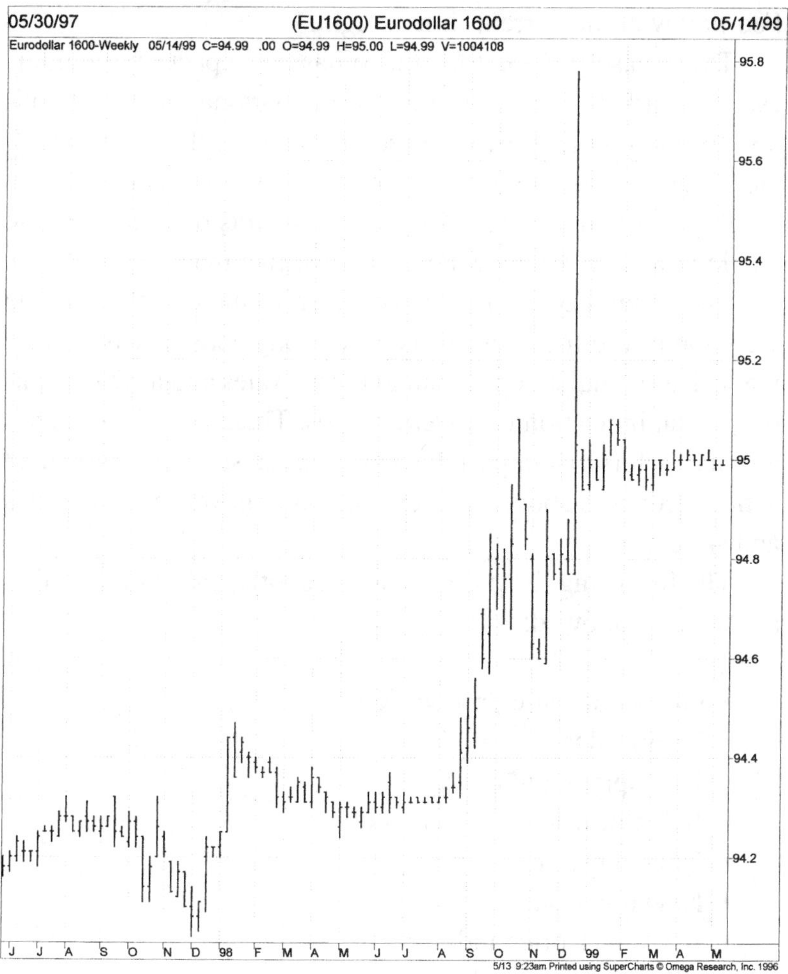

the money supply. Fed watching is a much-publicized sport, and you should have little trouble finding information pertaining to the Fed's actions.

Among the more technical indicators to watch is the Fed funds rate. This is the rate at which commercial banks lend to one another on an overnight basis. A high rate might mean the Fed policy at the current time is tight.

The Treasury Department also has an impact on the interest rate market. In order to finance the national debt, or to adjust for the normal operating requirements of the government, the Treasury will conduct auctions at various maturity levels ranging from 90 days to 30 years. The results of these periodic auctions will affect the general interest rate markets as well.

The general economic outlook also influences the way we view the future for interest rates. A strong economy is usually viewed as an indication of rising interest rates and a weak economy as an indication of lowering rates. There are of course additional factors that impact the bond market, such as specific Fed actions, concern about inflation, and other government policies and statements.

The following list presents other reports and indicators that are widely followed:

- Gross domestic product (GDP)
- Retail sales
- Unemployment rate
- Index of leading indicators
- Housing starts
- New home sales
- Consumer price index
- Producer price index
- GDP deflator
- Automobile sales
- Durable good orders
- Construction spending

FOREIGN EXCHANGE

Currency trading has existed as long as there has been more than one currency in the world. The major currencies being traded at the present time are the U.S. dollar, the Japanese yen (Figure 5.4), the British pound (Figure 5.5), the Canadian dollar (Fig-

FIGURE 5.4 Japanese Yen

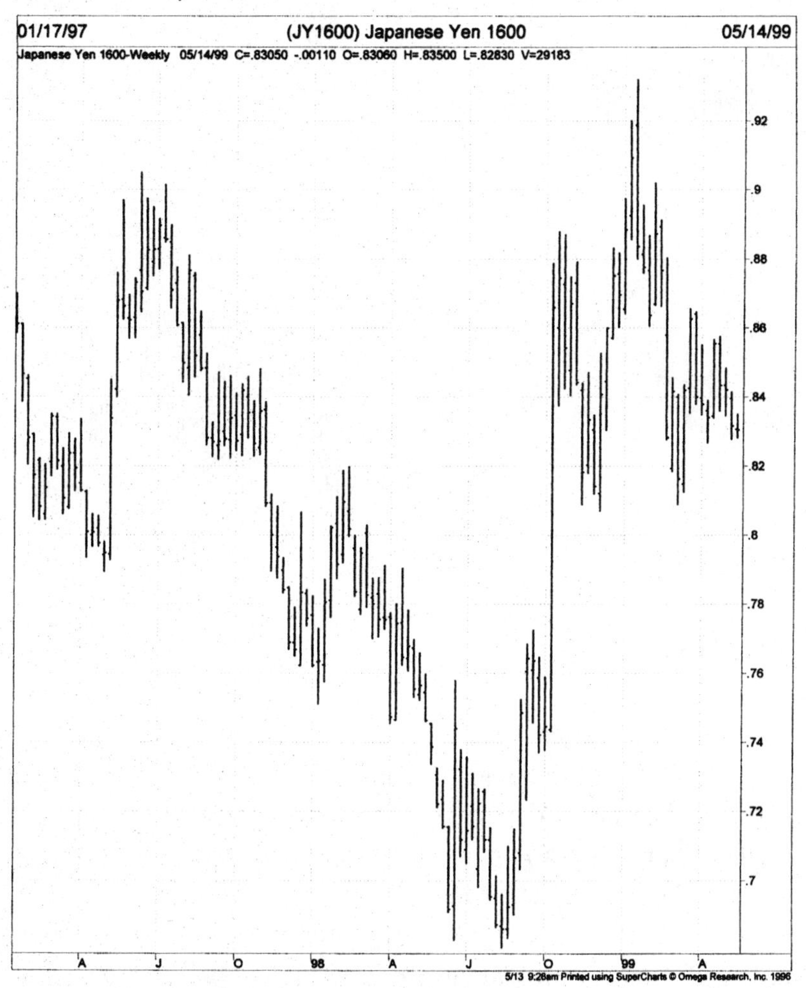

FIGURE 5.5 British Pound

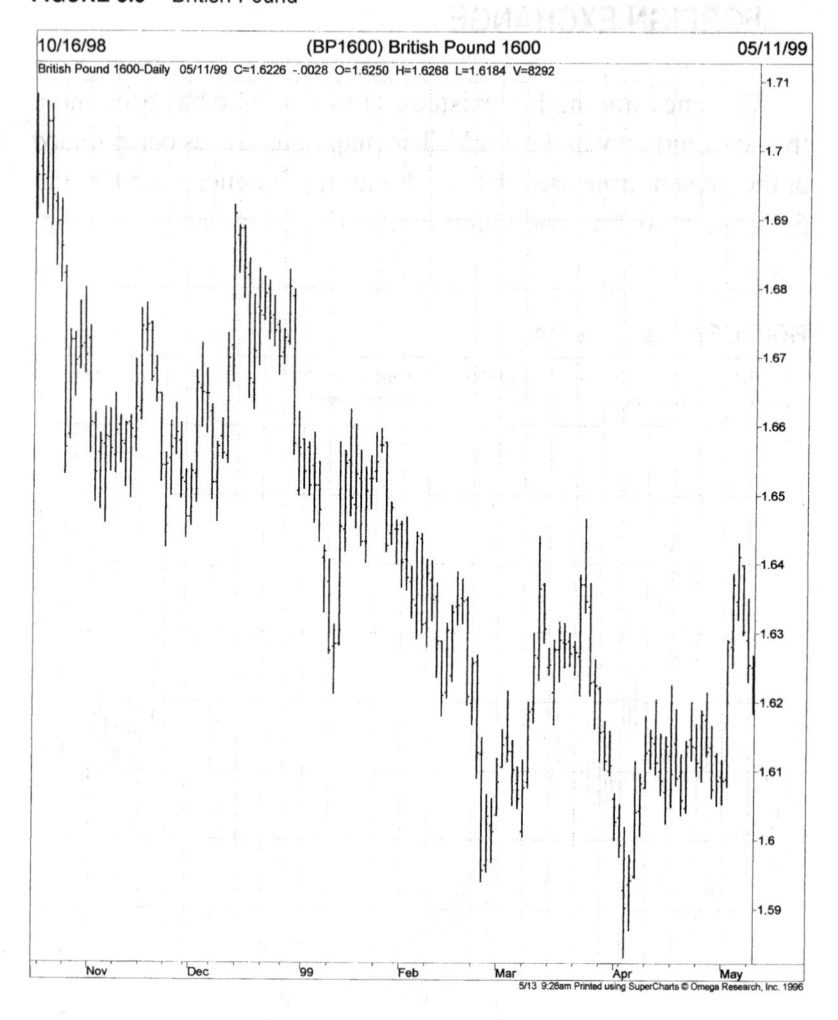

ure 5.6), the Mexican peso (Figure 5.7), the Swiss franc (Figure 5.8), and the European currency unit (Figure 5.9), which has replaced the deutsche mark (D-mark) in 1999. Access to the foreign exchange (forex) markets is through the interbank or on the International Monetary Market (IMM), a division of the Chicago Mercantile Exchange. Trading through the interbank market is the network of banks and financial institutions around the world

FIGURE 5.6 Canadian Dollar

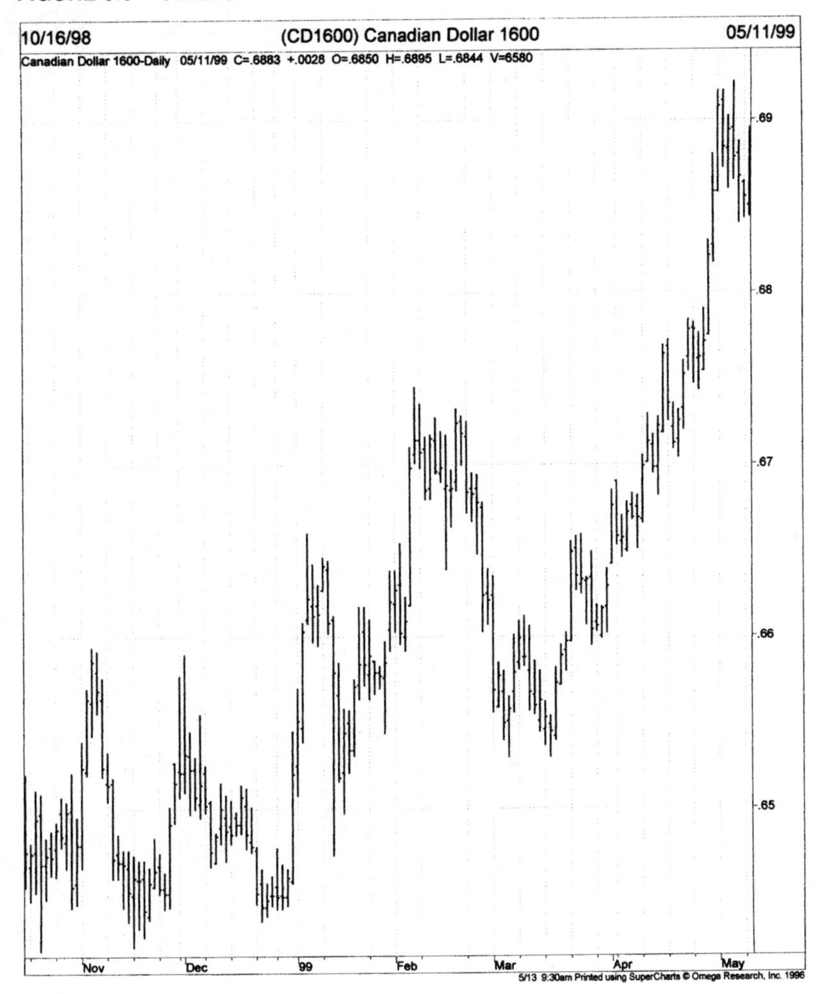

and requires a large amount of capital and a solid credit rating. The IMM trades the most active currencies in the world, which include the yen, the D-mark, the Mexican peso, Canadian and Australian dollars, the European currency unit, the British pound, and the Swiss franc. Of course, all of these currencies are traded in terms of U.S. dollars, and therefore the investor is buying or selling these currencies against the current dollar rate.

FIGURE 5.7 Mexican Peso

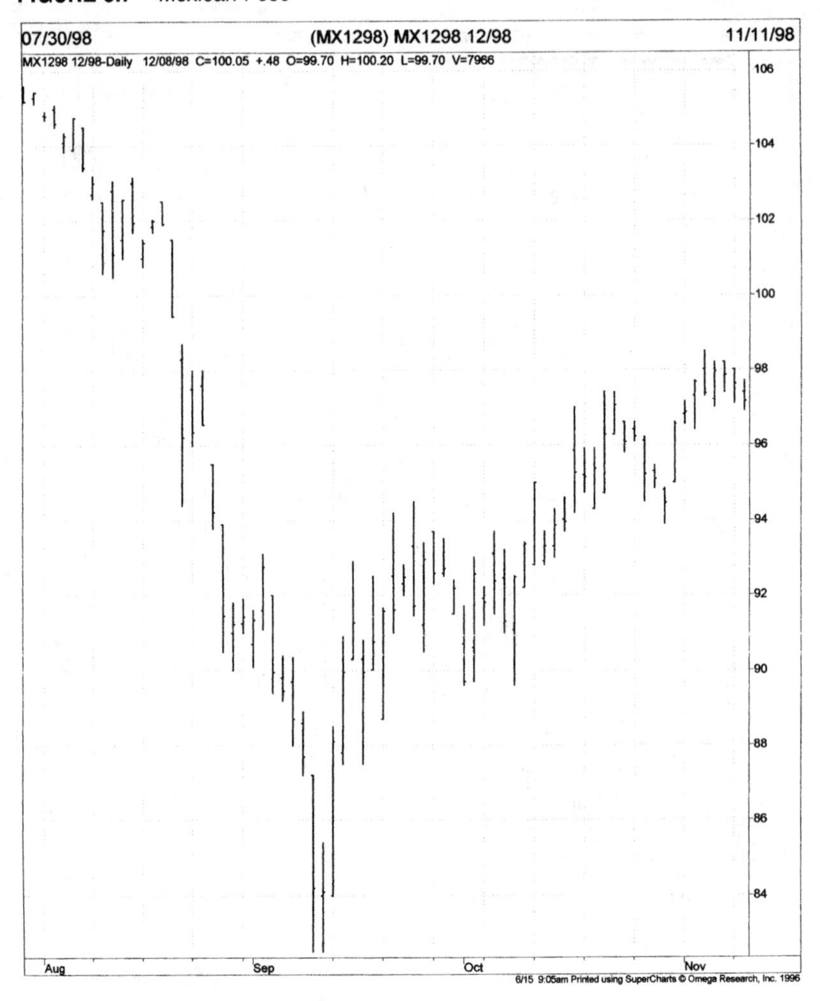

Fundamental Factors That Affect Exchange Rates

Balance of Payments

Balance of payments measures the amount of money that flows between two countries. These payments are generated by the sale of goods and services, investments, government pur-

FIGURE 5.8 Swiss Franc

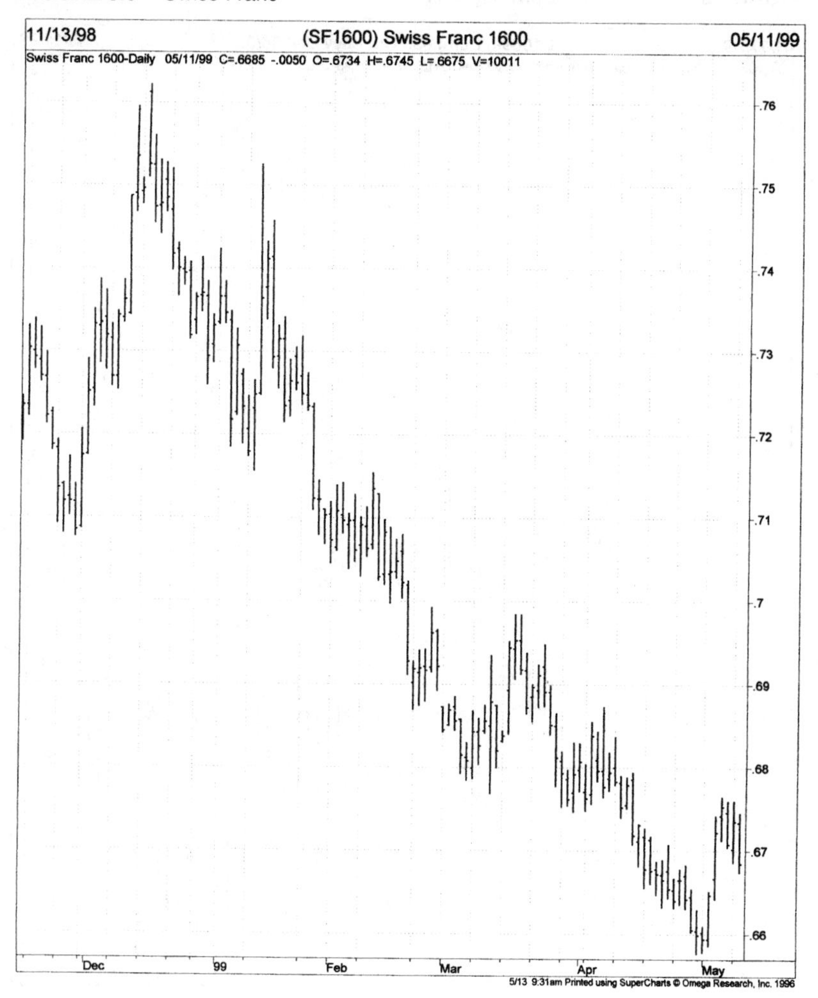

chases, and other claims and liabilities. A surplus of payment between the United States and another country tends to make the dollar stronger, and a deficit of the balance of payments would tend to make the dollar weaker. As in any other commodity, this is caused by more or less dollars being available as a result of the imbalance.

FIGURE 5.9 European Currency Unit

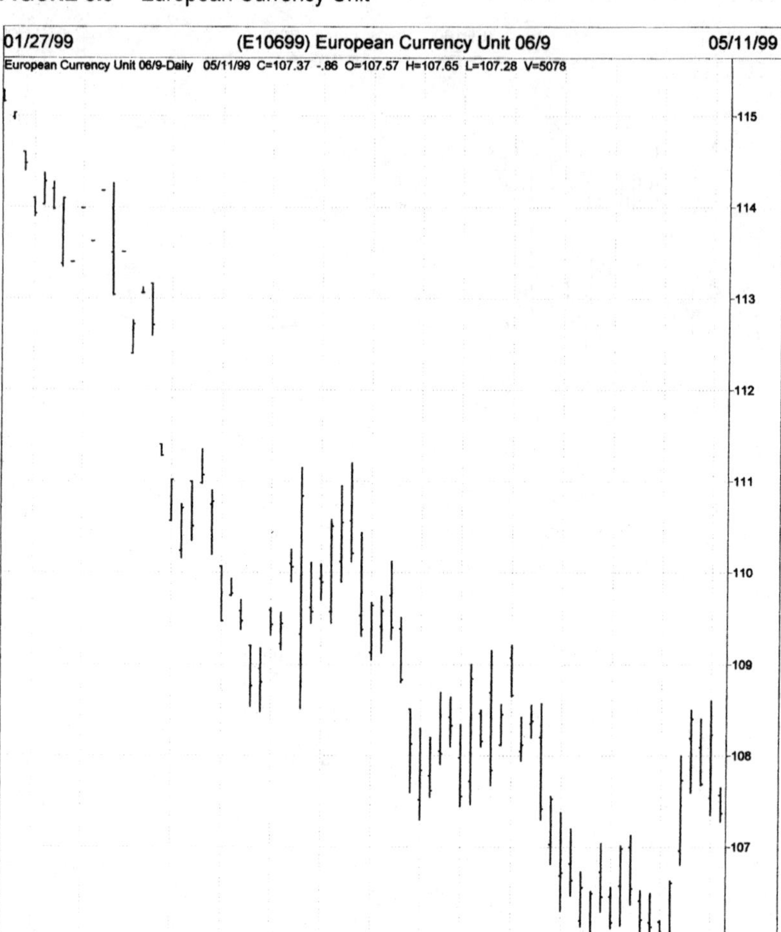

Interest Rates

If the interest rate in one country is greater than in another, then the currency of the country with the higher rate tends to be stronger. Arbitrageurs will constantly conduct transactions between the currency and debt markets in order to take advantage of the differences (spread differential) in the rate structure of each country. Although this is a highly specialized part of the foreign exchange world, it is important for you to be aware of the relationships that exist, if only in a general way.

Economic Considerations

The relative strengths and weaknesses of a country's economy can affect the value of each currency in relation to another. You must be wary of any conclusions you draw, because a strong or weak economy may have different results on a currency, depending on other economic or political factors at the time. If the U.S. economy is strong, but at the same time inflation is high or perceived to be out of control, the dollar may be weak. However, if the economy is strong, it may lead to higher interest rates that can make the dollar stronger. The point here is: There is no simple equation that you can use at all times based on fundamental analysis alone.

Politics

Political instability, elections, civil strife, and rightwing or leftwing extremist governments all impact the currency of a country. Political uncertainty is one of the driving forces in the movement of a currency.

Inflation

As with other economic considerations, inflation may have a wide range of effects on a country's currency. Inflation in the United States may make U.S. goods more expensive relative to another country's goods, which will decrease exports and increase imports and create a balance of payment deficit. However, sometimes inflation may be seen as leading to higher interest rates and can help strengthen the currency.

Psychology of Markets

Another major factor in the movement of world currencies is the impact of how the above factors and additional fundamental facts (generally known and unknown) might come into play. We have seen that most of these factors will affect the movement of currencies, but the direction of that movement will depend on the psychology of the marketplace; that is, what the overriding present attitudes foretell about the country's currency outlook for the future.

AGRICULTURAL MARKETS

Most interest in the domestic agricultural market is divided between the grain and livestock markets, which are traded respectively at the Chicago Board of Trade and the Chicago Mercantile Exchange. Other foodstuffs traded in New York include coffee, cocoa, and sugar.

Grains

The grain sector is generally broken up into three categories: the soybean complex, corn, and wheat.

The Soybean Complex

Soybeans, soybean meal, and soybean oil make up the soybean complex. Soybeans, which are not a grain but an oilseed, are grown largely to process into two by-products: oil and meal. Crushing the soybean produces these by-products. Soybeans futures and products are traded on the Chicago Board of Trade (see Figure 5.10).

Soybeans are a major cash crop in the United States and account for well over 50 percent of the world's production. Other major producers are Brazil, China, and Argentina. The worldwide use and implications of soybeans make this a market of international importance.

FIGURE 5.10 Soybean Futures

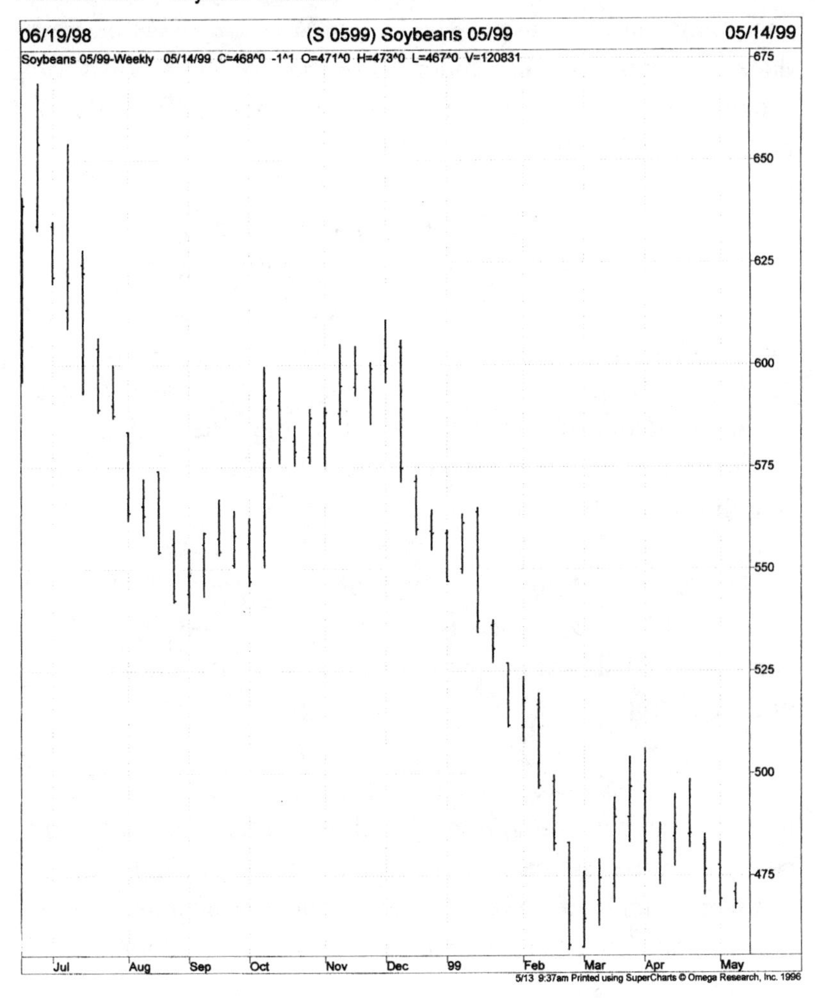

Soybean meal. Soybean meal is a major protein source for the poultry and livestock industry. The meal is exported from the United States, Brazil, and Argentina and imported into the European Economic Community, Japan, and other areas of the world. The bulk of the U.S. production is used in the domestic livestock industry.

Soybean oil. Soybean oil is used in salad and cooking oil, shortening, and margarine. The United States, as the largest producer, accounts for just under 50 percent of the world's total production. About 20 percent of the oil produced finds its way onto world markets.

Fundamental factors affecting soybean meal prices. The size of the animal population that consumes the high-protein feed as well as the price of competing feed sources are two of the major elements in determining price. The level of stocks available and estimates about future planting of soybean acreage are also factors to consider. Recently, the extent of international demand or lack of such demand has played an important role in driving the market.

Fundamental factors affecting soybean oil prices. The price of oil will be determined by such things as the price of the competing oil substitutes; butter, cottonseed oil, lard, and palm oil, for example.

Fundamental factors affecting soybeans. Of course, the demand for soybean oil and meal will have a huge effect on soybeans. However, soybean prices also are affected by the domestic and world supply of soybeans. Stocks available, planting acreage, growing weather, and even political events in other growing countries affect this supply.

Soybeans are planted in the spring in the United States and harvested in the fall. Soybean prices tend to reflect this basic fact and are usually at low ebb during harvest time. As the supply is used through the year, especially during the winter months, prices tend to rise. Other seasonal factors come from the fact that Brazil and Argentina, the next largest exporters, are growing their beans during our winter months.

Corn

Corn is used primarily as feed for livestock and is a leading cash crop in the United States. Although corn is grown around the world in China, Brazil, Russia, and central Europe, the United States is the largest producer. Corn is used mainly for beef and dairy cattle, hogs, poultry, and sheep. It also is processed into starch and used in breakfast cereal and as a sweetener. Corn is actively traded on the Chicago Board of Trade (see Figure 5.11).

Fundamental factors affecting corn. Because the supply of corn is the single most important factor, the size of planted acreage and the weather are the leading determinants in the price of corn. Recently, the exporting of corn around the world has taken on an increasingly important role. Other factors include the size of the livestock herds in the United States and abroad, the available stocks of corn, and the price of competing feed grains. In the past and possibly in the future, various government support programs that were designed to affect the price of corn also are to be considered. Such programs today are inconsequential, but you must be aware of government programs when they are proposed.

There is a seasonal pattern to corn prices: usually a decline into harvest lows in the fall and then a steady rise in prices into late summer.

Wheat

Wheat is grown and consumed all over the world. The wheat that is traded on the Chicago Board of Trade is soft red winter wheat (no. 2) (see Figure 5.12). However, other varieties of wheat also are deliverable at a premium, discount, or par to the soft red. Wheat also is traded on exchanges in Minneapolis and Kansas City but to a lesser degree. Wheat is either planted in the spring (spring wheat) or in the fall (winter wheat). The winter wheat

FIGURE 5.11 Corn Futures

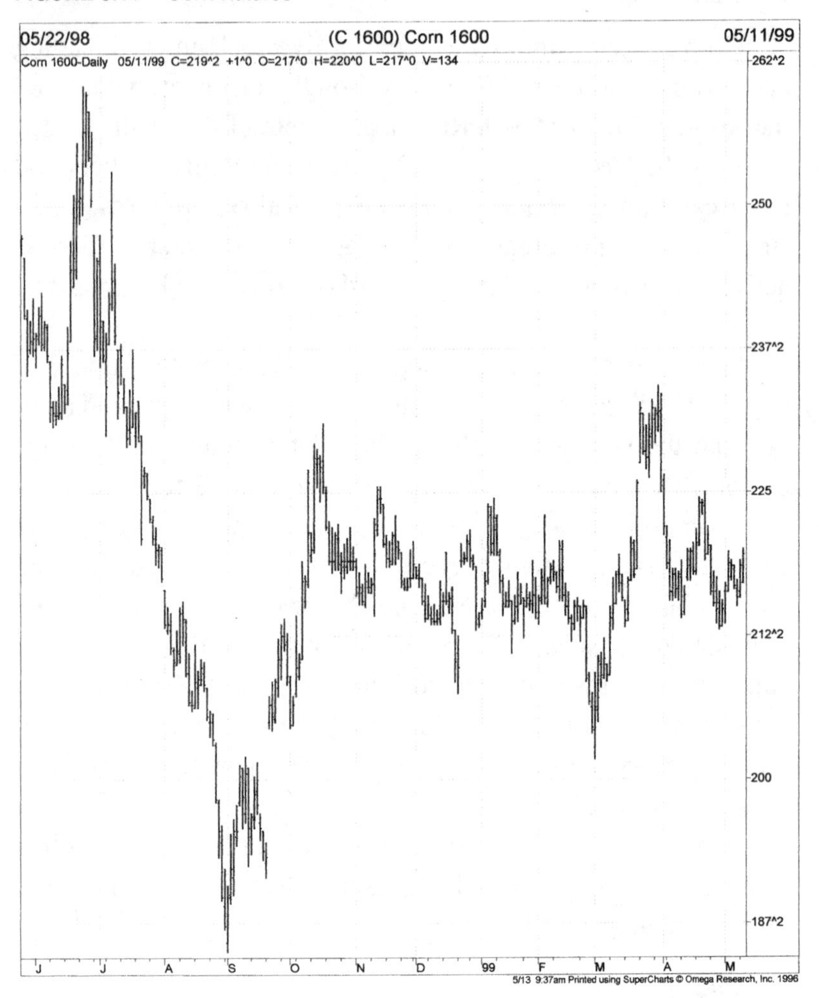

that is planted in the fall lays dormant under snow cover and is harvested between May and July.

Wheat demand comes primarily from exports, which account for up to two-thirds of the wheat production and domestic use. Wheat is milled into flour for making breads, pastas, pastries, and breakfast cereals.

FIGURE 5.12 Wheat Futures

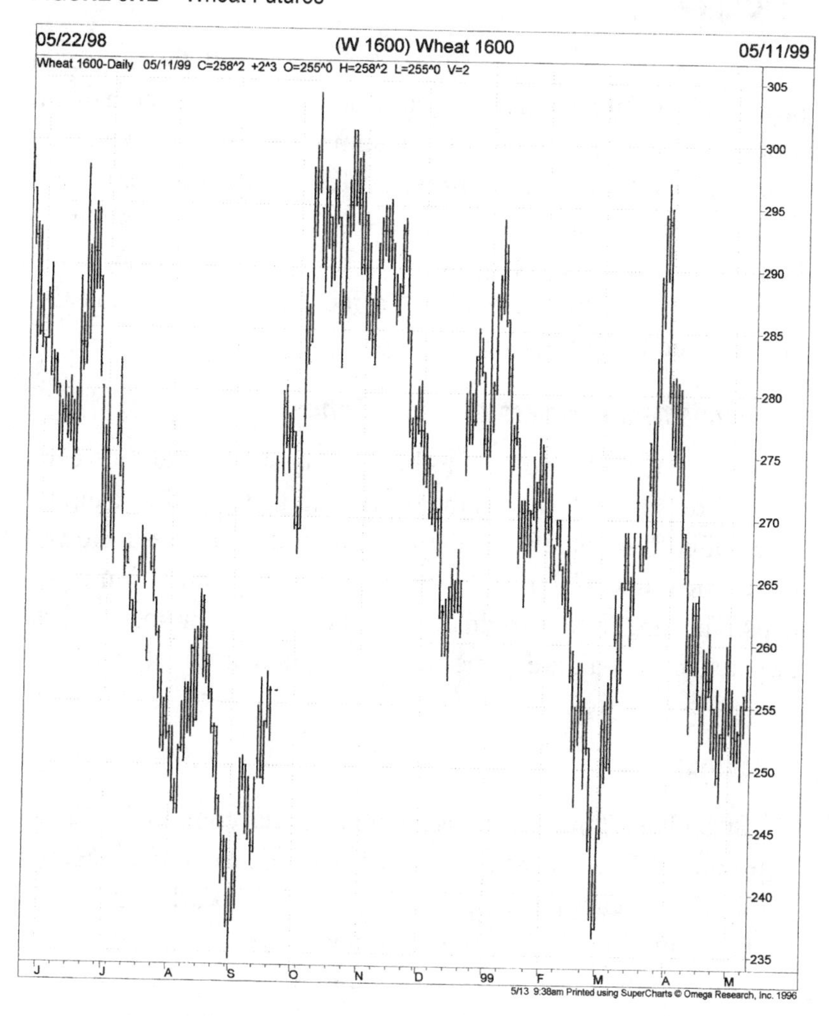

Fundamental factors affecting wheat. Worldwide weather is the dominant factor in determining the price of wheat. The demand for wheat is generally stable and predictable. Therefore, the supply of wheat, which is affected by weather and to some extent by political forces around the world, is very important.

Coffee

Coffee is an internationally traded commodity that is grown principally in the tropical and subtropical areas and consumed around the world. Coffee is the leading nonalcoholic beverage in the United States and Europe. Coffee's popularity can be attributed not only to taste but also to its properties as a stimulant because of its caffeine content. It is traded in London and in New York on the New York Coffee, Sugar, and Cocoa Exchange (see Figure 5.13).

Fundamental Factors Affecting Coffee Prices

The demand for coffee has been fairly stable over the years. Therefore, supply has been the overriding factor in the changing price of coffee. Weather is the most important factor, followed by political uncertainties, labor strife, and transportation problems. The rare blast of frigid air in South America or dock strikes, threatened or real, are some of the factors that affect coffee.

Sugar

Sugar has a long history as an international commodity. Sugar is produced from sugarcane or sugar beets. Sugarcane comes from the tropical and subtropical areas of the world, and sugar beets are produced in more temperate climates.

Most of the sugar produced is sold through long-term contracts. A small percentage of sugar is sold for short-term delivery and at spot market prices. It is this sugar that is traded in London and in New York on the New York Coffee, Sugar, and Cocoa Exchange (see Figure 5.14).

Fundamental Factors Affecting Sugar Prices

Sugar is a luxury item, and its use does reflect world economic conditions, particularly in the underdeveloped world.

FIGURE 5.13 Coffee Futures

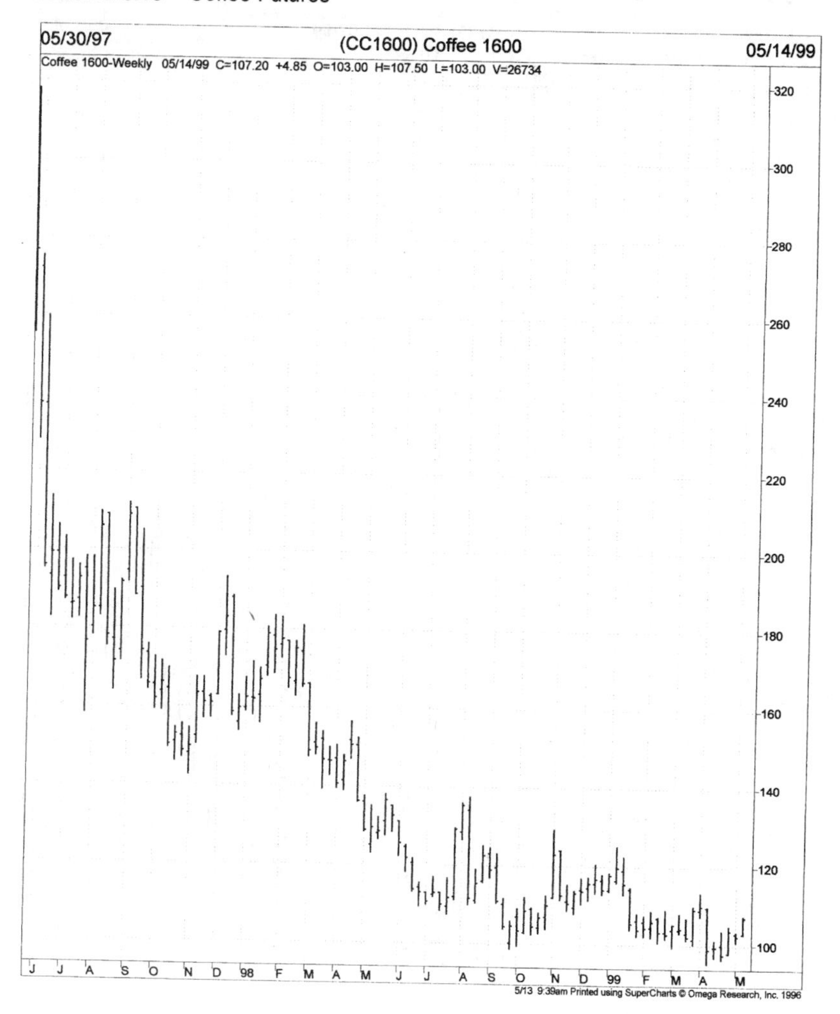

Price and competing products such as artificial sweeteners and other sweetening sources also can impact demand.

Supply is affected by weather, stocks available, political uncertainty, and transportation.

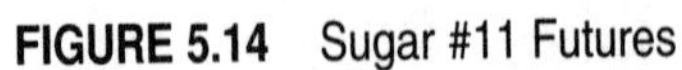

FIGURE 5.14 Sugar #11 Futures

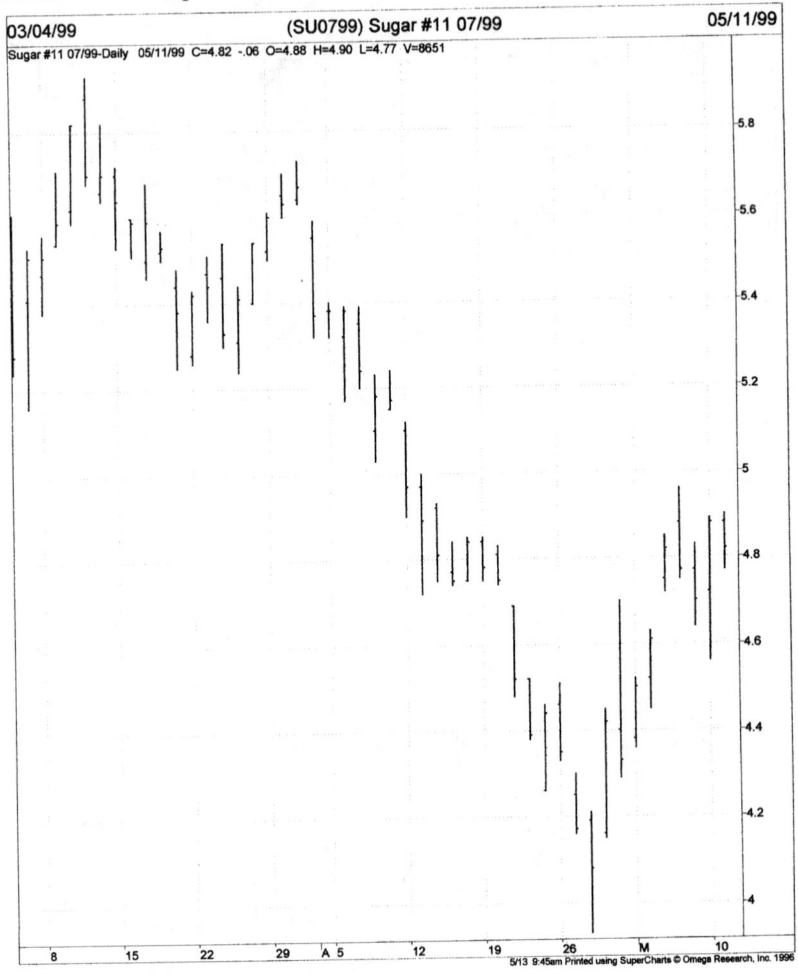

Cocoa

When the Europeans found out they could process the cocoa bean into a butter and add sugar and end up with chocolate, the world was never the same. The cocoa bean is grown in the tropics and subtropics of South America and Africa. It is an internationally traded commodity. It is traded in London and in

New York on the New York Coffee, Sugar, and Cocoa Exchange (see Figure 5.15).

Fundamental Factors Affecting Cocoa Prices

Demand for cocoa is relatively stable, so that supply becomes the issue in the movement of cocoa prices. Weather, political uncertainty, transportation problems, and stocks are all important factors.

FIGURE 5.15 Cocoa Futures

LIVESTOCK

The livestock quadrant is actively traded on the Chicago Mercantile Exchange with interest from producers, commercials, bona fide hedgers, fund managers, and large and small investors.

Live Cattle

Although cattle are raised throughout the world, most of the production is consumed within the same country. The beef industry is the largest agricultural product in the United States. Demand comes from home, restaurant, and institutional use. It is the most heavily traded livestock contract on the Chicago Mercantile Exchange (see Figure 5.16).

Fundamental Factors Affecting Cattle

The cattle cycle is a very long one taking almost three years from the birth of a heifer calf (female) to breeding, gestation, feeding of the offspring, and slaughter. The industry is separated into three areas:

1. The cow-calf ranch that produces calves
2. The feedlot that fattens the calves
3. The packer who slaughters the "fat" cattle and produces the cut beef

Demand for beef has remained relatively stable over the years with shallow dips and steady increases in consumption. Supply disruptions have an important effect and take a long time to turn around. Low prices can force liquidation of animals by ranchers, and the long cycle creates long-term effects on price. Very high prices encourage expansion, and the long cycle keeps that cycle going until prices are forced down again.

FIGURE 5.16 Live Cattle Futures

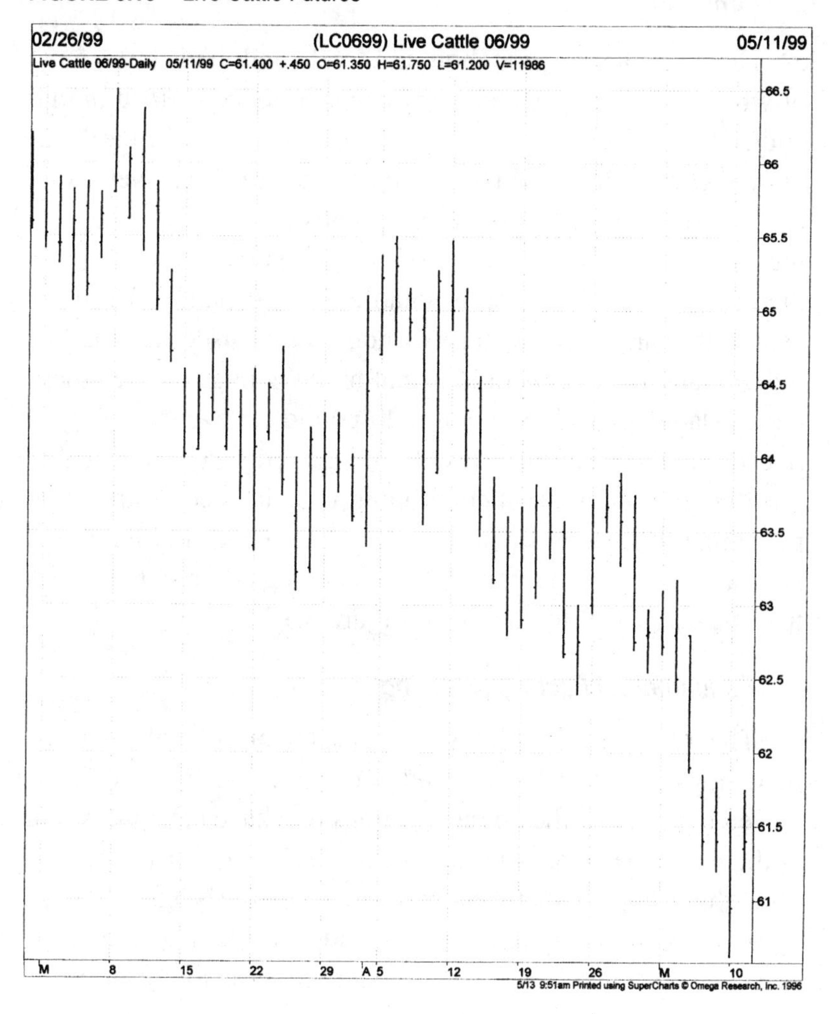

The government publishes total numbers of cattle throughout the country as well as monthly and quarterly numbers representing cattle on feedlots, cattle placed, and cattle marketed in the most recent period. The price and available supply of competing meat such as pork and poultry also can affect the price of beef.

Lean Hogs

Hogs are raised throughout the world and, like cattle, most of what is produced in a country is generally consumed in that country. The greatest numbers of hogs are raised in the Midwest states of Iowa, Illinois, Minnesota, Indiana, Nebraska, and Missouri. It takes about ten months from birth or farrowing to slaughter. The shorter cycle for hogs makes supply, and therefore price, much more volatile than for cattle. Until recently, the largest percentage of hogs were raised on small or individually owned operations that bred the hogs and fed them out to slaughter weight, about 220 pounds. Now, large corporate farms are creating vertically integrated hog factories that raise hogs in large numbers, hoping to reduce costs and raise profit margins. Hogs are now traded on the Chicago Mercantile Exchange. The contract traded is a lean hog contract that is actually a carcass of the hog (see Figure 5.17).

Fundamental Factors Affecting Hog Prices

The total number of hogs on farms, the number of sows (female hogs) estimated to be bred, the average size of the litters (seven to ten), and the amount of hogs that have been marketed in the recent past are important statistics. The government supplies these approximate numbers on a quarterly basis. These reports, called the pig crop reports, and some demand numbers, such as storage and usage, will affect the direction of prices.

PRECIOUS METALS

Gold

Gold has been a store of value for thousands of years. Although gold possesses some industrial qualities, its use as a

FIGURE 5.17 Lean Hogs Futures

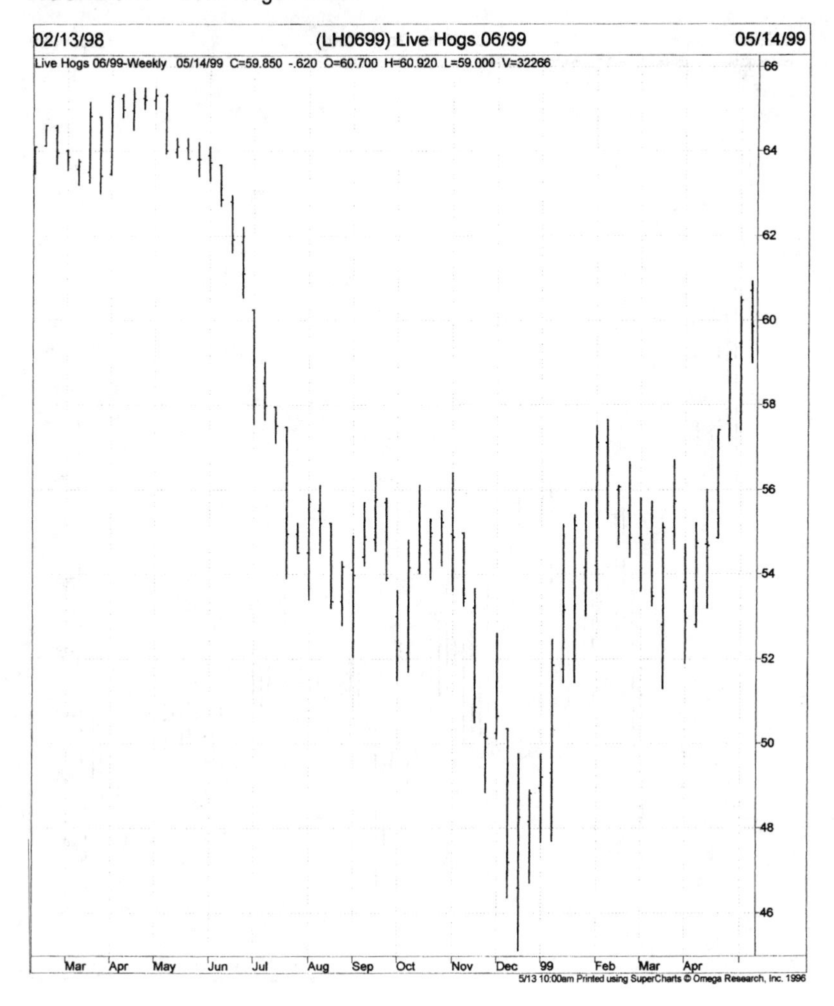

monetary substitute and in jewelry price it as a precious metal, not an industrial one. In 1971, the fixed rate of $35 per ounce was ended, and in 1974, U.S. citizens could legally own gold. Gold futures began trading in December 31, 1974, on several exchanges. The primary futures market is now the COMEX division of the New York Mercantile Exchange (see Figure 5.18).

FIGURE 5.18 Gold Futures

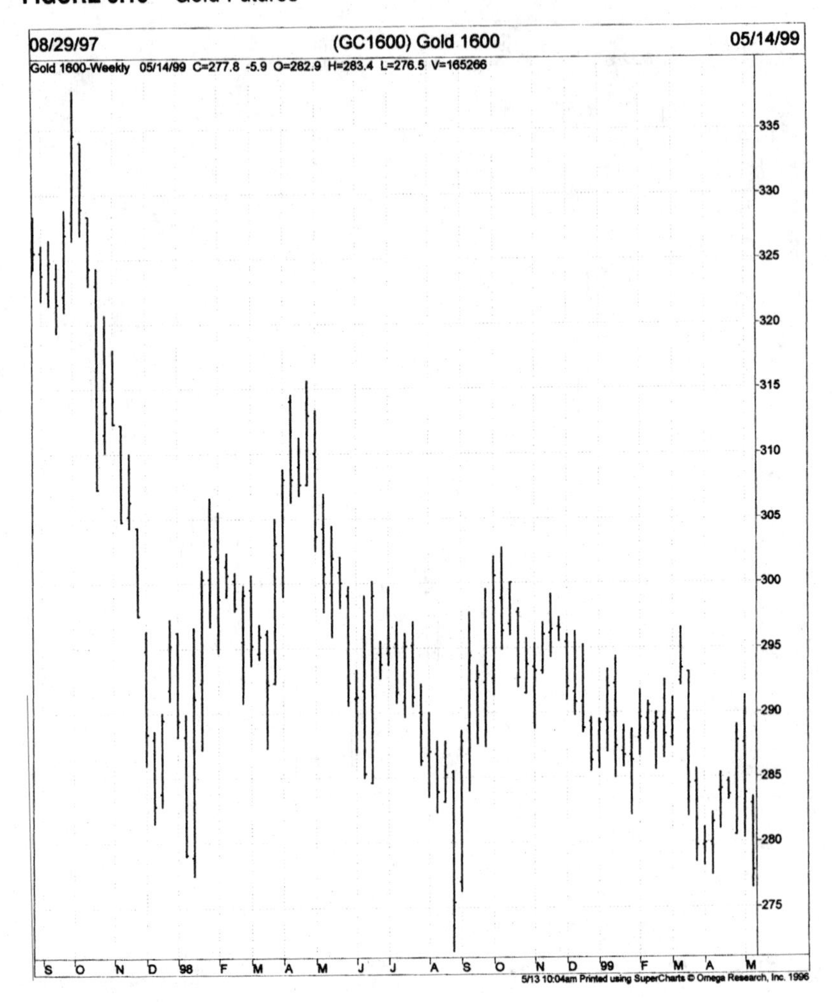

Gold prices, which were trading below $100, peaked in 1980 at $850 per ounce. Gold currently trades below $300 per ounce. South Africa and Russia produce the largest quantities of gold in the world, followed by Canada and the United States. Gold's industrial uses include dentistry and electronics. The major use of gold is in the making of gold coins.

Fundamental Factors Affecting Gold Prices

Mining numbers and industrial use play a minor role in the pricing of gold. Central banks, politics, inflation, war and peace, and interest rates are the factors most likely to move gold prices. Of all the markets in the world, gold could be the most emotionally charged and psychologically driven of all. There are few supply-demand equations that will give the investor the necessary clues. An astute reading of the world political and economic scene and daily newspapers is more valuable.

Silver

Silver, like gold, has been a store of value for thousands of years. Also like gold, silver does have some industrial uses, which have become much more important in recent years. Because of its particular properties, silver is used in electronics, computers, photography, and jewelry. Much of the supply of silver comes either as a by-product of the mining of copper, lead, zinc, and gold or from the recycling of old silver jewelry, silverware, and coins. Silver is traded on the COMEX division of the New York Mercantile Exchange (see Figure 5.19).

Fundamental Factors Affecting Silver Prices

Industrial use of silver is the primary factor in moving the price. For several years, the mined supply of silver has been below the industrial demand. The shortfall has been satisfied by the secondary sources of the metal. In 1980, the silver market traded up to $50 per ounce, driven by the speculative buying of the Hunt family. As a result of the extraordinary price level, a huge supply from secondary sources emerged. Jewelry and silverware made their way into the market.

FIGURE 5.19 Silver Futures

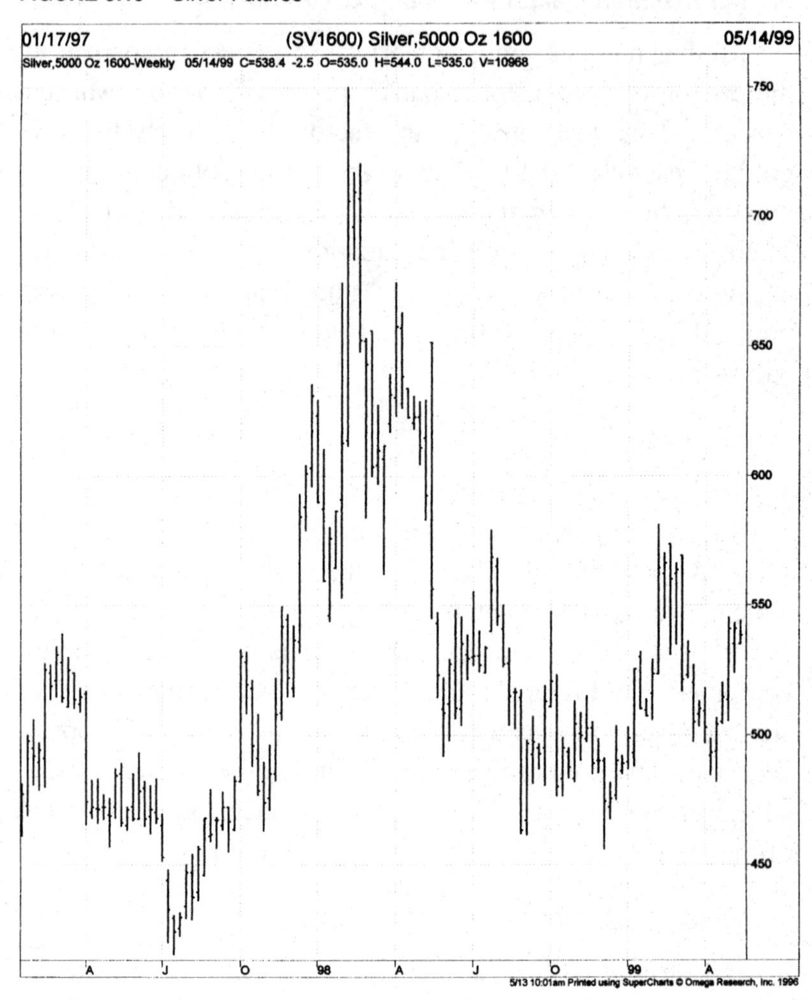

Copper

Copper is produced and consumed all over the world and has a long-established international market. Copper's industrial use comes as a result of its electrical conductivity, corrosion resistance, malleability, and strength. The copper supply comes mainly from Chile, Peru, South Africa, Russia, and North America. Copper is used widely in the electrical and telecommunications industry as well as the housing industry. It is actively traded in London and on the COMEX division of the New York Mercantile Exchange (see Figure 5.20).

FIGURE 5.20 High Grade Copper Futures

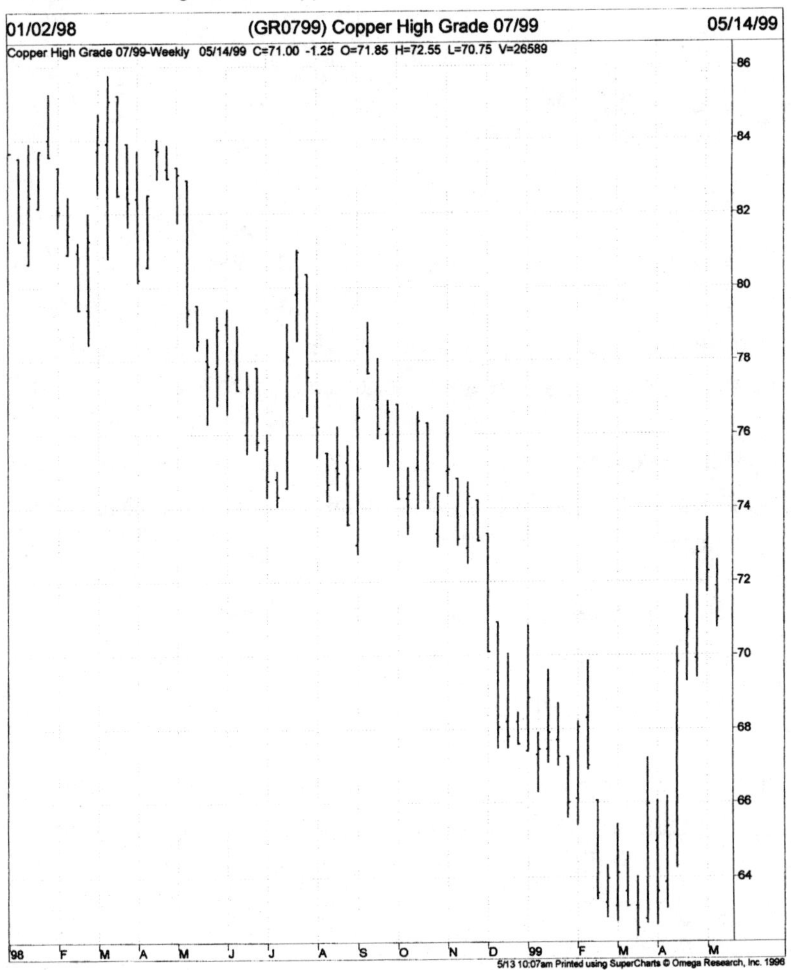

Fundamental Factors Affecting Copper Prices

Undeveloped countries mine much of the copper and on occasion supply can be interrupted by politics, economics, weather, or labor strife. Developed countries use much of the world's copper, and the strength of their economies will be very important to the demand side of the supply-demand equation.

PETROLEUM

Crude Oil

Crude Oil, until the mid-1970s, had a relative stable price history. In 1974, a cartel of mostly Middle East oil-producing nations (OPEC) set quotas on the daily production and marketing of oil and set off a new era in oil prices. Oil is extracted in many areas of the world, including the Middle East, Russia, the North Sea, and the Americas. Oil futures are traded in London and on the NYMEX division of the New York Mercantile Exchange (see Figure 5.21).

Fundamental Factors Affecting Oil Prices

Politics, the cartel, weather, war, and price can affect the supply of oil. The primary demand for oil comes from the refineries that process the crude oil into its consumable components, such as heating oil, gasoline, lubricants, and other industrial uses. Demand can be affected by cold winters, hot summers, economic conditions, price, and, to a lesser degree, competing energy sources.

FIGURE 5.21 Crude Oil Futures

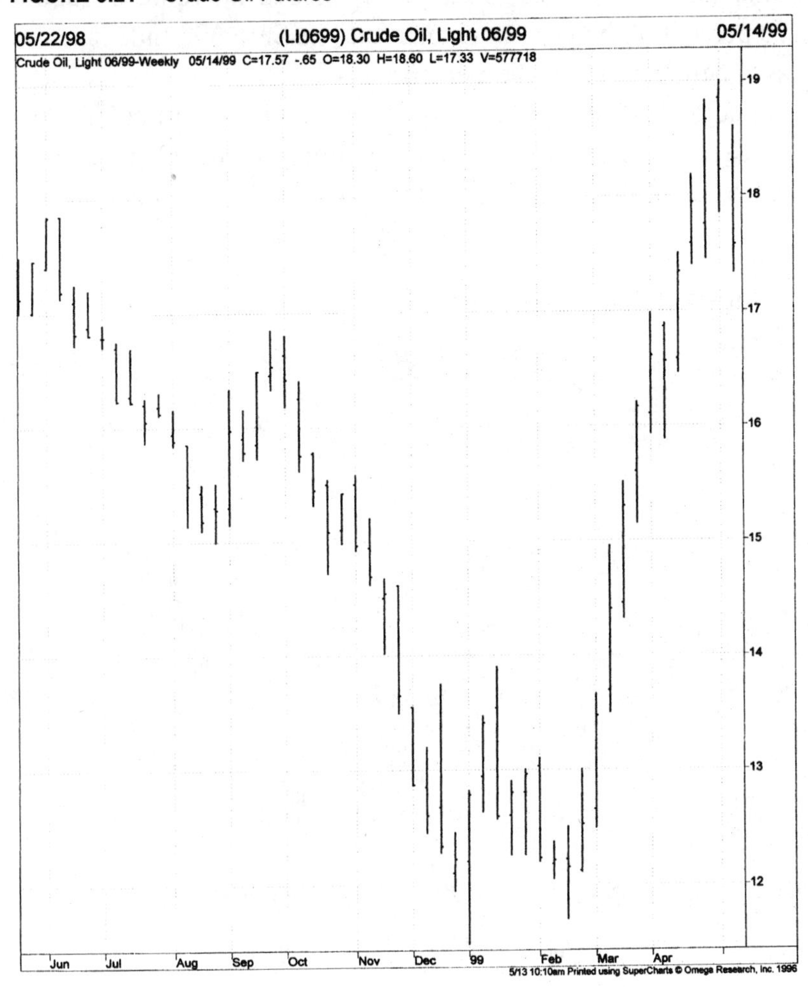

STOCK INDEXES

The first stock market index to be publicly traded was the Value Line Index in 1982. However, it soon was eclipsed by the S&P 500 Index futures contract, which is traded on the Chicago Mercantile Exchange's Index and Options Market (IOM).

This index consists of 500 large-cap stocks that represent about 70 percent of the U.S. stock market. The S&P 500 Index is used as a benchmark for the performance of the stock market as a whole and for individual money managers in particular. Currently, the index can be traded as a future on the IOM (see Figure 5.22), either in a full contract size or the E-Mini contract,

FIGURE 5.22 S&P 500 Futures

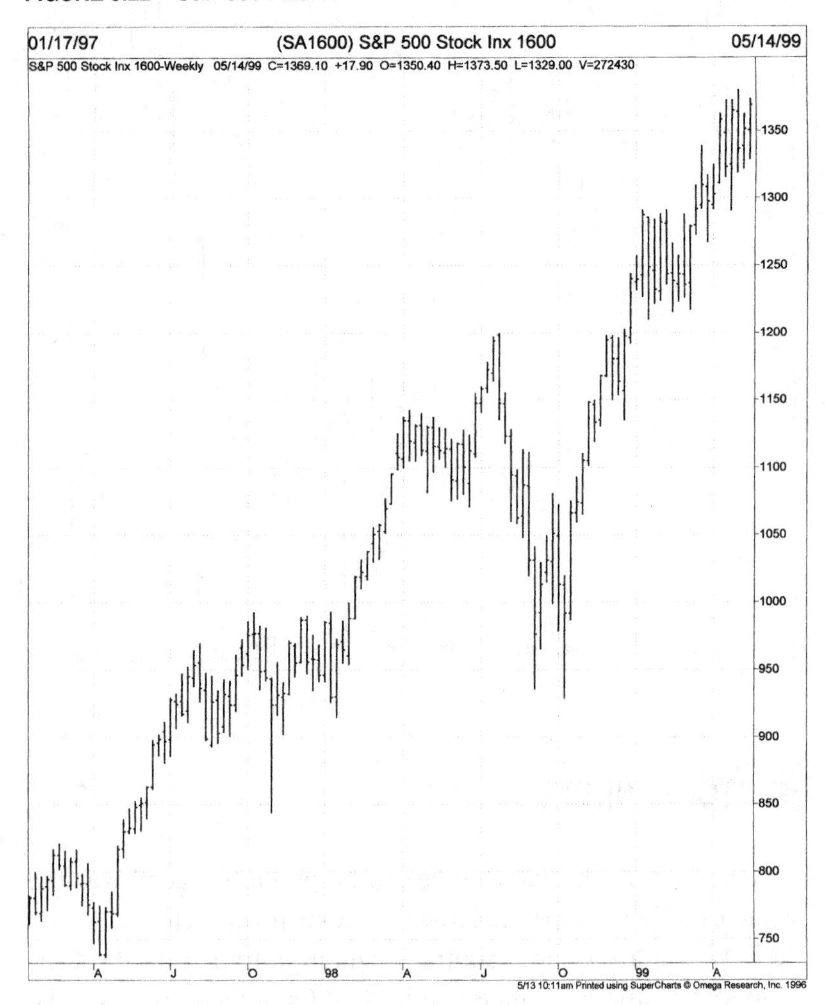

which is one-fifth the size of the full contract, or as an equity instrument traded on the American Stock Exchange. Its trading acronym is SPDR; hence the nickname "Spiders."

Fundamental Factors Affecting Index Prices

The S&P 500, which is composed of 500 large capitalization stocks, tends to reflect the general view of economic conditions as opposed to the condition of any individual stock. The economy, interest rates, inflation, the Fed, government, and the general sense of well-being by investors will affect the direction of the market.

6

PORTFOLIO MANAGEMENT

A portfolio manager controls risk through the use of diversification. By creating a "portfolio," an investment with many parts, you rule out the chance of making a killing and also eliminate the possibility of getting killed financially. By selecting a combination of investments that range from staid to risky, and by keeping the correlation of those investments as low as possible, you can achieve a rate of return higher than if you are restricted to all high-grade securities. The important elements of portfolio management are asset allocation and diversification.

ASSET ALLOCATION

The savvy investor knows the value of asset allocation. This is a process of determining how much of your investment capital should be allocated to any asset class. A well-rounded investment program should take 100 percent of dollars available for investment purposes and commit a portion of the dollars to several asset classes. For example, if you allocate 50 percent of your dollars to U.S. equities and 25 percent to fixed-income instruments like bonds, then the remaining 25 percent can be allocated to several of the asset classes mentioned in Chapter 5. These allocations will be different for each investor according to his or her needs and tolerance for risk. We believe that you should consider including as many of the global assets in your allocation formula as you are comfortable with. Global assets may include financial instruments such as stocks and bonds, foreign currencies, energy assets such as crude oil and natural gas, and agricultural products such as grains, coffee, cocoa, and sugar.

DIVERSIFICATION

Not to be confused with asset allocation, diversification is how you invest the equity in each asset class. For example, assuming the above allocations, your U.S. equity portfolio could be in 5, 10, or 50 different stocks. The fixed-income part of your dollars might have several different maturity dates. The remaining 25 percent of your overall portfolio might be invested in the metals, grains, currencies, or livestock markets.

This diversification within asset classes reduces the overall risk of your investment portfolio and allows for reasonable growth over time.

MONEY MANAGEMENT AND RISK MANAGEMENT

Although many traders use the terms *money management* and *risk management* interchangeably, we believe they are separate issues.

Money management refers to the overall use of capital as it relates to total equity committed to the markets. For example, if you commit $100,000 to your program, then you must decide how you will approach the risk on this total. You may allocate equity to different asset classes and then determine the maximum exposure for each of those elements. Or as many traders do, you may decide on the exposure of your equity on a trade-by-trade basis. Usually, systematic traders risk from .05 percent to 2 or 3 percent per trade. Discretionary traders very often expand those parameters; however, keep in mind that every successful trader has a money management concept in place.

Risk management refers to the way investors control the risk on each trade, both on an individual basis and as part of the overall portfolio. Many traders weigh the volatility of each market or security they are trading and adjust the risk for that particular market. Some take the standard deviation or the average range over some time frame or use full value to determine the risk. This is just a sample of the methods used; the various methods are endless. For many, the simplest approach to the problem of risk is to calculate exposure for each trade and then superimpose that risk onto the entire portfolio. This will give you individual and portfolio exposure each day. If there is a lesson to be learned here, it is that all successful traders have some mechanism in place that allows them, or forces them, to constantly evaluate risk.

TECHNICAL CONSIDERATIONS

You should keep in mind that technical analysis is not so much trying to find the profitable trade, but a tool to calculate risk and formulate a plan of action on a consistent basis that will maintain the level of risk you most desire.

Trend Identifiers

Remember the three primary methods of trend identification:

1. Linear, or trendlines
2. Moving averages
3. Channel breakouts

Simple trendlines are usually drawn from low to low to establish an uptrend, or from high to high to establish a downtrend (Figure 6.1). Variations on this theme are possible by using closes instead of lows or averaging daily ranges and using those points as references.

The oldest and best-known method of establishing a trend is the moving average (Figure 6.2). In its simplest form, a moving average is usually obtained by adding up a series of closes and dividing the sum by the number of days used in the series. The result is a smoothing of the series of numbers—and an effective method of trend identification. Many variations are possible, such as varying the number of days in the series, using an average of the daily range, using highs and lows, and even changing the value of the most recent days compared to the oldest days. The most obvious use of the moving average is in identifying that a trend is established when the close (or whatever variable you choose) is over (or under) the average, thereby signaling direction.

FIGURE 6.1 Trendline

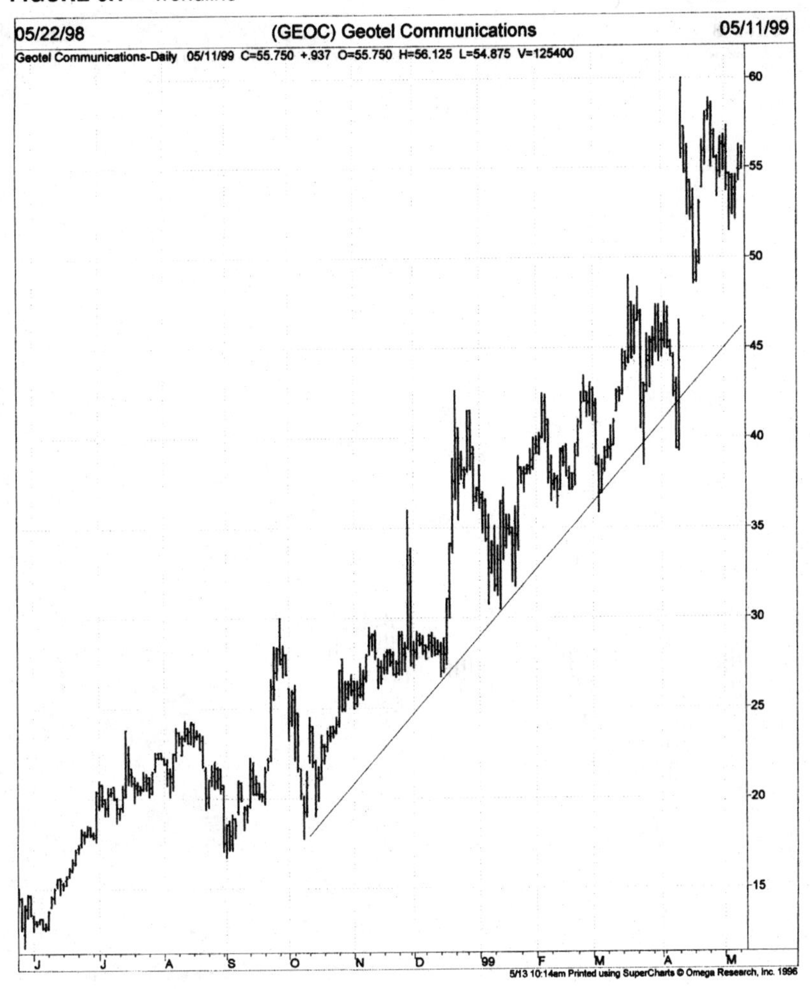

The channel breakout method can be used on its own or in conjunction with the other methods (Figure 6.3). We define a channel as a series of days or weeks that is contained within an area of highs and lows (or average of highs and lows). When a market moves through an area that has been established over a period of time, it then signals a trend.

FIGURE 6.2 Moving Average

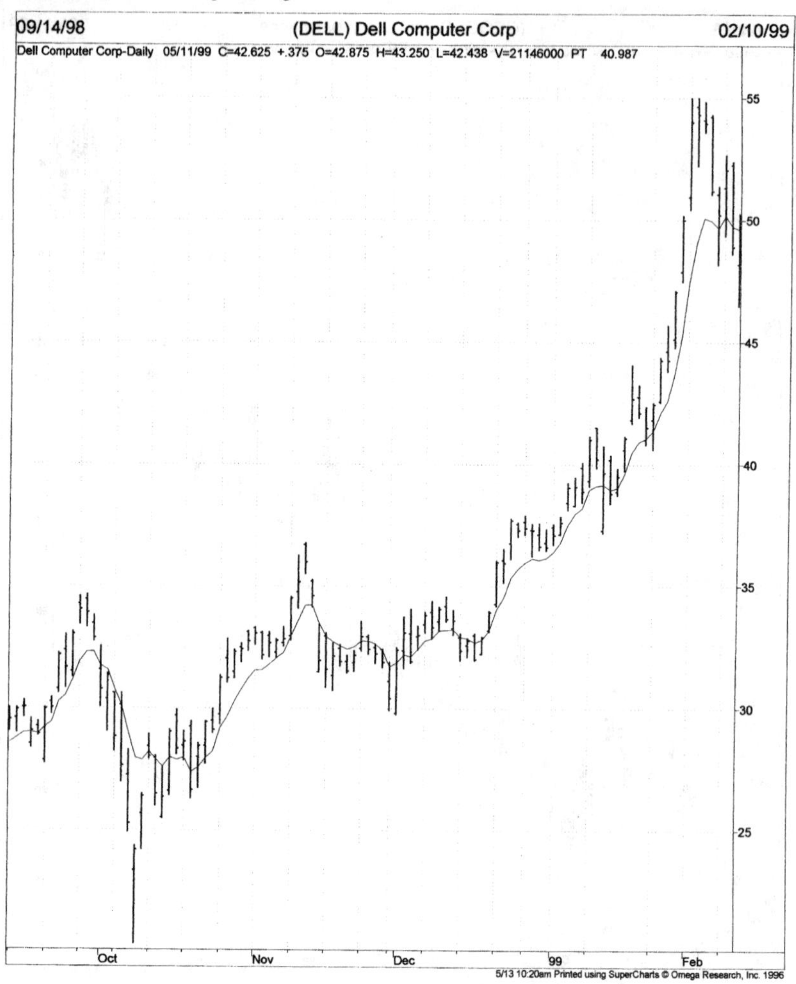

Use Trend Identifiers as a Risk Tool

The most difficult trade for most traders to make is when the market comes crashing down or rallies sharply to that trend-line, moving average, or channel top or bottom.

It is precisely at these sometimes climactic moments that risk is the smallest, most neatly defined, and—when taken—the

FIGURE 6.3 Channel

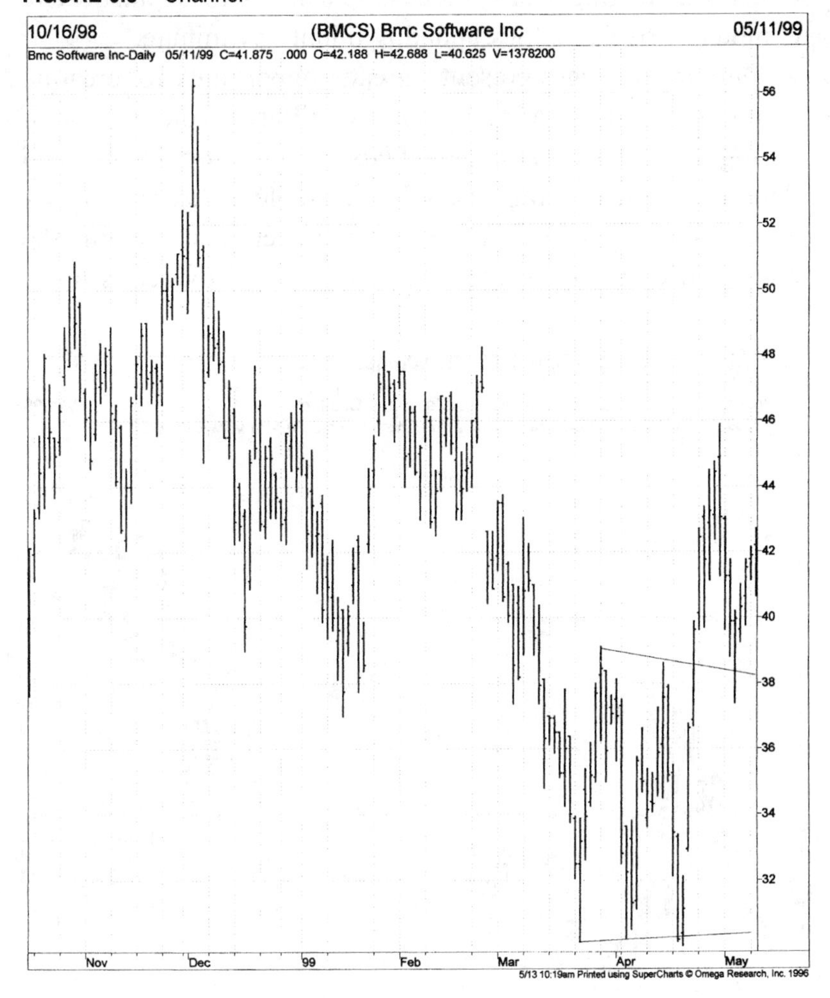

most consistent in results attained. For example, you may decide to define the risk as a close under the trendline that was used to make the purchase. Variations on this theme might include a filter of some percentage close above or below the trendline, or waiting for a low to be established and then buying with that low as the defined risk. There is an infinite variety of combinations, ranging from these simple ideas to sophisticated, computer-driven analogs updating minute by minute.

Moving averages present a greater opportunity for creating complex variations, as many traders will use a combination of averages as well as various methods of weighting the time and duration of each average used. For example, a fast moving average combined with a slower moving average can define the risk in several ways (Figure 6.4). The most obvious is if the

FIGURE 6.4 Fast and Slow Moving Averages

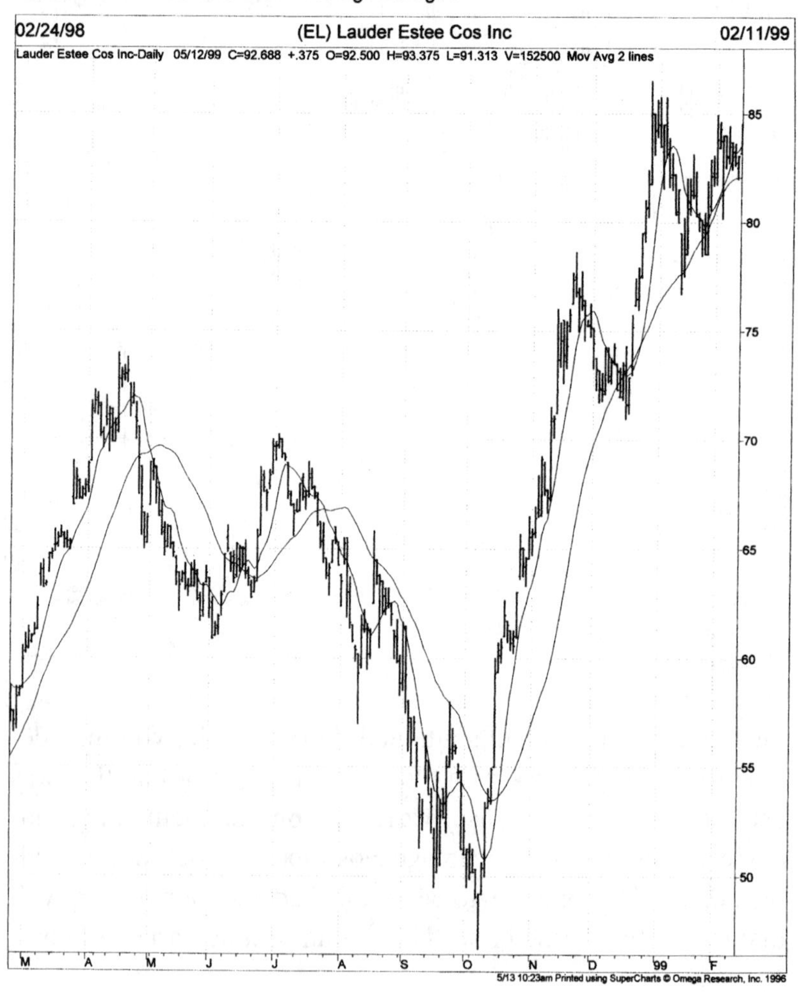

faster moving average crosses the slower moving average it may signal a change in trend. Another approach might be to measure how far the faster moving average moves above or below the slower moving average, and thereby give an indication of a possible overbought or oversold condition.

The channel also may be used in several ways to manage the risk of a trade. The simplest form would be exiting a trade that was established inside a channel as the market breaks out of that channel.

In summary, you need to be aware of the dual function of technical analysis as it relates to investing. Not only do technical, analytical indicators identify opportunity in markets, but also they just as importantly provide for circumscribed and calculated risk parameters.

Now, let's turn to our interviews with top traders, so that we can observe how they use technical and fundamental analysis as well as particular techniques and tactics they have developed over the years to profit from investment opportunities in various asset classes.

PART THREE

THE TOP TRADERS: THEIR SECRETS FOR SUCCESS

7

RICK SANTELLI

Mr. Santelli is a member of the Chicago Board of Trade and a senior vice president at Sanwa Futures. Previously, he was an analyst for Rand Financial Services and Drexel, Burnam, Lambert. He currently provides analysis and commentary on the interest rate sector for CNBC.

Q: Rick, can you describe how you first became interested in the market?

RICK: After completing my undergraduate degree at the University of Illinois, I came to Chicago. At the time, I was dating a girl whose father was a well-known pork belly trader who had been on the exchange since the 1950s. He was very busy, so I used to sit in the visitor's gallery for several hours watching him operate on the trading floor. It really captured my imagination.

Q: What was his name?

RICK: Laughton Lamb. You see, I just found the whole enterprise of trading and investing fascinating. I was planning to enroll in law school the following semester, but then thought, well, let me take a little time off. I became a runner for Shearson at the Chicago Mercantile Exchange. This was in 1979. After the first day working on the trading floor, I was hopelessly hooked.

Q: Well, you've taken quite a detour from pork bellies at the Merc! You're currently running a bond desk at the Chicago Board of Trade, away from the agriculture quadrant, tracking the movement and behavior of domestic and foreign interest rates. In addition, you're an analyst and commentator for CNBC focusing on the bond market. Can you talk a little about how you got involved in this sector of the market and then perhaps speak about your overall market philosophy?

RICK: You'll remember in the early 1980s when interest rates were in double digits and inflation was an obvious concern, Paul Volcker was on his way out, and the Reagan administration was coming in. At the time, I was trading T-bills, and I met Richard Sandor—one of the individuals credited with establishing the bond contract at the CBOT—when I joined Drexel. I was working on the Eurodollar desk, and an opening came up at the Chicago Board of Trade to work on the bond desk. Of course, at the time Drexel was a small firm. Remember, this was still prior to Michael Milkin and the junk-bond era. Nevertheless, it seemed like a pretty good opportunity, and I moved over to bonds. This was around 1984. It was at the time this market was starting to come of age. Liquidity started moving up tremendously, and bond options had just been introduced that broadened the general level of investor interest. At the time, the bond contract was about six or seven years old, and I felt I was a player in an emerging market sector.

Q: Can you describe your general approach to the bond market?

RICK: Keep it simple. Very early on I had a client who used to say KISS: Keep it simple, stupid. I mean, that was the way we would approach the bonds in terms of execution. Actually, I use a fairly complicated methodology to trade, but I think if I had to pick what I look at most, it would be weekly perspectives on the marketplace. It's my overwhelming belief that the

Friday trade creates the value with regard to current price structure. And most of the time in the bond market, the weekly highs or lows are extended on Friday. So, I really concentrate on Friday trends in trying to determine what's ahead for the market.

Q: Rick, are you saying that once the market establishes a direction on a Friday, there is a high probability it will continue that way, and as a trader you don't want to go against that trend?

RICK: That's exactly right. What we try to look at in the bonds is the rhythm of the market. You'd be amazed how often you will put the extreme of the week in early and you put the opposite extreme in late. In other words, on Sunday night or Monday, you'll put in a low and on Thursday night or Friday, you'll put in a high or visa versa. And if you know that that occurs with statistical reliability over a significant amount of time—that the range is directionally extended on a Friday—come Wednesday afternoon or Thursday morning, you look at where the current price is relative to the structure of the range of the week. It gives you significant insight into price direction. If 75 percent of the time bonds are going to extend that range, and you're much closer to the low end of the range, then I would be leaning towards looking for lower prices come Friday, given the historical reliability of the market's price action.

Q: How do you identify market opportunity?

RICK: I think it's important to understand that there are many tiers of activity occurring in the bond market. Of course, the tier that everybody likes to focus on is the new hedge fund and the large trading community. And, of course, you have the primary dealers in New York, who represent the most systematic order flow—that's almost a continuous order flow. And then you have everybody else, the large and small retail speculators. I don't like going with the herd mentality! I try to enter and exit the market based on perceived thresholds of pain for the "conventional wisdom" player.

Q: Does that make you a contrarian?

RICK: I think there's a lot to be said for being a contrarian. The problem of late is that there are so many contrarians that you almost have to take it to mean being a contrarian's contrarian. So, it starts to get a little ridiculous. But, in the final analysis, there are big issues that affect the market, and the *fundamentals* can't be ignored. It's knowing when those issues are driving the market, and when they are running out of gas in terms of their influence on the market, that I believe present the best investment opportunities.

Q: Do you have a basic market strategy you use?

RICK: If I had to pick one strategy that I would use most often, it would be: Always come up with a perceived trading range prior to the opening bell. And in truth, there are a lot of different methodologies that will do that. I think you have to have a plan before the market starts to trade and try to gauge what you think the high and low will be. I think if you don't have a specific perspective when you attack the bond market, you will flounder when emotions start to run high and things start to appear to be out of control!

Q: So, Rick, are you saying that on each independent trading day, you have a sense of what that trading range is going to be? You have a way of calculating the range, what you think the low and high end of the trading range should be based on historical price action?

RICK: Precisely. And there are a lot of ways I do it. If I had to point to a very simple way that anybody can follow, it would be a form of the Steidlmayer (Peter Steidlmayer) way of thinking; in other words, Market Profile. I also should add I don't believe that Market Profile (a method of identifying volume at specific prices) gives you the market direction or great trades all the time! But, knowing where the volume has been, knowing the amount of time the market spent in specific price ranges, and then factoring in where the perceived openings are can point you in the right direction. In other words, look for the range for the prior week and where you are relative to calendar events. Also, since Friday's are important, so are the beginning of fiscal quarters and fiscal years. Extending from that, constantly try to gauge where you believe the high and the low of price action will be based on its widest price movement in the appropriate time frame.

Q: To what extent do you rely on fundamental analysis? In other words, how much importance do you place on the actions of the Fed as it relates to monetary policy?

RICK: I would consider myself a technician, but I think that you have to be completely aware of all the fundamentals. And in the information age that we live in, it has to be a global approach that considers international interest rates and economic fundamentals: You have to be cognizant of monetary policy in the European Monetary Union. You have to be cognizant of monetary policy in the United States. You have to know where all the buzz numbers are going to be, whether it's employment or GDP (gross domestic product). You have to be cognizant of the part of the economy that's doing the best and the part that's doing the worst. Recently, manufacturing has been in the spotlight. There are certain highlight numbers from the commerce department, which move in and out of vogue in terms of their importance. You have to be aware of them and know the overall market expectations. Having said that, I think with all the market fundamentals that affect the bond market, eventually it all shows up on a chart. That is to say, ultimately I believe the technical chart shows you the price structure of the interest rate markets.

Q: So, you're saying that you're aware of the background of the interest rate market, the fundamentals and monetary policies that drive the market, but ultimately you believe the charts (the technicals) dictate the next price movement?

RICK: I think the chart is the best way to keep score of the fundamentals! I mean literally; I could make a list of 150 things we could look at on any given week in the bond market. And each one of them, whether domestic or global, is important. But, when I look at a bond chart, I'm going to have an immediate understanding of how the price structure interacted with the fundamentals. And the way we make money is not by guessing fundamentals, but by correctly analyzing how the market will respond to the fundamentals. That's why I strongly believe the bond charts continue to give you the edge in the markets.

Q: Can you elaborate in greater detail how you use the chart in determining the next market move based on your analysis of the market's technicals?

RICK: I'm a big fan of envelopes and bands. Basically, an envelope or a band is taking a series of moving averages and then taking percent additions and subtractions from those moving averages relative to various time frames. So, what I like to do is what I call fine-tune a market. That's how I pick the range.

I will look at a monthly, weekly, and daily chart with my envelopes. I'll look at the extremes and then try to fine-tune the intraday charts—60-minute, 30-minute, actually all the way down to 1-minute time frames—to try to see which way the momentum is moving.

Many times, significant market turns start in the 1- and 2-minute charts. And if you see this momentum start to move to higher time frames, and the bands or the envelopes are either contracting or expanding, you get a sense of momentum of price. I think that really is the key to my trading.

Q: When you're trading, do you find that you're moving from the larger time frame down to the smaller, or do you find you're moving from the smaller time frame in terms of the initiation of the trade to see if there's the possibility of an extended move over a longer time frame?

RICK: It really depends on the trends. For example, if the bond market is in a very bullish trend—as it had been prior to January 1999—I always look at the longer time frames first as part of a continuing/mature trend. If it looks as though these cycles are beginning to run their course, then I have other methodologies to gauge when the long-term trend-turns are coming, and I start focusing on the smaller time frames. In truth, considering my short-term mentality and given most of my clients are bond professionals operating in micro time frames, I probably spend 80 percent of my time looking at charts with 60-minute time frames or less.

Q: Sixty minutes or less but also cognizant of the larger trend, is that right?

RICK: Absolutely. I mean, it's logical that if you're looking at a year chart, a multiyear chart, or a monthly chart, the envelopes above and below the market are going to move much more slowly. It's easier to keep them in the back of your mind and know where the key trigger points are. And it's always those interesting days—a handful of days a year—where all of a sudden you get multiple time frames from the very long to the very short all lining up on a certain percentile above or below the curve price structure. And then you know that things are going to change!

Q: What changes or new developments do you see occurring in the bond market in the future?

RICK: The government does not have the need to issue as much debt. We are running surpluses. And most bond traders have really learned how to trade in an environment where the government is the big printer of securities. So, I think there are going to be other standards. It wouldn't surprise me at all to see monetary policy implemented through the purchase and sale of mortgage securities or other securities outside the Treasury. So, I think we have to begin understanding relative values.

For example, If less Treasuries are going to be issued and we have bear markets, the way they move lower in price relative to corporates or agencies or mortgage backs is going to be different from the recent past. There's going to be a basis or spread relationships that actually may present considerable opportunities to savvy investors.

Q: How so?

RICK: I think even as the government is issuing less debt, the appetite to put this capital to work in fixed-income products is growing exponentially. So, I think trading spreads, which has always been my second favorite way to trade markets, presents real opportunity. It's a little safer. And I think it's interesting to calculate where fair value is relative to a varied fixed-income benchmark. If I were a new investor, I would certainly pursue this area of analysis.

Q: Could you talk a little bit about spreading as an investment strategy? How do you use spreads to hedge your risk?

RICK: A great example of this is what happened in the fall of 1998, when the capital markets started to break sharply. The credit market also started to melt down. The way that was recognized first was by the players who had a good sense of how many basis points value should exist, say, between high-graded and low-graded corporate securities and other government sovereign securities against U.S. And if you were watching closely, the fact that all of a sudden the spread started to widen dramatically was a very good indicator that you wanted to be long in the Treasury market. That's because end users at any spread over Treasuries aren't going to buy debt from Russia or debt from the Ford Motor Company. There was a dramatic shift in credit perception. And again, the biggest and the best trades are in developing major shifts in perception.

Q: How can an ordinary investor capitalize on that kind of shift of perception?

RICK: Well, it brings me back to my weekly mentality, which is to say, my approach to the markets. I think once a week, preferably after Friday closes, investors ought to sit down and map out several things. I think you should look at a series of spreads. Look at where the 30-year benchmark rate compares to other sovereigns, or if it's the 10-year that is more actually conforming to outside duration or maturities outside the United States. And look at how the German 10-year, the Japanese 10-year, and the U.S. 10-year are priced for the close of the week. Did their spreads narrow or did they widen?

Also, look at issues within the country, and I would pick a basket of very-easy-to-track indexes such as the Lehman or Goldman index. They have corporate bond indexes and mortgage indexes. And just get a sense of where value is and begin to monitor changes.

Also, I think it's very important to track volume. Of course, many investors tend to overlook something that simple when they look at weekly moves. If you get big moves with small volume or small moves with very large volume, this is very significant. It is important to understand the importance of volume and its impact on markets.

Q: Rick, how would you characterize your overall market philosophy?

RICK: I think it's too easy to say what we all have heard: Keep your losses small and let your winners ride. I think we live in an information age where riding the winners means so much less today than it did five years ago, and profoundly less than ten years ago. Today, trends in markets just play out differently.

Q: Do you mean that sometimes you'll get an entire trend played out in four or five trading days?

RICK: Yes, absolutely. I guess my philosophy would be to keep my trading fluid, to have an investment philosophy that is fluid. Never fault yourself or your strategy for having dramatic but calculated changes in short periods of time. The market is bigger than all the players. If you have a strong conviction that the market is changing, you have to be fluid enough to implement your strategy: make a change and don't become married to or inhibited by what was the conventional way of thinking about the market the day before!

Q: How do you personally calculate risk?

RICK: Very simple. To me, every investment is 2 to 1. I try to look at everything in a 2-to-1 scenario. I want to make twice as much money as I want to risk. And I want to always try to give myself the edge when it comes to the trading decision. In other words, there are two things at work: You try to be a picker of trades where, let's say, you're picking five or six out of ten winners, which I think is very possible if you do your homework. And having said that, if you're making twice as much money as you're losing on your winning trades, you want to have a very simple formula. On paper you draw what you're going to risk, what you're going to make, and how accurate you think your style is. And if that works, you can make money in the markets.

I think the problem is not having an investment plan as it relates to risk and money management and trying to make very important capital preservation decisions in the marketplace without being cognizant of your historical pattern. If you look at your trading over a year, your biggest winner has to be of a certain size compared to your biggest loser. And if these very simple quotients don't work out, it's a losing proposition and you must reformulate accordingly.

Q: Beyond the usual clichés, what do you think makes for a successful investor?

RICK: Most important is knowing when not to trade or be invested in a market. I really think that the market opens every day—and it's such a simple thing but such a big issue—and there are many times when it just doesn't behoove an individual, especially in the Treasury area, to trade. For example, quarterly refundings are terrible times to trade. Even some of the monthly auctions and big issuance days aren't good days to trade, because there are underlying tones to market activities based on issuers, underwriters, and primary dealers that will mask or cover up what's really going on. And I think especially if you're a technician, and you're looking at short-term charts, those times can be very misleading.

I personally like to trade days where the market is trading in a specific range. So, the first thing I do every morning is try to pick a range. I guess my second activity—and this usually is after the market has traded for a half-hour or so—is to assess if I'm in a defensive or offensive market. A defensive market is more of a range trade, and I always think that's the best opportunity to make money. You see, the market that only goes in one direction doesn't afford you any mistakes. The market's going to open on the lows and close on its highs, and unless you're a position trader, that's a tougher market to trade. But it all comes down to individual style and what suits your temperament and personality.

Q: What do you think is the single most important thing that you learned about trading the bonds, and how do you utilize that knowledge on a day-to-day basis?

RICK: I think that's changed. In the early part of my career with the bonds, it was knowing how to interpret the Fed. Then, if you knew how to read what the Fed was doing, you could make money in bonds. Mr. Greenspan has really implemented an open-door policy, so that you don't need to be as aware of the inner workings in Washington. I think the best way to capitalize now would be to join the crowds as much as you can. You see, being a contrarian is great. Initially, if everybody's buying, understand what's going on! It doesn't mean you have to buy with them. What it does mean is you have a better place to sell. If the crowds are selling, go with them. Don't buy it initially; wait until the regular crowd sells it and then look to buy it. What I try to do is understand the crowd mentality, and my approach to how I want to trade the market has more to do with execution: I will not execute with the crowd!

I guess that's my philosophy on bonds and I think that's the way to trade, especially as we get more and more access into the marketplace. The competition becomes much fiercer. Let's face it, I think the reason hedge funds got in so much trouble in 1998 (i.e., long-term capital) is because they looked at U.S. markets as the big leagues and at overseas markets as the farm teams. It's easier to make money if you're a good player with a lot of capital in the farm system. But, it caught up with people. Now we have all the really smart players concentrating more in the United States, knowing when to leave it alone and when to trade aggressively. Remember, there are slow days of range trade, when it behooves you to look at where your best band levels are and where the best volume has been of late. This information gives you a real edge. I'm always cognizant of where the highest volume price is over the past year, over the past month, and over the past week. In the bonds, for example, for all of 1998 the high volume price was 120.07. It's just very important to know that.

Simply being aware of that fact allows you to know where long-term price structure value is. It's really very simple. As you move towards value, you lose momentum. As you move away from value, you build momentum. That is probably the single most important secret of price structure. If you can identify those opening and closing opportunities of momentum, I think you will find it profitable to trade.

8

JOANNE PEKIN

Mrs. Pekin is president of Pekin, Singer and Shapiro, a securities brokerage and investment management firm.

Q: Joanne, can you describe how you first became interested in the stock market?

JOANNE: I started on the switchboard at Mesirow Financial (a Chicago-based financial services company specializing in dealing with institutional clients). Today, they are clients of ours.

My husband worked in the back office, and when Mesirow went to self-clearing, all the wives came down to help out. They stuck me on the switchboard. After I cut off the firm's two largest clients, I was off the phones and became one of Richard Mesirow's gofers. During this time, I fell in love with the market, became registered, and went back to school. I had a degree in economics, so it wasn't that removed!

Q: Which markets do you concentrate on now?

JOANNE: We look at stock markets and bond markets.

Q: Can you describe your general approach to the market?

JOANNE: We start out by thinking about what is going to happen in the world and how we can profit from those events or conditions. And then we are bottoms up instead of top down in our approach.

Q: Can you elaborate on that?

JOANNE: Sure. In the 1980s when it became clear, at least to us, that interest rates were going to fall and that inflation was over, we decided to buy those beneficiaries of falling rates. In particular, we loaded up in the early 1990s on CitiCorp when the banks were all hysterical. In general, we try to think what's going to happen and how we can make money from it.

Q: What is your time frame generally when you look out? Do you look out five years, ten years?

JOANNE: Three to five years. It's been very hard to be a value investor in the past six months because the speed of ascent of various entities has been beyond conventional expectations. Certain stocks have behaved like commodities. If you think that stocks are going to adhere to their traditional pattern of making 12 percent approximately a year, it forces you to be long term in nature. And I think the past six months have put everything on its ear. Just look at those .com stocks!

Q: Joanne, how do you identify market opportunity?

JOANNE: Let me give you an example. Today, everybody's petrified of the small or medium cap stocks. And in truth, they certainly have underperformed for the past three or four years. There's fear in the marketplace. But fear brings value. So, if I were to say to you where do I perceive an area that has the most fear now, I would say it would be the small or medium cap sector. And there are obvious opportunities there to start accumulating a long-term position.

Q: So, you would view that as a buying opportunity?

JOANNE: Right.

Q: On the basis of evaluations, PE ratios?

JOANNE: Yes, and cash flow. And you can find small steel companies selling at three times cash flow. When you mention them or look at them, people just throw up their hands.

Q: Do you look at a company's management?

JOANNE: Absolutely. We usually try to contact management. The best situation, of course, is when the management owns a significant piece and they're sitting on the same side of the table as you. In the past three, four, or five years, let's say, management has acquired ownership of significant pieces of small or medium-size companies, and with the popularity of options as a compensation issue, the stock price has meaning to management. I mean, 15 years ago the guy at AT&T who sat on the board of directors didn't care whether the stock went up or down!

Q: Can you talk about some of the homework and research you do when you've identified a sector of mid caps or small caps that you believe offers financial opportunity?

JOANNE: Well, let's take what's happening in the entertainment world. One thing that Americans do particularly well is exporting their culture. And because the entertainment industry is exploding with energy and opportunity, the people who produce the content are sitting in the driver's seat. So, you look at those companies that are producing content, like Seagram's, for example, which is a company we're interested in. Unfortunately, it's up four points today. But, here you have a heavy management ownership. Bronfman has redone the company. He's got the cash flow from liquor, he's leveraged himself up, and now he's got cash flow to pay down his debt. And, he's got content to sell. Certainly, Disney would be another company that has content we believe presents ongoing opportunity.

Q: What is your homework when you identify a Seagram's or a Disney?

JOANNE: Well, we look at the cash flow numbers very carefully, because these companies don't have earnings. They have cash flow. And that's the whole secret. I mean, Disney is certainly not in the same class as Seagram's, but do they have the cash flow to unleverage themselves and produce satisfactory returns for the investor? You must be able to answer that question categorically. In the case of Seagram's, you're certainly sitting on the same side of the table as Mr. Bronfman, who clearly wants Seagram's stock to go up, too!

Q: Would you characterize your approach as being entirely fundamental or do you use a technical focus? How do you use technical analysis with your basic fundamental ideas to buy a particular company or sector of companies?

JOANNE: Well, the perfect fit is when the stock makes sense fundamentally and also looks good on the chart. I was trained as a very young girl on a point and figure and also on bar charts. I spent years of my life putting the little *X*s in by hand.

Q: So when both the fundamentals and technicals click in at the same time, you buy?

JOANNE: Right, then you know. And, of course, Seagram's is a classic. I mean, if you look at a point and figure chart, it's all there.

Q: How would you characterize your overall market philosophy?

JOANNE: We're basically value investors. But, we will buy growth. We're very long term in nature, and we try to buy growth at a reasonable price. And inherent in that is the understanding that it takes time for investments to work out.

Q: The Warren Buffett approach?

JOANNE: Yes. I've always made the most money by being patient. We've been in such a long-term bull market, and in the final analysis the patient investor has made the most money!

Q: How do you calculate risk when you enter into an investment, and what in general terms is your concept of capital management?

JOANNE: I have thought about this a great deal, and in essence, I don't know how exactly to characterize risk. There's no risk when no one wants something; there's great risk when everybody wants it. I think risk is a very individual thing. Fundamentally, it's a psychological decision as well as a financial decision, and certain people stomach risk better than others.

Q: When you bought Seagram's, for example, you had an underlying concept of the company. You saw certain things that you found fundamentally attractive, then you looked for confirmation on the price chart. Have you ever had the experience where the market didn't gratify your expectation?

JOANNE: Yes, of course. It has happened to all of us.

Q: When you find that the current price chart doesn't reflect your initial thinking, do you use the chart to develop a stop loss point or do you wait for the fundamentals to change?

JOANNE: We basically wait for fundamentals to change. The problem is that we have so much more volatility in the stock market than we ever had, even three to five years ago. I mean, things move in a day the way they used to move in years. It's incredible! You can be absolutely killed on the charts, and the next day it goes right back up.

Q: Are you saying that you really have to wait for a fundamental change to adjust or change your position?

JOANNE: Yes, you've got to be patient. Stocks have become like women's clothes: they go in and out of style. And, of course, if you wait for something in your closet to come back, it eventually does. You just have to hold onto it long enough, given it's a justified purchase to begin with.

Q: But as you know, stocks don't always come back, even though that hasn't largely characterized this market.

JOANNE: No, well, so far the smaller mid caps haven't moved that much. And the past six months have been very narrow. And Internet stocks someday are going to blow up. And maybe we'll all stand on our chairs and applaud. I just think that ultimately value investing is the smartest approach.

Q: What would you say are the essential ingredients of a successful investor in your terms?

JOANNE: Capital, guts, patience, and homework.

Q: What is the most important thing you've learned about investing over your long career as a money manager?

JOANNE: The market always surprises you!

Q: We assume what's implied in your comment is that you have to be prepared for those surprises, is that correct?

JOANNE: I think as an investor there are certain things you have that are permanent, that eventually it does come down to numbers. On the other hand, the psychological aspect of investing ranges continuously between fear and greed. And the fear part lasts longer than you think it should, and the greed part lasts longer than you think it should. The things that might have worked five or ten years ago don't necessarily work now.

Q: I guess what you're saying is that you need to be adaptable also.

JOANNE: Yes. I certainly don't think any of us thought after the October minicrash that we would have the kind of raging bull market we are now observing.

Q: You're talking about October 1998?

JOANNE: Yes. Even in the '87 crash, the market laid there and quivered for four, five, or six weeks before it went up. These are incredibly dynamic markets!

Q: Do you use any mathematical models when you're trading?

JOANNE: No. The other thing I think worth noting is the speed of the market; we are ratcheting up at increasing speed. The market moves are just unprecedented. They go up fast and they go down fast now. The commodity market is the same way, isn't it?

Q: In some instances, though not nearly as dramatic.

JOANNE: But, in the glory days of the commodities markets, I think you would get those kinds of moves. Of course, with the .coms you really see a perfect example of how equities have been transformed into trading like commodities. Evaluations aren't there.

Q: Exactly. How can you talk about PEs? There are no Es! So, Occasionally it feels like you're really trading pork bellies in stocks clothing!

In closing, would you say that for you the keys to successful investing are capital, guts, and good research?

JOANNE: And patience. You've got to be willing to take an opposite stand to be successful and be patient about it if your homework's right. That, in essence, is the secret to profitable investing.

9

JEFFREY SILVERMAN

Mr. Silverman is a long-term member of the Chicago Mercantile Exchange, where he served on its board of directors. A graduate of MIT, he is one of the largest market makers on the trading floor, where he trades for his own account.

Q: Can you describe how you first became interested in the markets and what appeal they hold for you?

JEFFREY: I think that from a very young age the market held a very great appeal for me. I just loved observing and following markets and being part of them. Investing was always something I've wanted to do. I would like to add something else: Until I started to work, I'd experienced a lot of what I view now as difficulty dealing with persons in authority, particularly women in authority. And I disliked the idea that my grade on an exam, or my evaluation in a course, particularly English, was a subjective measure of what I did and didn't really mesh well with what I thought I deserved for my efforts. I was always interested in a career that would compensate me based on some objective standards.

By process of elimination, I thought I could involve myself in essentially two fields: sales, where there was a measure of how well you were doing based on how much you were selling and the commission percentage, or trading, which was my first love, where your evaluation for your efforts is fairly immediate. I ended up getting started in this business on the sales end and gradually turned to trading.

I didn't have any money to begin with, so I figured the easiest way to get started was on the sales side, where I could be involved in markets and gain experience while I developed my understanding of the marketplace.

Q: Today, your main markets tend to be agricultural, the livestock sector in particular. For a guy who comes out of MIT, this is not the most likely career destination. How did you get involved with these markets and what continues to interest you about this sector in particular?

JEFFREY: When I started in the futures markets, there were something like 30 commodities traded all together, 15 domestic and 15 international markets. And, the government was heavily involved in the grain market with surpluses and subsidies, and that meant having to figure out what the next government program was going to be. So, I crossed that off my list because it was a subjective kind of thing, and there were politics involved. When it came to understanding people and their motives, I was mystified at that time.

Some of the international commodities that required good statistics, such as sugar, coffee, and cocoa, were also difficult to trade. I thought the commercials had better access to information, supply and demand data and such, and better inside connections. So I crossed those off my list. It boiled down to the domestic commodities, in particular livestock, where the production economics were accessible and fairly widely known.

You just had to look at the basic philosophy of the market. The commodity market shouldn't return to the producers over the life of the production cycle; the four-year hog cycle or the six-year cattle cycle shouldn't give the industry more than basically a breakeven. And so, I started thinking about the production side and the full dynamics of this market.

Everything would feed back on the other, and to me it was just that simple. Strangely to most people, it looks totally impenetrable from the outside. But to me, it was like a well-oiled and jeweled clock. Everything fit together logically, and there was a logical progression of conditions and events. High prices leading to more production, which led to low prices, and those were things I could understand!

Q: Based on your mathematical and statistical background, did you feel that the market was more penetrable from that perspective in terms of developing a quantitative analysis of the cost of production?

JEFFREY: I thought that was part of it, and the other thing is that I am extremely pragmatic. I was interested in what worked, not what was theoretically possible or what should work. And, there were plenty of data, and unlike the stock market cycle that might last 10 to 15 years, the commodity market cycle was just a couple of years. I thought in a compressed business cycle time frame I could learn far more about markets, and in far less time. It's like in college where you learn how to learn, and if you end up in an area with lots of information coming at you, you can separate the wheat from the chaff. You also can end up learning a lot about yourself as an individual: What's your tolerance for risk, how greedy do you get, and how out of control do you allow your emotions to get?

Q: How would you now describe your general market approach?

JEFFREY: I try to have a fundamental value approach to commodity markets when they're priced at a low within a specific time period and everybody's losing money. I'm looking for the turn in the cycle when prices are going to have to go higher to discourage the demand that's been built up and to encourage supply and vice versa.

I don't really look at the charts except as a history of prices, so that I can look back at various times and try to put in monitoring checks to a position, given the fundamental and price information and to see how news follows prices.

Most traders get frustrated with fundamentals, because they mix up, in their minds, market news with basic fundamentals. News follows the fundamentals.

Take the guy on the floor who's a wire service reporter. He has two cards filed on his desk, bullish quotes and bearish quotes, and it's like a debate. If the market goes up, he goes to the bullish card file and picks out five or six quotes that sound good, elaborates on them, and blends them together to form a story. I have always felt that news followed the market. In essence, my job as a trader was to figure out what everybody's going to want to buy before they know they want to buy it. I want to buy it and sell it to them when they've got to have it!

Q: How do you identify market opportunity?

JEFFREY: Well, for one thing it's fairly easy to look at something and say, my God, the price of this particular commodity at this moment is very low. Take hogs, for example. The price is low based on the cost of production and historical pricing of that particular commodity.

Q: Can you walk us through how you form your judgments about the market, how you use a mixture of fundamentals and technicals?

JEFFREY: The technician looks at the price action and sees something happening. He doesn't know that there's necessarily a fundamental reason. In fact, he doesn't care if there is. I start with the known fundamentals and try to discriminate between what everybody knows and what I call surprises, the things that may or may not transpire. I try to find situations where all or a large portion of the potential surprises are favorable to my intended positions.

Q: Do you develop this into a quantitative model or is this a discretionary judgment that you make?

JEFFREY: Well, I've tried to come up with a price impact. I take last year's prices and try to understand what the known fundamentals should do to the price levels. Then I look at what potential surprises are there in the thoughts of the magnitudes to those surprises and what the impact might be. And, I try to set up a situation where if I'm wrong and the surprises don't materialize, I won't get hurt. But, if I'm right and there are some good surprises, it could turn out to be a pretty dandy trade.

Q: When you decide you're wrong and the fundamentals aren't clicking in or having a price impact that you thought they should in the market, how do you measure that you're wrong? Is it a price amount? Is it a technical stop point? Or, is it that you just don't see the fundamentals materializing as anticipated?

JEFFREY: It's because I'm losing more money than I'm willing to invest on the trade, more than I planned to risk. I say to myself, there's something going on here that I don't understand, at which point I get out and approach things again with a clear head.

Q: In a past interview *(The Innergame of Trading),* you presented a very interesting idea about approaching the market from the perspective of a 10,000 contract trader. Can you elaborate on that idea?

JEFFREY: I think one of the most dangerous things people can do in the marketplace is to constantly switch their opinion. It's so easy to pick up the phone and change your mind, and everybody starts as I did, as a one or two contract trader. The one and two contract trader has the flexibility, the ability if you will, to change his or her mind in an instant. Get in on a whim, get out on a whim. It's Friday. I'm going away for the weekend. I don't want to worry about this. So, I'll get out. I can always get back in on Monday. Traders tend to lose their good trades that way because they're always taking profits too soon.

And then there are the transaction costs. Despite the fact that I have a membership and have lowered my commission costs as far as they can go, and I execute some of my own trades to lower the cost even further, there's still a large transaction cost for making lots of transactions. And, I think there are only so many good decisions in me; that is, I don't think I can be right on every zig and zag in the marketplace, so I tend to want to trade much longer term. Part of the reason for this 10,000 contract trader rule is I try to force myself around the corner, to think far ahead. I look at the market from the perspective of someone who is in it for the long run. This is a very important point.

I was reading Ron Chernow's new book, *Titan* (Random House, 1998), about the life of John D. Rockefeller. An observation was made about Rockefeller that he had the ability to look far ahead and around the corner. Imagine yourself as a really large speculator who's got to turn an ocean liner in the middle of the ocean and change course. If you try to think like that proverbial 10,000 contract trader, you're sticking your hand in the fire providing the liquidity in buying the market when no else wants it. You're selling out of your positions when everybody wants it. And, you may or may not be right on your timing, but at least you've got a chance to be somewhat more in tune with the bottoms and the tops. Then going back, looking at price charts, and trying to decide when you got into things and when you got out of things, this too improves your performance.

It just became clear to me: You've got to be willing to buy things when it's the most emotionally painful to buy. A friend of mine was talking about the cattle market and an old Miller beer commercial. It's Miller time and they're cracking open bottles on the back of a pickup, only they're not popping the lids, just knocking the necks off on the side of the truck. This is the time to get out!

Q: How do you use price charts?

JEFFREY: Really, as a history of what has happened over time, the relationship between one commodity and another: hogs and corn, cattle and corn, hogs and pork bellies, hogs and cattle. I try to isolate areas where there are extremes and where there's value. Someone once said, "Don't diddle in the middle." If you can find a commodity near a price extreme, have a reasonable chance of catching a real serious wave of pessimism, and can hang on for awhile until a wave of optimism hits the market—that presents opportunity. And, if you take the money and stand back until there's another obvious wave of optimism or pessimism to take advantage of, you will find you can do pretty well.

Q: How would you characterize your overall market philosophy?

JEFFREY: Without sounding too flip, I'd say: Get a hunch and bet a bunch and then go to lunch!

Q: And you live by that dictum?

JEFFREY: Well, you live by the sword, you die by the sword. What you always have to be watchful of is the time you feel like reaching around and patting yourself on the back, telling yourself how smart you are. That's when you should be reaching for the phone and getting out of your position. "Pride goeth before the fall." There's no saying more ingrained in the minds of successful commodity traders. When you start feeling really good and really smart, that's when the market's going to teach you some lessons that you should have remembered.

Another thing worth mentioning is that trading is addictive. The highs and the lows are both addicting. A friend of mine and I were talking, and I don't know how he knows about addiction and gambling, but he asked me this question: What's the second greatest thrill for a compulsive gambler? I don't know, I said. Losing and not being able to cover.

You know visions of kneecaps being broken and getting thrown in a river do not appeal to me at all! But, I know I'm absolutely compulsive and in love with trading. I don't feel alive unless I've got an opinion on the marketplace, and I've got it expressed, and my positions are moving up and down or at some meaningful level that holds my attention. It's just part of my psyche.

Q: Based on your long experience with markets, what do you think is the essence of a successful trader or investor?

JEFFREY: I think it boils down to being an extremely pragmatic, hardworking student of the marketplace. You've got to come with a background of intelligence, to be observant of the markets. You've got to be psychologically cognizant of yourself: your own emotions and the emotions of the people around you. You've got to have a good memory of what's happened in the marketplace and in your own psyche, and be constantly learning about the market.

The market is constantly evolving. It's really the sum total of all the participants, whether they're producers, consumers, or representatives such as meat processors or handlers of the commodities. As an investor, you must recognize that everybody evolves over time, and your job is to be a little smarter and evolve a little faster and stay a little ahead of the curve. And, I guess it boils down to the essence of human evolution in the sense that humans have survived because they have the ability to walk upright, carry tools, and use them effectively. We didn't fall out of the sky as the rulers of the universe! We were weak little things and survived by our wits.

Q: What do you think has been the most significant thing the market has taught you about yourself?

JEFFREY: I think the most significant lesson from the marketplace is that at some time you are just going to be totally wrong. And when you are, you've got to get out of the market, preserve capital, take some time off, clear your head, and be able to admit that you were wrong. No matter how smart you are and how good a track record you have, there's going to come a time when everything's goes to hell and you'll need to have humility.

Q: How do you enter those periods?

JEFFREY: Not well. I'm still very stubborn. I hang onto positions probably too long when they're against me and probably a little too short when they're going my way. When they asked Bernard Baruch the secret of his success, he said, "I always sold too soon."

Q: He did okay.

JEFFREY: Yes, he did all right.

Q: So, the key then, is to sell too soon.

JEFFREY: I'll agree to that and just add, don't get in too early!

10

DICK STOKEN

Mr. Stoken is a long-term Chicago Mercantile Exchange member and currently heads his own trading firm, Strategic Investments.

Q: Can you describe how you first became interested in the market?

DICK: Well, that goes way back. I have always been interested in trading and finance. I studied at the University of Chicago at a time when the prevailing academic view was that you couldn't beat the market. And so I went to my finance professor, Dr. Ketchum, who was a fairly well-known economist. He told me that in fact he knew of many people, personal acquaintances, who were making money in the stock market.

This was in 1958, the year I graduated from college. Dr. Ketchum told me to try to get a job at a brokerage house. I walked down LaSalle Street and went from wire house to wire house, and the major questions at that time were: How much money can you bring into the firm? and What country club do you belong to? Of all my friends and relatives, I thought with luck I could put together $5,000.

The only firm willing to hire me was Merrill Lynch. I believe at the time there was a six-month to one-year wait before you started the training program. In the intervening time, a friend of mine discovered the Chicago Mercantile Exchange. He started telling me all about it, and I got excited. At that time, the Merc was just a small exchange—butter, eggs, and onions. It was before currencies or financial instruments.

So, I went on the floor and went into the executive office. Edward Harris was the president. I got on the floor before the opening and all of a sudden the opening bell rang. I stood there and marveled—hardly anybody was younger than 45 years of age. I saw these men—at the time I called them "little old men"—running into the pit. They were jumping on each other's shoulders and screaming, and I thought, my God, this is for me! I raised the $3,800 to buy a membership. I borrowed $2,000 from the clearinghouse I traded through and only really had to come up with $1,800, which was a lot then!

Q: Dick, how many different markets do you trade today?

DICK: I trade almost everything. I'll trade anything from the wheat and corn and soybeans to pork bellies and hogs to Japanese bonds and stock indexes.

Q: Are you trading both domestic and international markets?

DICK: Yes.

Q: How would you characterize your general approach to the market?

DICK: Let me first say my trading approach has gone through many changes and refinements over 40 years. But, what I try to do now is coordinate technicals and fundamental data wherever I can. I say wherever I can, because obviously you can always determine technicals; fundamentals are a bit trickier. After a long period of time, I've worked up fundamental models that work pretty consistently in several markets. On the other hand, there are several markets that seem to elude me, at least as they relate to fundamental models—in particular, currencies and gold.

Q: Which markets do you find work best with your fundamental models?

DICK: Grains and livestock.

Q: Traditional commodity markets?

DICK: Yes. That and equities.

Q: How do you use your fundamental model, let's say, when you're trading grains?

DICK: With grains I start with just working supply and demand factors. I begin there to get a basic feel. And it's easy, because the grain market really lends itself to that kind of analysis. You have government reports and can monitor the supply and demand coming at you. This allows you to be a step ahead to see when the markets are a little too high or a little too low in the context of an overall fundamental situation. As far as weather goes, it's hard to stay a step of ahead! But in general, supply and demand factors are very useful.

Q: Do you look at the relative prices of corn to wheat or meal to beans?

DICK: No, I don't. I mean, once in awhile when those commodity relationships get way out of whack, a bell goes off and I say to myself, okay, I'm going to start watching the spread. But, in general, I try not to.

Q: So, you try to analyze each grain market as a discreet market?

DICK: I try to watch grains more or less as a whole market sector, because most of the time each component market will trend together. Corn and beans usually trend very well together, and wheat is often fairly well correlated, too.

Q: If you're bullish grains, can you see yourself being long beans, corn, and wheat at the same time, or do you generally try to just stay in one commodity?

DICK: I sort of model it so that I'm ready to do all three, or especially two of the three. Then, if I see one of them picking up relative strength, or one of them having fundamentals that are much more bearish or bullish than the others, I will go ahead and shift into that particular market. Right now, the bean fundamentals are much worse, generally more bearish.

For example, I have a ratio where I try to have 66 percent of my money in beans when I'm bullish and 33 percent in corn. Now, because of the fundamental outlook, if I was long, I would have 80 percent in corn and only 5 percent in beans.

Q: How do you identify market opportunity?

DICK: I try to model the markets into three categories: bullish, neutral, and bearish. I try to identify a zone where fundamentally there is an opportunity. Actually, my opportunities come up when I'm well in the zone of bearish or bullish. Sometimes, when I'm watching these markets, I'll see something that will jump out at me. An interesting example from the livestock sector is hogs. For years, in the pig crop report, production hardly advanced more than 4 percent or 5 percent beyond the previous year. And all of a sudden, in 1998, it stuck out at 7 percent or 8 percent, approaching 9 percent more than a year ago. For me, that was a sign of something that was going to dramatically affect the market.

Q: So, how do you interpret that data?

DICK: I would interpret it as extremely bearish. It stuck out from the previous government reports of the past 10 to 15 years.

Q: Once you've identified opportunity, do you have a basic market strategy how to enter the market?

DICK: Yes. For one thing, I do not like to go against the technicals. What I have done is develop a technical model that is trend following. And I do not like to go ahead and fade that (take an opposite position); I wait until that model is in sync with the overall fundamental picture. Built into the model are short-, intermediate-, and long-term indicators. But, if the long-term model is in a particular direction, I won't enter a position until I have additional confirmation.

Q: Specifically, how do you use your fundamental analysis in conjunction with your technical analysis? There must be times when your fundamental model is telling you to go one way, but the technical model is indicating a different kind of market.

DICK: Definitely. I have different ways of working it out in different scenarios and in different markets.

Q: Speaking about grains, how would you use fundamental data in conjunction with the technicals in determining market entry?

DICK: A good example would be the grain market in 1993. My fundamental model pointed down, but my technical models gave some very strong signs of going up. What I did in that case was wait for my most powerful major long-term signal to turn.

Q: And you followed the fundamentals?

DICK: No, I followed my long-term technical model, which I allowed to overrule my fundamental model.

Q: In your long experience in trading markets, do you think the fundamentals or the technicals lead?

DICK: I think fundamentals usually yield the first sign, but there are so many signs it's hard to really know how to follow through.

Q: But, on a long-term basis, would you say that when you have determined the fundamental shift—that is, you get a long-term fundamental signal—you are willing to go with that?

DICK: Not until I get corroboration of the technical model.

Q: So, you need the confirmation of the technicals?

DICK: Right. At one point in my career, I didn't, but now I find a statistically more significant result by waiting for additional confirmation.

Q: Which markets do you think hold the most potential in the future as you look at all the markets that you are currently trading?

DICK: I would have to be a little bit more biased toward the financials. I think financials have a much stronger future for investors, especially when I look at some of the foreign markets and particularly at European markets such as the DTB. I also think gold is going to come back to life in the next three to four years.

Q: Are you bullish on gold?

DICK: Yes, on a very long-term basis. Right now I recognize it is in a cyclical down. I think it can be a very exciting market.

Q: What do you think will drive the gold market in the years to come?

DICK: Inflation will return. And, looking back from 2019, we might ask why we didn't get into gold, because the writing was on the wall.

Q: You have been in this business for a long time and of late have observed an unprecedented interest and excitement about the stock market. Do you think this bull market is going to continue, or do you think we have finally reached the top of the mountain?

DICK: Well, having been in the business for so long and having seen both bull and bear markets, it's hard to be anything but bearish—and frankly skeptical about what's happened. But I must add I've been skeptical now for close to two years! And it might be another two years before this market does finally top out.

Q: How do you approach the equities market?

DICK: I have a pretty good fundamental model on equities. By the way, it's still bullish.

Q: What does your model take into consideration?

DICK: I look at interest rates and rates of inflation. As far as I'm concerned, those are the two key things.

Q: Do you look at PE ratios?

DICK: No. It's all background stuff that tends to build up feel for the market, but I don't really have that built into my model.

Q: You don't focus on it?

DICK: No. But I do take into consideration the political cycle, in particular, a 15-month political cycle that ends the year of elections. Most analysts who watch the political cycles focus on the year of the election. Mine is a little different.

Q: So, when you go into equities, you're not actually analyzing the management of a particular company? That doesn't come in at all?

DICK: No, I go ahead and trade the indexes.

Q: How would you characterize your overall market philosophy?

DICK: In some ways, I've gotten a lot more conservative and a lot more humble being in the business a long time. I would say, though, my main objective is to focus on the long term. That way, I can focus on the fundamental side of markets and stay with something I know I'm not going to have to change my mind about over a period of time. Take the Fed, they don't move on interest rates because the last quarter's economic growth was too high or something like that. They know that if they want to make a move, they will be able to stick with that move for six months, a year, or more. And that's basically my philosophy. Before I'm ready to make a move, I want to feel that the technicals are setting up and that there's something behind them, that fundamentally the position has legs.

Q: So, when you go into a position—whether it's grains or equity or livestock—you're going into it for the long run? It could be a year or two or longer?

DICK: Yes. But, I might get out of the position on a tactical basis; I might see the technicals turn on an intermediate basis or something like that. And I might get out of the position—not go the other way but get out or lighten the position for awhile and then at a more advantageous time come back in.

Q: Do you ever find yourself in a position that goes against the long-term trend of the market you're trading?

DICK: No, I try not to.

Q: How do you calculate risk?

DICK: I started out with the basic philosophy of cut your losses and let the profits ride. But that has evolved into something much more concrete. What I try to do now is stay in the direction of the trend, at least until the intermediate indicator turns against me. Also, if I have several positions on, I try to get negative correlations in many of the different market sectors.

Q: You try to have the diversification of your portfolio working for you in the long term, is that it?

DICK: That, and then I add in a very conservative money management margin technique. For instance, if I trade a T-bond, I'll allocate $16,000 to do one T-bond contract. That allows me to sustain a pretty adverse move without really cutting into my equity that much.

Q: How much do you allow on an adverse move?

DICK: Until the trend turns. I don't want to do a dollar amount; I'll wait until the trend gives me a signal. Let's stay with the T-bonds, for example: The T-bonds are roughly 12 percent of my portfolio. And I've got a $16,000 margin, so that even if I take a hit of $8,000, it's only 6 percent of my total portfolio.

Q: Which would be a very large move in the T-bonds.

DICK: Yes.

Q: And will that usually indicate to you very quickly whether you're in a changing trend?

DICK: Usually, it will. Plus, I have the negatively correlated markets working in my portfolio.

Q: What do you think makes for a successful trader?

DICK: I'd say a certain amount of self-confidence, but not too much because then it gets in the way. Also, a certain amount of mental agility and flexibility are essential, as is the ability to focus and learn something and be able to implement it into your overall strategy.

Q: Would you characterize yourself more as a trader or an investor?

DICK: I'm still a trader. I think an investor is exemplified by someone like Warren Buffett.

Q: Somebody who's very long term?

DICK: Yes, because you know that eventually I'm going to play both sides of the market. Going back to bonds, I'm going to be long and I'm going to be short the market.

Q: In 40 years of trading experience, what would you say is the single most important thing you've learned?

DICK: I would say that there's always a tomorrow. No matter how bad today is, there's always a tomorrow. No matter how good today is, there's always a tomorrow. And, I always try to keep that in focus.

Q: Can you talk about the role of discretionary trading in your market approach? To what extent do you either override your models or are you tempted to second-guess a trading model?

DICK: I try not to. I used to do that a lot more, but I have found that over time I didn't do a very good job of overriding it.

Q: Does intuition come to play at all in your trading?

DICK: It used to more, but now I've kind of given it up. I think I'm a loser on intuition!

Q: What do you think is the most important thing you've learned in terms of systems development?

DICK: Stay away from things that are too popular, because if they're too popular, generally they're not going to work. And the second thing is: Keep in mind your own biases. You're going to bring your biases into it. For instance, you're going to immediately start out; if you're going to look at a system and want to go way back, you're going to look at a system that didn't blow up in 1987. So, you already built that bias into your system! You've got to really try to overcome that and all other biases and start out with strategies that can be tested for an extended period of time.

Q: How far back do you go when you're testing a new idea?

DICK: I go back as far as we have records!

Q: Do you have any other ideas about what would make for a successful investor or trader?

DICK: Patience, I think, is very important. And the ability to manage your emotions; it's so easy in this game to go both ways, to get overly depressed when things are going wrong. And it's also easy to go the other way and get arrogant; so you need to keep that in check.

Q: It's interesting that you mention the importance of managing your emotions, because you are now a systems trader and, as you mentioned a moment ago, pay little attention to intuition. So, the managing of emotions is the ability to stick to your model and not be distracted. Is that what you mean?

DICK: That too, but part of it is to monitor that feeling that you're some sort of Godlike figure.

Q: Getting divine premonitions about the market?

DICK: Yes, and that you really know everything. Sometimes it's hard not to!

Q: Are you saying it's hard even though you have a model and a system? Do you find your emotions coming into play?

DICK: I find I'm able to execute okay, but let's face it, there are times I have to talk to myself.

Q: It's funny, because people generally assume there are two clear-cut categories of traders: the discretionary trader and the systems trader. We're not saying these are correct perceptions, but there is the perception that the systems trader somehow is purely unemotional.

DICK: It's just part of the whole process of investing. Emotions come into play. Even if you have good models and systems, you must monitor your response to markets. We may be traders and investors, but we're also human beings!

11

DAVID SILVERMAN

Mr. Silverman is a long-term member of the Chicago Mercantile Exchange and International Monetary Market, where he serves on its board of directors. He has traded foreign currency markets and currently day trades equities.

Q: How did you first become interested in the market?

DAVID: I started working at the Chicago Mercantile Exchange during my summer vacations from the time I was a teenager through my college years. After college, I went to law school for a year and ultimately decided that I didn't want to become a lawyer. I was reading the *Wall Street Journal* every day and wishing I were involved in the market rather than studying civil procedures. In fact, I cut classes regularly to come to the exchange and just stand on the floor, fill out charts, and do things related to the markets. If I had not left law school on my own, I would have been asked to leave eventually. And, I would have ended up a trader *later* rather than sooner!

Q: Was it the market action that fascinated you?

DAVID: Yes, and the fact that the early '80s were a very exciting time. At the exchanges in Chicago, there was a lot of opportunity. The barriers to enter were very low. I think you could get started at the time with just a few thousand dollars in your trading account. There were even special memberships for younger traders that were only a few hundred dollars a month. So, it was very easy to start. I borrowed I think $5,000 from my dad, and that was everything I had to my name. Just a few years later the barriers to enter got very, very high. So, I was in the right place at the right time.

Q: How did you first get involved in currency markets?

DAVID: The kind of membership I had at the exchange allowed me to trade a number of different products. And the main product to trade was Eurodollars, which at the time was a rather quiet market. It was a far cry from what it is now—the biggest interest rate futures contract in the world.

At the time, foreign currencies were very active and you had to trade a minimum number of Eurodollars before you could trade currencies. I gravitated toward the currencies because there was more opportunity there. And at some point, I started doing all my business in currencies and then purchased a full trading membership.

By that point, I was established in the currencies, mostly because it looked like there was more opportunity there. The traders who did make a commitment to the Eurodollar market ended up becoming extraordinarily successful over the years, because they built the market and had an initial foothold there. Currencies were a wonderful place to be for the period of time I was there.

Q: Did you trade the currencies on the floor for many years?

DAVID: I was in various currency pits for probably 15 years.

Q: Are you still trading the currencies today?

DAVID: Yes, but no longer in the pit.

Q: How would you describe your general approach to the market?

DAVID: Not being on the floor changes things a lot, because what you look at when you make a trade as an off-floor trader is very different. You're not so concerned with the physical aspects of the trade; you're not hearing the bids and offers and not watching the body language. That kind of action doesn't come through a computer screen. And so, you have to look for different sorts of market clues. The kind of trading typically done in the pit is very short term and based on factoring in trader emotion. You don't think about the market in the same way you do when you're off the floor and have more time to analyze and then react.

Q: In other words, when you're on the trading floor you're basically trying to scalp the market and get quick short-term returns.

DAVID: Right. And oftentimes, you're not so much responding to the macroeconomic data as you're really responding to what the trader standing in your immediate area is bidding or offering. You may be completely bearish on the market and still give him a bid for a substantial quantity of the product, because there's an opportunity there in the very short term.

Q: How has that changed your approach since you began trading off-floor?

DAVID: For the first couple of years, being off the floor was a real handicap. The scalping approach is almost impossible to use successfully off the trading floor. We're going to talk about Nasdaq Level II, which is a different story entirely, and that approach typically won't work very well in currencies. There's slippage. There are execution costs. There's just the inability to be connected to the market in the same kind of physical way. In my opinion, scalping is really the wrong approach for someone who's off the trading floor. I mean, some days I would trade a couple thousand contracts on the trading floor, and it's inconceivable to me that I would take such an approach off the trading floor! That's not to say that you can't make a lot more money trading far fewer contracts—you certainly can, but it requires a different methodology.

Q: What do you do off the floor that's different?

DAVID: Off the trading floor, you tend to be more analytical than you are on the trading floor. You tend to pay attention to external factors, more of the macroeconomic data. Now I read the papers more carefully and listen to the fundamental information. I have time to call people at other computers and other desks—in New York and overseas—in order to get their views on the market.

Also, because I'm not required as a market maker to respond instantaneously every time there's a bid or an offer, I have the time to be analytical, to sit in front of a charting machine, if I like doing that, and spend a good portion of my day analyzing charts.

Q: How do you personally identify market opportunity?

DAVID: The best market opportunity for an off-floor trader is a trending market. Whether you use simple moving averages or have some sort of esoteric formula that you've either bought or created on your own, a trending market is the easiest type of market for the off-floor trader to trade.

Q: Does that characterize, in general, the way you would approach the market?

DAVID: Yes. Because of the slippage and the execution problems, you're going to get chopped to death in markets that move sideways. What you want to look for are markets that are trending. And, to the extent that you have the ability to trade lots of different things, you can see them as a generic trading vehicle rather than saying, "I can only trade currencies because I've got an IMM seat and I'm a currency trader." You're really able to move wherever the interest is in the world! Thanks to the technology, you have the ability now to trade lots of different markets, 24 hours a day. I mean, if you want to trade European interest rates, you can. When I started in the 1980s, it was deutsche marks or Eurodollars and that was pretty much it.

Q: Would you say your basic market strategy is always to go with the trend as opposed to taking swings out of the market and going contrary to an established trend?

DAVID: Well, that's the goal, but you screw it up a lot! And sometimes, you think too much. Ideally, you want to be on the trending side of the market and catch a long-term move.

Q: So, in a bull market you're always trying to buy breaks, and in a bear market you're always trying to sell rallies.

DAVID: Right.

Q: Would you buy rallies in a bull market?

DAVID: Yes, sometimes; that is, if the market seems really strong and the volatility is such that you think there'll be a big follow-through. But, one thing that I try not to do is chase the market too much. I try to look at the market in terms of the number of levels it moves at a time. That sort of approach can serve you really well if you are trying to follow the trend. Let's say, for the sake of argument, that you think the market's going *X* number of points, and when it comes back 50 percent, let's say, that's where you want to be buyer, or maybe 75 percent. Whatever your approach, it really doesn't matter. You could say, I'll buy it when it comes back 10 percent. The key is to be consistent and base your actions on statistically reliable testing.

Q: Do you quantify the standard deviation of a particular move and then at a certain percent try to buy or sell the market?

DAVID: Right. I would say not formally, because I'm not a systematic trader. I know lots of people who have actually quantified those things, put them in their models, and they don't really have any trading decisions to make per se; their models make the decisions. Mine is a lot less formal. That's also residue from being a floor trader for 15 years.

Q: It's more intuitive, and at the same time, it's based on your day-to-day experience over several decades about how markets trade, in currencies particularly, is that correct?

DAVID: Absolutely. You want to try not to be a buyer at the top of however many levels you think it's moving up, even if it goes higher from there and you miss that trade!

Q: Is a level a standard deviation?

DAVID: Again, I'm using a very informal standard. I think that's probably a fair comparison, but there's a specific definition to standard deviation. And I'm probably trivializing the definition, if I say my levels are standard deviations. They're not. They'll also change from time to time, based on my subjective interpretation of what's going on in a particular currency market.

Q: Is your level based on observation of what is the typical or usual move within a particular time frame that the D-mark or Swiss franc has made based on historical price action?

DAVID: Yes, and every market has a different characteristic.

Q: And a different personality?

DAVID: And a different personality, and you try to learn them over time. The ones I trade allow me a good intuitive sense of what the levels look like, although they may be changing. Even to the extent they change, I'm more on top of those changes in markets in which I'm active.

Q: In fact, you have to adapt. I mean, particular currency markets have a certain personality for a time and then change. You just have to be aware of how they're changing and why they're changing to trade them effectively.

DAVID: Actually, last summer someone told me to take a look at the agricultural markets, which I never trade. I looked at them, and they looked like they were going down, so I got short not thinking about levels or anything. They looked lousy on the chart, and I think they went significantly lower in two days. I got out because there was a profit; there was no other good reason to get out particularly, and they went down for another five days. That was a market where I did well, but not as well as I could have, because I really didn't have a good sense of that sector's trading characteristics.

Q: To what extent do you rely on fundamental information for trading the currencies?

DAVID: Certainly a lot more now then when I was on the trading floor. You have to be aware of what's going on: Listen when Greenspan talks and try to read between the lines. Understand the significance of a German finance minister getting fired or resigning, as occurred recently. Watch money supply figures and think about changes in the European economic structure that have had a huge effect on money flows and on all sorts of relationships between the different currencies. To trade currencies, you really have to be in tune with the underlying market fundamentals.

I also try to keep up with publications like the *Economist,* which is an excellent source. I also like *Risk Magazine,* and I read the *Wall Street Journal* every day, as well as *Investor's Business Daily* and the *New York Times.*

Q: Do you read the front pages or just the business pages?

DAVID: Especially with the *Times,* the front page often has a lot of information about Europe that is useful. But it's real easy to find page 17 in the C section of the *Journal* and read about the currencies.

The people who really are good at currency trading read other things and try to see what really is going on; they don't just react to what everybody else is reading. And, that's where you can distinguish yourself from the crowd. I mean, sources like CNBC are important, and you've got to listen to them—I actually have one of my television monitors tuned to CNBC all the time—but I use them as a counterindicator. I look at them as a fade. If it's on CNBC, you pretty much want to go the other way!

Q: To what extent do you rely on technical indicators? And which indictors are you using for trading currencies?

DAVID: I like moving averages, because they're really simple. I use CQG for Windows, and it's a real simple function to program in, simple to understand and visually very clear.

Q: Do you use multiple moving averages or just one?

DAVID: It depends on the market—and on whether I'm looking for a really long-term move or just day trading. Moving averages are simple to use. The average person who's just trying to follow a trend and not be in and out of the market 100 times a day probably would be very well served by looking at charts with moving averages on them.

Q: Which moving averages would you recommend—the 18-day or the 30-day, for example?

DAVID: Again, that's obviously contingent on what sort of risk tolerance you have for being in the market. Someone who is not going to trade very much and is really looking for a long-term trend may want to look at a 30-, 45-, or even 90-day moving average. If you traded S&Ps, it would have kept you long for the past three years—and you'd be very wealthy!

Q: When you say you use moving averages, are you waiting for the shorter ones to cross over the longer ones, or are you just looking at a particular moving average in isolation?

DAVID: A little bit of both. I do look for the crossovers, but I tend not to look as far out as a 60- or 90-day moving average; that's a little bit too far out on the horizon for me. I may put them on the chart just to see what they look like, but they're not all that relevant to my trading. I'm probably looking at 3-, 7-, or 14-day averages mostly. I look for where they cross over or if they don't. And again, their simplicity and their movement make a lot of sense to me.

Q: Do you also look at moving averages on smaller time frame charts, a 60-minute chart, for instance?

DAVID: I've done that. But, because of slippage and execution costs, I question whether the detriments with the slippage and execution costs are worth making the trading decision. Even if you make the right trading decision as a result of that, you're going to pay something for being in and out of the market as often as it's going to require you to be.

Q: Basically, you're looking at moving averages daily, and you're not that interested in intraday time frames, is that right?

DAVID: Right; that is, with the moving averages. It doesn't mean I don't trade for a shorter period of time, but I don't use moving averages to initiate a short-term trade.

Q: What changes or new developments do you see occurring in the currency markets?

DAVID: Obviously, the most important thing that's happened recently is the change to the European economic structure. In the next couple years, the sterling likely will join the rest of the European countries. And, the idea that there will be one currency where there were 11 or 12 before is an extremely important change. All those currency interrelationships will have disappeared, and there will be an obvious impact on interest rates and various global stock markets.

The individual currency trader of the '80s and '90s will no longer be a force. In the final analysis, in my opinion, he or she will not be very important to the marketplace. However, there still will be opportunities for savvy market players.

Q: How would you characterize your overall market philosophy?

DAVID: I don't try to hit home runs. I don't like the term because everybody uses it, but I think it's descriptive. I'm also not "betting the farm" to try and make lots of money on any specific trade. In every trade I make, I consider the risk inherent in the trade, so that no individual trade, or series of trades, will eat up so much of my trading capital that I won't be able to come back and make another trade tomorrow.

Q: How do you define your risk and your money management parameters? Do you do it as percent of equity?

DAVID: Yes. It's actually very simple. In my case, it's really just a percentage of equity. I know how much capital is in my trading account, and I know how much I'm willing to lose on a particular trade. That defines for me how many contracts I can put on and how far the market can move against me at any given time. And, I will put a stop in the market, and if I'm out, I'm out, and then I reassess. That allows me to make many trades without ever really getting hurt. I would have to make 30 or 40 losing trades in a row before I would have to figure out how to do things differently. And that's never happened to me before, and it's almost inconceivable to me that it would happen.

Q: Would you say that holds true for your currency trading as well as your equities trading on Nasdaq Level II?

DAVID: It's similar, but the methodology in trading Nasdaq stocks on a Level II system is completely different. As a general philosophy, you don't want to lose a lot of money on any particular trade, because it will obviously impact on your ability to make more trades. And the more trades you can make if you've got a good trading system, the larger the percentage of chances you'll be successful. So, the general philosophy is the same, but in terms of actual method it's really not.

Q: How did you first become interested in Nasdaq Level II, and what are some of the practical things that you're doing with it on a day-to-day basis?

DAVID: I had read and heard about electronic communication networks, or ECNs, for a couple of years. And I saw that the growth of these ECNs was dramatic. They only have been around for a couple of years, and the amount of business being transacted on them is absolutely astounding. When I started looking into how business is done on ECNs, I found Broadway Trading in New York. It is, at least in my opinion, the most successful of the day trading ECNs. Imagine a few hundred traders at a few different locations, all of whom are sitting in front of computers every day and acting effectively as market makers, using a proprietary system of Datek, whose retail broker is called Island. Island is one of nine ECNs, and it allows you to participate in the order flow that comes through Nasdaq on its Level II system. Literally five minutes after seeing this system, I knew they had replicated what I had done for 15 years as a trader on the exchange floor.

It was the first time I had seen such a thing, and I've seen a lot of systems out there. It's even better than trading in the pit because of the ability of the small trader to actually have preference over the market maker. And, there's such an incredible flow of information through the system that if you can learn how to interpret it, you're far ahead of where you would have been in the pit just listening to the bids and offers!

Q: Are you looking for trend or are you looking to trade as you did in the pit, to catch the quick moves in the market?

DAVID: Nasdaq Level II trading is really more like pit trading. You're looking for eighths and quarters, and in the Internet stocks, you're looking for more because you're risking more. But if you're trying to trade these things with a moving average because you want to make $25 over a couple of days in some stock that's hot, you don't.

It's very exciting. You sit there and you eat the glass; I mean, you get in that computer monitor and you don't even know what time of day it is. It's an incredible surge you can get, because they have managed to replicate the trading floor so that you get an even break with the professionals.

Q: Whether trading currencies long term or trading Nasdaq Level II for short-term market moves, what would you say are the essential attributes of a successful trader or investor?

DAVID: Risk management is very important. You always have to be able to come back and make another trade. A lot of people in the business don't necessarily like comparing trading to gambling, but it is very much like gambling. Someone who puts everything on red might have a big payoff, but the casino's always going to win in the long run. If you keep putting everything on red, eventually it's going to come up black. And so, what you want to do is try to put yourself in a position where you have the odds of the casino, even if it's only 51 percent. If you can stay in the game long enough, using meaningful risk management techniques, you will make money in the long run, almost by definition.

Q: What about the importance of psychology?

DAVID: I think it's probably the most important component of trading or investing. You can sit down and write a model and never make another trading decision. But, you have to go home every night feeling good about what you're doing. And a lot of times you're going to lose money, or you're not going to make as much as you think you're going to. You must always be cognizant of the psychological side of trading.

Also, remember that the learning process never ends. You'll have times when you really think you're on a roll, but don't get too excited about it, because it's probably going to come to an end, at least for some period of time. Also, don't get too despondent when things are going poorly.

Sometimes you may have to step aside and look at what you're doing. Analyze if your approach is robust enough. Is it effective in this market? Are your risk management techniques reasonable? And if they are, and you happened to have made a series of losing trades or had an extended period of drawdown, that's part of the business; you just have to live with it.

Q: The market always looks worst at the bottom!

DAVID: Right. Absolutely, and if you look at studies about how much trading takes place at the bottom or tops of markets, it's very small. In essence, that's where the greatest opportunity is. With the right psychological approach and well-defined risk management, in my experience, opportunity always presents itself!

12

DAVID HELD

David Held is a long-term member of the International Monetary Market who specializes in trading bonds and Eurodollar futures. He is an analyst and broker for professional and institutional clients in the interest rate sector.

Q: Can you describe how you first became interested in the market?

DAVID: I was really more or less thrust into the marketplace. I was straight out of the air force and looking for a job. My cousin at the time was a vice president at Shearson at the Board of Trade, and he got me a job as a runner.

Q: So, you started off carrying orders into the trading pits?

DAVID: Yes, running the orders back and forth, preparing the trading cards. I did whatever needed to be done.

Q: In which markets were you first involved?

DAVID: At first the grains—corn, beans, wheat, and such.

Q: Did you ever trade the grains?

DAVID: No, not at all.

Q: Now you're involved in the Eurodollar?

DAVID: That's right.

Q: How long have you been in the Eurodollar market?

DAVID: Eight years now. Before that, I was arbing bonds and silver and gold at the Board of Trade. Then, I came over to the Merc and started arbing currencies and S&Ps. When the Eurodollar pit was getting started, I just naturally moved over to that market.

Q: What is your general approach to the market?

DAVID: Basically, I try to define important areas of support and resistance. I also try to identify where I think the stop orders are going to be, in order to determine if the market will accelerate away or hold at those levels. In addition, I look at the cash screens and watch how the 30-year bonds are trading.

I also watch what the key order fillers and dealers in the pit are doing, where they are willing to buy and sell, and again I try to put it all together in the context of what's going on in the cash market. When I see the cash market start to get hit, and if I see the bonds starting to slip, I usually go with them. Basically, all the locals in the pit—that's what they're watching. Those are the two main indicators: watching the cash and the price movement in the bonds.

Q: Do you usually have a macro point of view of the market?

DAVID: Yes, I do. When I come in every morning, I look at the overnight trades and try to calculate what is happening with the long bond.

In particular, I'm looking at the overnight range. Let's say the range was 121 even to 121.26; once I know the range, I establish a halfway point, or what I like to call my pivot point. And that's where I decide if I'm going to be a buyer or a seller. If I'm above the pivot point, I'm a buyer. If I'm below that pivot point, I want to be a seller of the Eurodollar market.

Q: Do you wait for the market to come to your pivot point?

DAVID: Yes, that is the discipline. I always wait. But sometimes on the opening, you might be through the pivot. Let's take an example: If 121–01 is your pivot, and you already traded 121–04—05 when the bonds open—then I have to be long. So, I will buy 04s or 05s. And now my stop—my double down stop—will be that 01 pivot. When I come back down through it, I'll be stopped out of my longs and will reverse and go short. I know I'm going to lose three or four ticks on that trade, but I'm already short because I'm going to double down and will now be in what has the highest probability of being the next market move.

Q: What happens if the market crosses back above your pivot?

DAVID: Then I'm jumping back and forth, going back and forth. And I'll do that (try to buy the market) three or four times and then give up. In essence, I will have learned my lesson for the day. It's a choppy market, and I should stay out!

Q: Basically, what you've learned is that the market is just too choppy to trade that day, that most probably it's a nondirectional day.

DAVID: That's correct. If the market doesn't give me a clear direction early in the morning, I'll basically stay out and wait until the next day.

Q: When you're trading the market on a day-to-day basis, are you also analyzing projections of interest rates over the next 30 days, or the next 60 days?

DAVID: Oh, absolutely. I'm always looking at that. I consider what Greenspan's thinking; I look at various rates, checking for any discrepancies.

Q: How do you identify market opportunity?

DAVID: Being in the pit, I watch who are the market makers. Is there quality buying or selling going on? If Goldman's coming in buying 5,000 at a crack, I'm going to have to buy the market. I'm not going to fade a quality buyer!

Q: You're looking not only at the volume of the buying but also at the quality of the buying, is that correct?

DAVID: Definitely. If it's coming through someone like Goldman Sachs, Smith Barney, Dean Witter, something like that, yes.

Q: Do you have clients also?

DAVID: Yes, mostly professional and institutional traders.

Q: Do they rely on your analysis and market feel?

DAVID: Yes.

Q: Also, do you inform them of the quality of buying or selling at any given point in the market?

DAVID: Constantly. I continuously update my people about who's doing what in the market and, at the same time, inform them about changes with various spread relationships. Many clients will play the market that way. If they are bullish, they will sell the nearby option and buy the deferred. And if they are bearish, they will buy the nearby option and sell the deferred. It's just another way to take a market position in Eurodollars.

Q: Generally speaking, will your clients have a double position on out rights (longer short positions) and spreads?

DAVID: Yes. Generally, they will have multiple positions on, depending on what they are trying to accomplish in the market. Interestingly, I trade the 30-year bond for myself. I use my expertise in Eurodollars, which is a short-term instrument, to develop ideas about trading a longer-term instrument.

Q: How would you characterize your approach to the market?

DAVID: In general, I would say that I'm a short-term trader and long-term analyst. For myself, I look to catch small market swings, but I always have a longer-term view that I trade from. Being a floor trader for so many years has given me a certain trading mentality: I pretty much hit and run in my trading so that I don't get caught in a meltdown position! It suits my personality to approach the market on a day-to-day basis. But for my clients, I provide a much longer-term perspective, which works quite well for them.

Q: To what extent do you think you rely on fundamental analysis?

DAVID: I always monitor Greenspan's statements, trying to figure out what will be the next decision taken by the Fed. Also, what is being said between the lines is very important! Be aware of who's coming out that day and talking, and what are the market expectations for the various reports that are constantly coming into the market.

Q: Are you looking at reports and crunching numbers?

DAVID: Well, you've got to know what the market is looking for in the more important reports like unemployment, inflation, and GDP (gross domestic product).

Q: Money supply?

DAVID: That is not as significant as it used to be.

Q: From a fundamental point of view, what do you think most drives the market that you try to be aware of?

DAVID: Alan Greenspan. He is the market! You must be on top of anything that comes from the Fed. For example, watch the wording he uses, even though he's not coming out and saying something definitive. Listen closely in order to understand his intent and to know which way the Fed is leaning. That's a huge factor.

Q: To what extent do you rely on technical indicators?

DAVID: I read all the charts—daily, weekly, and monthly—regardless of whether I'm taking a short-term position. As they say, the trend is your friend, so until you break the trend, don't buck it. I'll trade short term but with the trend.

Again, the technicals help me form an opinion about the market. I particularly like using a nine-day RSI (relative strength index). The basic idea is that if the RSI is below 20, you want to buy it because it represents an oversold condition. And if you're above 80 on the RSI, you're looking to sell the market because it's an overbought condition. But there have been days when it's gone below 20, below 10 even, and the market has continued to sell off. So, you really have to use this indicator in conjunction with price action.

Q: As you're going through the longer-term stuff—the daily, weekly, and monthly price charts—are you also looking at the shorter time frames? Do you look at 60- and 30-minute charts as well?

DAVID: I'll look at a 30-minute bell curve (market profile) that I keep on the trading desk to get a sense of the market.

Q: Are you also using a market profile?

DAVID: Yes, and it helps a lot for the short term, because it establishes fair value and let's me know where to get long or short. It also is a confirmation at times of my pivot numbers.

Q: Are you looking at where the fair value is in the Eurodollar market?

DAVID: Yes. And if the market comes under fair value, I'm selling it. Above fair value, I'm a buyer.

Q: What do you look at for your long-term analysis?

DAVID: I'll look at 100- and 200-day moving averages. If you break those averages, the market is in for a sell-off.

Q: What changes or new developments do you see occurring in the Eurodollar market?

DAVID: Electronic trading is coming in June of 1999, and we'll see how that goes. Right now in the S&Ps, the E-mini is side by side with open outcry, and that works pretty well. I believe it should work just as effectively for the Eurodollar contract.

Q: Do you think execution will be more effective for the smaller investor off the electronic platform?

DAVID: Absolutely. But I also think open outcry will always have its place.

Q: How would you characterize your overall market philosophy?

DAVID: I'm very conservative. I mean, I'm not going to try to hit a home run every day. I'm going to chip away day by day; the market teaches me something every single day.

Q: So, you're looking to hit singles on a day-to-day basis.

DAVID: Yes. If I can make a couple of good trades each day, I'm happy. If you're looking to hit home runs, you better be able to take the big losses, too!

Q: So, basically you're just looking for steady increments.

DAVID: Exactly. If I can make a few good trades to cover commission and costs and put a couple of bucks in my pocket each day, I'm satisfied.

Q: Would you say, then, your overall philosophy about the market is just to approach the market on a short-term basis?

DAVID: Yes, and this sounds like a cliché, but just to let my profits run and take my first loss, which as the saying goes is the best loss. I find that philosophy works very well for me. It also can be very profitable over time.

Q: In your opinion, what makes a successful trader or investor?

DAVID: Someone who's very disciplined. You need discipline to succeed at investing. I mean, you see a lot of traders who start out very brash, trading large, and six months later they're clerking for somebody else, or they're gone. They never developed an understanding, or appreciation, or respect for how the marketplace works.

You need to respect the market. It's kind of like the respect I learned in the military. You must have that same overriding sense of respect for the market. The market will always bring you back to reality. And if you respect it and do your homework, you'll be rewarded. But it requires effort, discipline, persistence, and patience.

You must research as much as you can. If you can, come down to the trading floor and actually take a look at what goes on. There are a lot of traders in offices behind screens that have never been on the trading floor, and they think they know what's going on!

It's very eye-opening and humbling to see the market in action. One other thing about preparation: I get in about 5 AM every morning, a good two hours before the market opens, and I look at what Singapore did, what happened overnight in Tokyo, reading everything I can about the market. I read *Bridge News,* the *Wall Street Journal,* anything and everything—whatever comes out to make me able to compete. After I read everything, I'm right only about 50 percent of the time! You must do your homework and stay disciplined and, as the title of your book says, then and only then will you become a savvy investor!

PART FOUR

DIGITAL DAY TRADING

13

COMPETING WITH THE MARKET MAKERS

The digital age of financial investment has arrived. Individual traders and investors can now bypass brokers and enter the formerly rarefied arena of the major Wall Street players with just a PC, strengthened by their own knowledge and trading ability. This chapter presents some of the basic elements of what you need to know for electronic intraday trading for small price increment. For a more detailed discussion, we refer you to *Digital Day Trading* by Howard Abell.

The securities markets as they exist today are composed of two distinct systems: the specialist system and the market maker system.

SPECIALIST SYSTEM

On the New York Stock Exchange and the American Stock Exchange, a specialist system is used; that is, each stock traded on the exchange is assigned to a specialist who is expected to maintain an orderly market and also keep a book of resting orders above and below the current market. The specialist not only bids and offers for others but also steps in during volatile price movements and uses his or her own capital to take the opposite side of either an excess of bids or offers. Of course, the price at which this occurs is determined by the supply and demand of the stock at that moment. For example, if a favorable earnings report is released for XYZ, and there is an influx of buy orders, the specialist will use a combination of sell orders from the public, the book of resting orders, and his or her own capital to accommodate all the buy orders for XYZ. The price of XYZ will be determined by the sell orders available, and when those are exhausted, the experience and judgment of the specialist. I am sure we have all either seen or experienced a stock that opens several points above its previous day's close. This is the specialist attempting to find an appropriate price level.

MARKET MAKER SYSTEM

The Nasdaq and over-the-counter (OTC) markets are traded through an electronic network that brings together market makers, brokerage houses, and traders. This system gives everyone the opportunity to "see" the market by its display of bids and offers and by the size of those bids and offers to all who want to participate.

Currently there are three levels of available service:

1. *Level I* provides real-time quotes that reflect the best bid and offer and their sizes. Brokerage houses and the majority of investors who are looking for the most recent quotes use this level of service.

2. *Level II* differs from Level I in that it shows not only the best bid and offer by size but also the depth of the market. Depth refers to the market that exists behind the best bid and offer. It may show two or three other bids or offers at the best price and then will show the next best bid or offer for several levels up and down from the last price.
3. *Level III* has all the features of Level II and is used by market makers. It allows the market maker to constantly update the quotes for the securities they trade.

The Level II trading screen is your window to the world of securities markets. It gives you real-time information, such as stock quotes, bids, offers, volume, time of sales, and much more. Learning what information is available and when and how to use that information are key to beginning the process to successful digital day trading. There are several software companies that produce the Level II information, and we do not make any judgments about them. However, for purposes of illustration in this book we are using information from TradeCast, Inc.

Customized Windows in Level II TradeCast Software

Customized windows on your screen include:

- Blotter window
- Stock window
- Ticker window
- Time of sales window
- Board views window
- Top ten windows
- Fundamental data window
- Order entry window

The Blotter Window

The blotter window comprises three panes: an open position pane, a summary pane, and a trades pane. The open positions pane (Figure 13.1) keeps track of your current open positions and is customizable with 25 different pieces of information that you can display in the format that suits you. A summary pane (Figure 13.2) contains information about the current day's trading, such as equity, margin, P/L, number of trades, and realized and unrealized profit and loss. The trades pane (Figure 13.3) allows you to view all trades, today's trades, open trades short positions, long positions, and completed trades.

FIGURE 13.1 Open Positions Pane

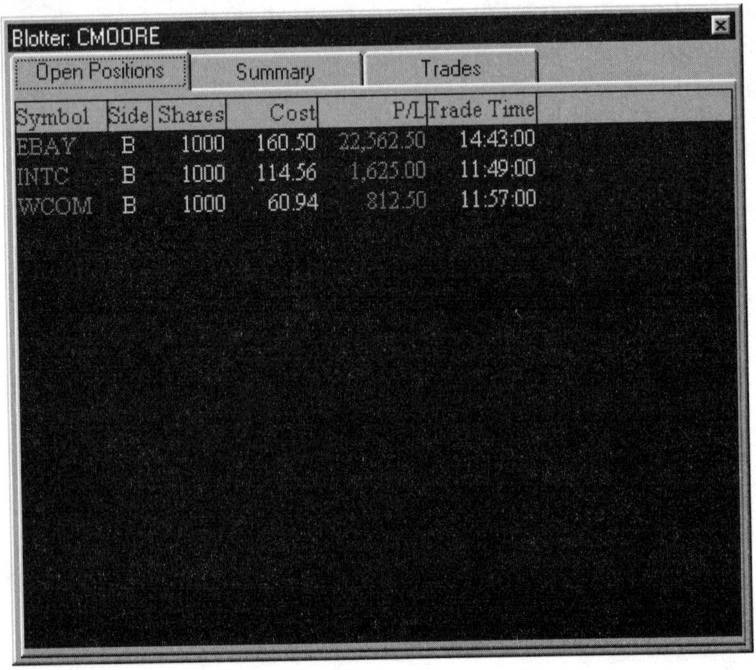

Blotter: CMOORE

Open Positions | Summary | Trades

Symbol	Side	Shares	Cost	P/L	Trade Time
EBAY	B	1000	160.50	22,562.50	14:43:00
INTC	B	1000	114.56	1,625.00	11:49:00
WCOM	B	1000	60.94	812.50	11:57:00

FIGURE 13.2 Summary Pane

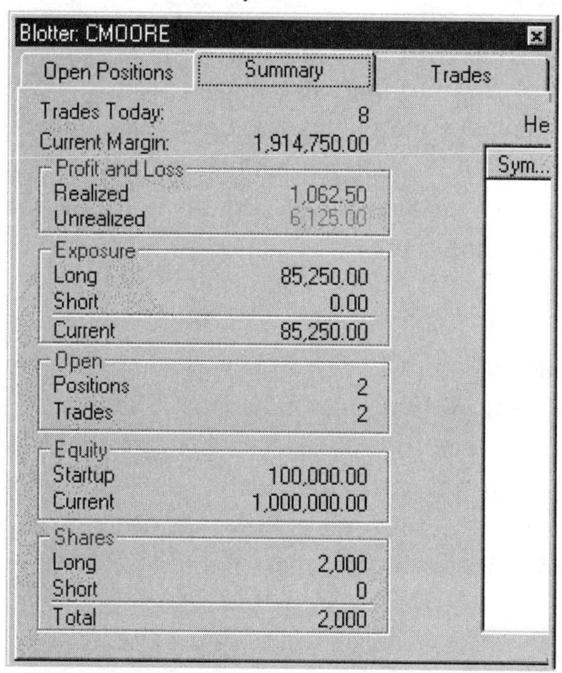

FIGURE 13.3 Trades Pane

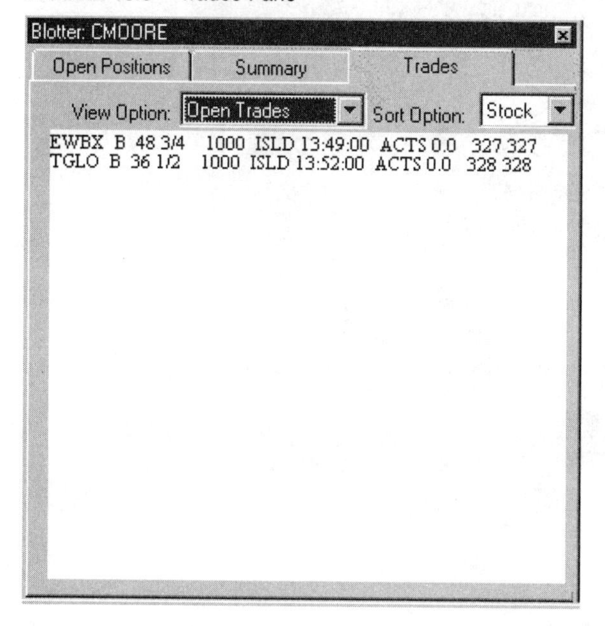

The Stock Window

The stock window (Figure 13.4) is an all-purpose window that supplies most of the information available from Level I and Level II. This includes individual stock symbols, quotes, bids and offers, various ECNs, and market maker information. This window also can be customized and usually serves as the centerpiece of your trading screen.

Ticker Window

The ticker window (Figure 13.5) will keep you updated on price changes in several different combinations. The position ticker will display changes to those stocks that you hold as open positions. A long ticker will display only those stocks that you are currently long. You also have the ability to add any stock you wish to follow merely by clicking on its symbol in

FIGURE 13.4 Stock Window

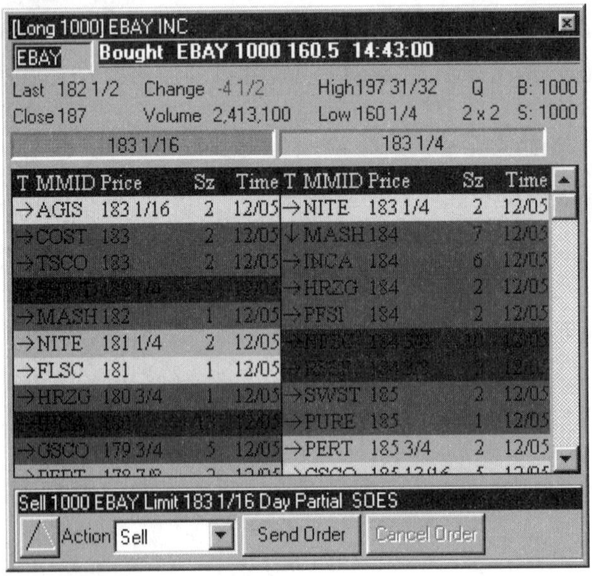

FIGURE 13.5 Ticker Window

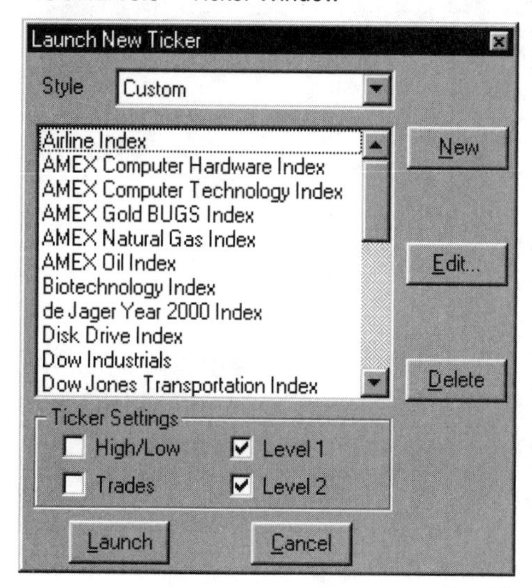

the stock window and dragging it to the ticker window. The ticker gives you a continuous update of any number of stocks you are currently interested in.

Time of Sales Window

This window displays the actual time of the sale of a stock, its bid or offer, and the number of shares traded. Some traders use this window to get a good idea of price sequence (Figure 13.6).

Board View Window

The board view window (Figure 13.7) is similar to the blotter window and will list as many symbols as you like, along with information such as bid, offer, high, low, close, last size, time, change, and volume. You may customize several board windows if you wish.

FIGURE 13.6 Time of Sales Window

INTC

Time		Price	Size		
14:27		101 1/16	200	Q	
14:27		101 1/8	400	Q	
14:27		101 1/8	500	Q	
14:27	a	101 1/8	30	Q	
14:27	b	101 1/16	5	Q	
14:27	a	101 1/8	30	Q	
14:27	b	101 1/16	10	Q	
14:27		101 1/8	300	Q	
14:27	a	101 1/8	30	Q	U
14:27	b	101 1/16	10	Q	U
14:27		101 1/16	100	Q	
14:27		101 1/16	100	Q	
14:27	a	101 1/8	30	Q	
14:27	b	101	10	Q	
14:27		101	30000	Q	
14:27		101 1/16	3500	Q	
14:26		101 3/32	1000	Q	
14:26	a	101 1/16	30	Q	
14:26	b	101	10	Q	
14:26		101 1/16	200	Q	
14:26		100 5/16	200	Q	X

FIGURE 13.7 Board View Window

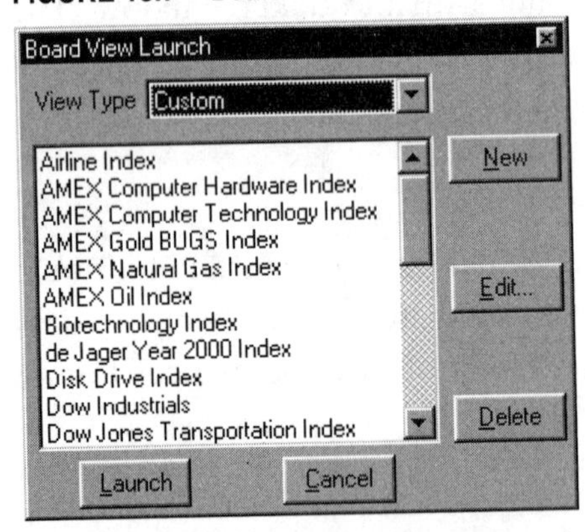

Board View [Disk Drive Index]

Symbol	Bid	Ask	Close	Open	Last	Size	Time	Change	High	Low	Volume
APM	7 1/16	7 1/8	7 1/2	7 3/8	7 1/16	200	11:20	-0 7/16	7 3/8	7 1/16	89,500
HMTT	12 9/16	12 5/8	12 1/2	12 1/2	12 5/8	200	11:19	0 1/8	12 7/8	12 1/2	15,900
HTCH	32 5/8	33	32	31 3/4	33	1,300	11:18	1	33 1/4	31 3/4	177,600
IOM	8	8 1/16	7 13/16	7 15/16	8	500	11:20	0 3/16	8 1/8	7 7/8	1,337,100
KMAG	10 13/16	10 15/16	10 15/16	11	10 7/8	500	11:20	-0 1/16	11 1/4	10 7/8	223,900
QNTM	20 7/8	20 15/16	21 5/8	21 7/8	20 7/8	1,000	11:20	-0 3/4	22	20 7/8	800,900
RDRT	16 9/16	16 5/8	16 15/16	16 7/8	16 9/16	100	11:20	-0 3/8	16 7/8	16 1/2	196,600
SEG	31 13/16	31 15/16	32 3/8	32 11/16	31 15/16	1,000	11:20	-0 7/16	32 11/16	31 7/8	523,300
STK	33 1/8	33 3/16	33	33 7/8	33 1/8	2,300	11:20	0 1/8	34	32 3/4	218,000
WDC	15 1/2	15 9/16	15 3/4	15 7/8	15 9/16	500	11:20	-0 3/16	16	15 7/16	313,100

Top Ten Windows

Top ten windows (Figure 13.8) give you the opportunity to monitor the big winners and losers during the trading day. The categories are for each individual exchange or market and include:

- Gainers/Losers
- Percentage gainers/losers
- Volume
- Nasdaq small cap gainers/losers
- Nasdaq small cap percentage gainers/losers
- Nasdaq National Market System composite (NMS) gainers/losers
- Nasdaq NMS percentage gainers/losers
- Nasdaq NMS volume

Fundamental Data Window

This window (Figure 13.9) displays fundamental information that is not displayed on any other windows. Some of the information includes:

- Rank
- Beta

FIGURE 13.8 Top Ten Windows

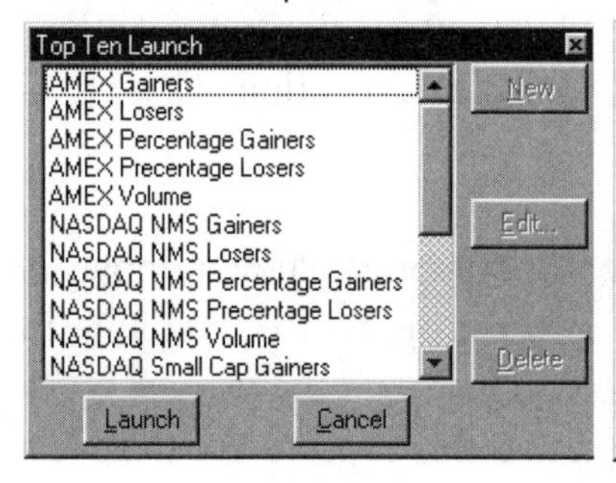

NASDAQ NMS Gainers

Symbol	Name	Change
BCST	BROADCAST.COM INC	7 1/2
EGRP	E*TRADE GROUP INC	6 13/16
GEEK	INTERNET AMERICA INC	10 1/8
INTC	INTEL CORP	4 13/16
MALL	CREATIVE COMPUTERS IN	11 13/64
MZON	MULTIPLE ZONES INTL IN	18 3/8
NSCP	NETSCAPE COMMUNICAT	8
UBID	UBID INC	44
VRSN	VERISIGN INC	9 15/16
YHOO	YHOO	4 7/8

FIGURE 13.9 Fundamental Data Window

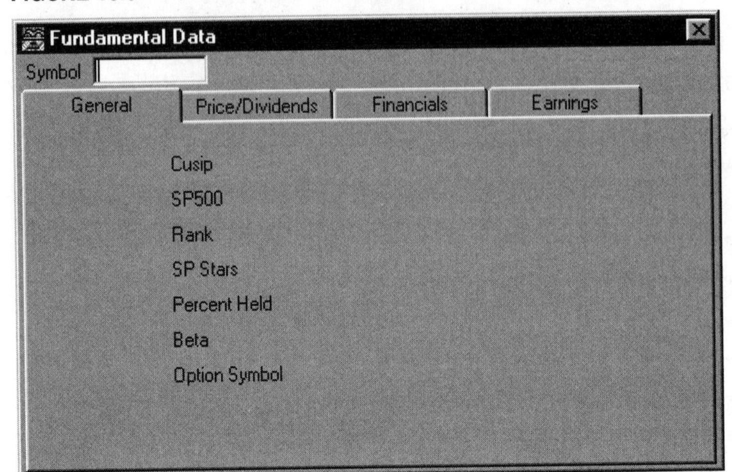

- Price-earnings ratio
- 52 week high/low
- Year high/low
- Average daily volume
- Dividend rate
- Earnings
- Earnings comment
- Financial comment
- Earnings estimates

Order Entry Window

This window (Figure 13.10) lets you see the status of your pending orders. It also displays a list of executions as well as message logs.

The overview of the Level II capability shown above is merely an introduction to the information that is available to the trader. The flexibility of the windows and the various ways to manipulate the information make this a powerful tool. It's

FIGURE 13.10 Order Entry Windows

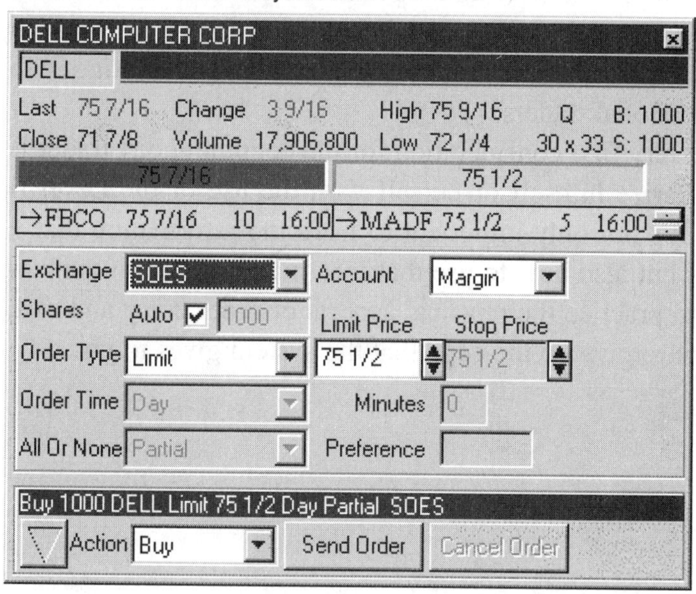

DELL COMPUTER CORP
DELL
Last 75 7/16 Change 3 9/16 High 75 9/16 Q B: 1000
Close 71 7/8 Volume 17,906,800 Low 72 1/4 30 x 33 S: 1000
75 7/16
75 1/2
→FBCO 75 7/16 10 16:00
→MADF 75 1/2 5 16:00
Exchange SelectNet
Account Margin
Shares Auto 1000
Limit Price
Stop Price
Order Type Limit
75 1/2
75 1/2
Order Time Use Specific Mi
Minutes 5
All Or None All or None
Preference
Bid 1000 DELL Limit 75 1/2 For 5 Minutes All or None SelectNet
Action Bid
Send Order
Cancel Order

this information and technology that allow you to enter and exit markets, gather the latest information, and keep tabs on hundreds of stocks and that puts you on an equal footing with all professional traders.

The very first consideration for the beginning day trader is to familiarize himself or herself with the use of the Level II screen. It's not only important to learn the information that it conveys but also how to use that information. Next, it is mandatory to practice the physical aspects of order entry and exit, so as not to give up the edge that the system gives to you.

PART FIVE

CAPTURING THE REAL EDGE OF MARKETS

14

WINNING VERSUS LOSING

In the final analysis, we believe being a market savvy investor comes down to this: discipline, focus, optimism, and confidence.

DISCIPLINE

Discipline is a purely psychological characteristic. For some, it is inborn, but for most traders and investors it is acquired along the way. Discipline is literally the ability to refocus attention at the moment of decision away from one's normal fears and associations. It is the mental skill to overcome the trader's natural need for control and certainty, which is always beyond reach, and a genetic aversion to pain (taking losses). It is teaching oneself to visualize and to hear and feel imagery and associations that enhance market performance, as well as internalizing a belief system that assumes a successful trading result.

Pat Arbor, chairman of the board of the Chicago Board of Trade, had this to say: "The essential characteristic required for successful trading, bottom line, comes down to one thing—discipline. Discipline is the way you handle yourself no matter what else is going on around you. Having it results in success. Lack discipline and you're a loser."

Jack Sandner, former chairman of the board of the Chicago Mercantile Exchange added this:

> "Discipline means many different things to people but I think its main ingredient is focus. They say traders have a nice life. They come in at 8:30 and they're gone at 1:00. You see their expensive cars going down the expressway! What people don't realize is that a lot happens before the bell rings and a lot happens after the bell rings. The other thing people don't realize is between the opening and closing bell a tremendous energy is expended in focus, if you're any good at what you do. I don't know one trader that's any good that doesn't really focus 1,000 percent every second on what he's doing, and is consumed by it! And the traders that don't are lazy; they'll make money sometimes, but eventually they'll get caught. I think it takes a tremendous attention span and focus. If you don't then the discipline can't follow. You can't be disciplined unless you focus, because it's too easy to look away and rationalize."

FOCUS

The optimum performance state for the successful trader and investor is characterized by the following: physical relaxation, psychological calm, a feeling of positive expectation, energized demeanor, active engagement, alertness, effortlessness, anxiety management, and being in control. It is in fact a unified experience of heightened focus, where the trader feels totally relaxed, confident, and automatic in his or her response.

Traders who have experienced this level of focus often refer to it as being "in the zone." They report feeling "relaxed and loose," "an inner quiet and calmness," "intensity," or "having fun and letting go."

Donald Sliter, one of the largest independent floor traders of the S&P 500, had this to say: "I'll tell you what; I get in a zone. I'll trade thousands of S&P contracts in a day, and I'm just moving in and moving out, feeling great, eating up everything in sight. I get in the car in the morning and I'm juiced. I can't wait, especially on number days or on expirations. I get so pumped up sometimes. . . . Just the idea that each day is going to be different, that I'm in control of my own situation, my own destiny, every single day. There's nobody to answer to. Everything you do you're either rewarded or spanked for."

The savvy investor also must understand viscerally the influences and impact of his or her state of mind on decision making and maintaining investment discipline.

OPTIMISM

Optimism is being constantly in a frame of mind that allows you to have a positive expectation about yourself and the market opportunities. It is only as a result of adopting a system of empowering personal thoughts, beliefs, and attitudes that well-analyzed trades and market opportunities can be automatically and effortlessly executed.

Bruce Johnson, president of Packers Trading, had this to say about the role of optimism: "I always say to myself in the morning I'm going to have a good day. And even if it isn't good, I always kind of look on the bright side of everything. I'm really the eternal optimist, which I think is essential. I mean, it's the key ingredient in being a good trader. Staying positive allows you to make good investment decisions."

An essential aspect of optimism is a willingness and commitment to continuously strive to improve. Jeffery Silverman summed it up this way: "You must be willing to work hard and know yourself. You must spend the time; you must study the characteristics of successful traders. You must study your own mistakes. You must study the mistakes of others around you. Increasing levels of sophistication will point you in the direction of understanding who you are."

CONFIDENCE

Confidence is the investor's ultimate bet on his or her own abilities. It is the profound belief in self that Tim McAuliffe, a top trader, expressed in an interview with us when he said: "With three seconds left on the shot clock, I want the basketball. I'm not going to pass it off or hesitate, because in a real sense as a basketball player or as a trader, I believe there is no one in the world in this instant who can do a better job!"

Jack Sandner expressed the importance of confidence this way: "You have to have a tremendous confidence in yourself and your ability, and that trading is a cycle like everything else is a cycle, and at the end of the term it will turn your way if you have confidence in yourself and do all the right things."

RISK VERSUS REWARD

As we have seen in the interviews with top traders, all calculations of risk management take into consideration the following characteristics:

- Define your loss.
- Trade aggressively at your well-calculated points of entry.
- Focus on opportunities.
- Consistently apply your proven system.
- Be highly motivated.
- Don't overtrade.
- Never average down.
- Take small losses, big profits.
- Have no bias to either side of the market.
- Preserve capital.
- Think in probabilities.
- Always trade in a highly positive and resourceful state of mind.
- Act in certainty.
- The market is never wrong.

The key point here is that successful investing is a direct result of a well-disciplined approach of calculated risk taking that once again assumes the following:

- The successful investor effectively manages emotion.
- The successful investor is aware of overcoming the pitfalls of crowd psychology.
- The successful investor understands his or her conscious and unconscious motivations.

- The successful investor risks an appropriate percentage of the overall portfolio.
- The successful investor acknowledges personal abilities and limitations.
- The successful investor is systematic and consistent in approach.
- The successful investor stays emotionally balanced during winning and losing periods.
- The successful investor resists trades that are outside a defined risk parameter.
- The successful investor is open to calculated risk opportunities.
- The successful investor is analytical and disciplined in every stage of the investment process.

As you read again each item in the list of principles of successful risk taking, ask yourself the following questions:

- How does all this relate to me?
- How do I personally experience risk?
- What physical symptoms do I experience?
- What emotions do I have when taking risk in the market?
- What do I hear in my mind's ear?
- What sensory imagery do I experience?
- What specific recurring anxieties do I experience?
- What am I thinking when I take a loss?
- What do I believe about the market and myself when taking a loss?
- What self-defeating attitudes do I possess that I can overcome?
- How can I incorporate all of these principles into my current trading system?

CREATING AN EXPECTATION FOR TRADING SUCCESS

"Nature's way is simple and easy but men prefer the intricate and artificial."

—Lao-tzu

The peak performance expert, Dennis Waitley, writes: "If it's going to be, it's up to me." All triumphs and tragedies in the market and elsewhere begin with taking responsibility for your own actions. There is an old saying: "The psychologically rich keep getting richer and the psychologically poor get poorer." Investors who are open-minded and flexible in their approach can't help but improve. It's the result of their natural commitment to themselves and their passion for trading. When Jack Schwager interviewed Ed Seykota for *Market Wizards* (New York Institute of Finance, 1989), he asked him what a losing trader can do to transform himself into a winning trader. Seykota's response was right on the mark when he answered: "A losing trader can do little to transform himself into a winning trader. A losing trader is not going to want to transform himself. That's the kind of thing winning traders do."

Edward Toppel, the author of *Zen in the Markets* (Warner, 1995), stated that successful investing boils down to the following seven simple rules:

1. Never add to a loser.
2. Only add to a winner.
3. Let profits run.
4. Cut losses fast.
5. Don't pick tops.
6. Don't pick bottoms.
7. Let the market, not your ego, make the decisions.

It is obvious by now that what makes trading and investing so difficult is learning how to apply these rules consistently and profitably. Toppel writes:

> "There is something within each of us that has a power over our minds that prevents our acting according to what we have agreed is the proper course of action. That something is present in all of us and is very powerful, more powerful than anything I know. Those who rid themselves of their egos are rewarded greatly. They are the superstars of their fields. In the markets rewards come in the form of profits. In the world of art masterpieces are the results. In sports the players are all-stars and command enormous salaries. Every pursuit has its own manifestation of victory over the ego."

In *The New Market Wizards,* Jack Schwager writes, "Understand that you are responsible for your own results. Even if you lost on your broker's tips, an advisory service's recommendations, or a bad signal from the system you bought, you are responsible because you made the decision to listen and act. I have never met a successful trader who blamed others for his losses." Schwager, who interviewed dozens of Wall Street's and Chicago's most successful traders and portfolio managers, concluded that although the methods employed by exceptional market professionals are extraordinarily diverse—some were pure fundamentalists, others employed only technical analysis, and still others combined both approaches—specific commonalities were abundantly clear. Schwager's observations and recommendations for attaining what he termed "Market Wizardom" are the following:

- Be sure that you want to invest in the market. It's common for people who think they want to trade to discover that they really don't.

- Examine your motives for investing.
- Match your method to your personality.
- It's absolutely necessary to have an edge.
- The type of method is not important, but having one is critical.
- Developing a method is hard work. Shortcuts rarely lead to trading success.
- Be realistic in your investment goals. Virtually anyone can become a net profitable trader, but only a few have the capability to become supertraders. For this reason, it may be possible to teach trading success, but only up to a point.
- Good money management and risk controls are essential. Never risk more than 1 to 2 percent of your capital on any trade. Predetermine your exit point before you get into a trade. And, cut trading size down sharply during losing periods. If you lose a predetermined amount of your initial capital, stop trading until you regain confidence in your trading.

ADDITIONAL POINTS EVERY MARKET SAVVY INVESTOR MUST KNOW

- You must have an investment plan.
- Discipline is essential.
- Independence of thought and action is critical. You must be able to make your own trading decisions.
- Confidence—the top market professionals believe they've won the game before they begin.
- The possibility of loss is inevitable and must be factored into every investment decision.
- Trade only when you feel confident and optimistic. Keep in mind the importance of your state of mind.

- Patience is essential. Waiting for the right setup or high-probability trade greatly increases your chance for a successful result. As one seasoned investor put it: "Guard particularly against being overeager to trade in order to win back prior loses and revenge trading is a sure recipe for failure." Patience is important not only in waiting for the right trades but also in staying with trades and investments that are working.
- Vary position size according to market conditions and volatility.
- Consistency is more important than being right.
- Catching just part of a market move is just fine. The fact that you are not going to capture the entire trend is no reason not to make the trade.
- Maximize gains, not the number of wins.
- You must be able to make uncomfortable investment decisions; in other words, execute what is right, not what feels comfortable.
- Open-mindedness is a common trait among all the top traders. As one trader put it: "The mind is like a parachute; it's only good when it's open."
- If you are looking for excitement, don't invest.
- Top traders know how to identify and eliminate stress in their trading. The calm state of mind of the investor is essential for trading success.
- The market can be beat.

"The reason a lot of people don't recognize opportunity is because it usually goes around wearing overalls looking like hard work."

—Thomas A. Edison

15

LEARNING TO BECOME A MARKET SAVVY INVESTOR

"The trader is like a Masai warrior who each day must 'face the knife' and hunt the lion with only spear and bare hands. His success will come from relying on his own wits and instincts at the moment of truth, embracing risk as his ally to achieve the desired outcome."

—Robert Koppel, *The Tao of Trading*

Investing presents many challenges, but as with most things in life, persistence and patience, confidence and competence, and above all willingness to pay the price will give you the desired result.

In *The Alchemy of Finance* (Wiley, 1994), George Soros writes:

> "Values are closely associated with the concept of self—a reflexive concept if ever there was one. What we think has a much greater bearing on what we are than the world around us. What we are cannot possibly correspond to what we think we are, but there is a two-way interplay between the two concepts. As we make our way in the world our sense of self evolves. The relationship between what we think we are and what we are in reality is the key to happiness—in other words, it provides the subjective meaning of life."

Remember, capturing the real investor's edge involves the following:

- Personal discipline based on hard work, independence, and patience
- Love of investing—making the process fun
- Well-defined risk management
- Total acceptance of losing as part of the process
- Understanding and acting on your motives
- Developing a personal strategy that works for you and fits your personality
- Maintaining a positive state of mind

It's just that simple—not easy, but simple. Anything else is distraction.

Miyamoto Musashi wrote the *Book of Five Rings* in 1643. It is one of the most important texts on strategy emerging from Japan's Bushi (samurai) culture. Its insights were designed for leaders in all professions who were in search of individual mastery and personal excellence. Musashi advises the following:

> "Think of what is right and true.
> Learn to see everything accurately.
> Become aware of what is not obvious.
> Be careful even in small matters.
> Do not do anything useless."

KNOW YOUR GAME PLAN

As we have emphasized throughout *The Market Savvy Investor,* in investing it is essential that you understand your particular game plan. Some additional advice:

- Rehearse your investment ideas mentally—consider the best time to enter and exit.
- Practice an open, flexible, nondefensive state of mind.
- Practice patience in all things; it will improve your trading and investing.
- Pace yourself physically and emotionally.
- Trading and investing are not about proving something—to yourself or anyone else.
- Condition yourself regularly for investment success by being a keen observer of markets and start to think about them as a market professional.

BECOMING A SUCCESSFUL INVESTOR

Choosing to become a successful investor is like undertaking any important change, and to succeed specific conditions must be fulfilled. Three characteristics of successful investing are:

1. Knowing your outcome
2. Developing a plan of action
3. Reevaluating and retooling

Knowing Your Outcome

You must have an end point in mind. It's important that you know exactly, in detail, what you want to accomplish in quantifiable and verifiable terms: "I want to become a successful investor and for me this means . . ." and "I know I'm successful when . . ."

Developing a Plan of Action

You must develop a program, a personal strategy to accomplish this end, based on homework, hard work, and discipline.

Reevaluating and Retooling

Successful investing, like success itself, is not a single mountain to be climbed or a static thing to be possessed. If you want to succeed at trading or investing, you must view it as a process, a continuously changing dialogue of the mind, fraught with peril but offering great rewards. So you must be able to adjust to changing conditions. When things work, use them; when they don't, discard them and move on.

There are untold riches to be gained by being able to discern between winning and losing strategies, and by acting accordingly. Have you ever observed a toddler in the process of learning to walk? The child employs a host of strategies before he or she is successful. You must view success at investing with the same perspective of flexibility and persistence.

WHAT ALL TRADERS AND INVESTORS SHARE IN COMMON

All investors, from the novice to the most highly successful, have three things in common: They lose, become frustrated, and at times feel lousy and experience stress and disappointment. Top investors, at varying points in their careers, undertook to develop personal strategies for overcoming these types of setbacks. They taught themselves specific, though varying, methods for getting around potentially disabling psychological bends in the road, techniques and strategies that you can learn, too. Wanting to become a winning trader or investor in psychological terms is not very different from choosing to make any significant improvement in your life (getting in shape, for example). It requires a four-part process.

The Four Cs of Investing Success

1. Commitment
2. Conviction
3. Constructing new patterns of behavior
4. Conditioning

Commitment

All significant change begins with a strong overriding motive to succeed. Picture the intensity of Michael Jordon. Top-performing traders have a commitment to overcome any hardship or setback to achieve their goals. They also are not afraid to be engaged.

There is a wonderful story about a poor overworked guy who goes to church and prays, "Please, Lord, let me win the lottery." A week goes by and nothing happens. That Sunday, the man returns to church and once again prays, "Dear Lord, would it really hurt you if I won the lottery?" Still there is no winning number. Six months pass and the man, determined to win the lottery and having great faith in the power of prayer, returns to church and in his most impassioned, supplicating voice, looking heavenward, begins, "Oh, Lord, if only you could let me win this week's lottery." Suddenly, he is interrupted in mid-prayer by a divine voice that emanates from the church rafters. "John," begins the voice, "you gotta buy a ticket!" It's the same with investing: If you want to succeed, you have to buy a ticket. Commitment is that ticket.

Conviction

Have you ever observed young children pretending to drive their parents' car? They bounce up and down, to and fro in front of the steering wheel. They believe their movements will dictate the movement of the car, but the car stands still until someone puts a key in the ignition. When it comes to operating in the marketplace, developing a system of beliefs that fosters excellence is the ignition necessary to fire up the engine of great trading. It's critical for you to possess a range of positive beliefs about yourself and success in the market to achieve optimum results. As Bruce Johnson put it: "You gotta believe the market exists just so you can make money!"

Constructing New Patterns of Behavior

If you want to lose weight, you have to stop consuming french fries and ice cream sodas. There's no way around it! You must interrupt old patterns of behavior by substituting new ones. If you have trouble taking losses in the market, buying when everyone else is selling, or catching a breakout, then guess what you have to do to become more successful? Top investors have developed techniques for constructing new patterns of behavior that empower them to act decisively and automatically. So can you!

Conditioning

Finally, once a new pattern of winning behavior has been substituted for a losing one, it is not enough to apply this new approach just once. You must condition yourself to buy breaks/sell rallies/buy your numbers, to trade your system. In short, you must discipline yourself, virtually condition your nervous system to act automatically and unemotionally. Discipline does and will produce confidence and ultimate success.

ONCE AGAIN: CAPTURING THE INVESTOR'S EDGE

Investors always speak of "getting the edge." This is particularly true of top investors. However, to a person, top investors understand that the edge has little to do with the common sense or conventional notion of getting a good fill in the market or being stopped out exactly at your price. And it makes little difference if these investors employ fundamental or technical analysis, whether they are day traders or position themselves for the long pull. The idea that was repeated time after time by the top traders we interviewed was that an edge is essential. Their edge is the overriding ability to be resilient to whatever the market sends in their direction: weathering difficult times, even long periods of drawdown, and being able to maintain unassailable confidence in themselves at all times. For these top performers, trading is a game; and, although methodologies vary widely, they all shared in common a burning, unquenchable desire to become successful at trading and investing often at significant personal and professional expense.

Other commonalties in capturing the edge include:

- A personal discipline based on hard work, independence, and patience
- A love of trading and investing
- Well-defined risk management
- Total acceptance of losing as part of the trading process

These are the points you need to remember:

- *Fully understand your motives for trading and investing.* Once you know what your motives are, examine them carefully. Most traders and investors trade in a constant state of conflict. It has been our experience that many people who think they want to trade, really don't. In addition, your motives should include a strong need for personal independence, which is crucial.
- *Develop a personal strategy that works for you and fits your personality.* If the system doesn't feel right, you're going to lose before you even start.

- *It has to be fun.* We can't stress this point enough. Investing, literally, has to feel good, which is to say, you must be in a frame of mind that allows you to enjoy the process effortlessly, to be resourceful, and to make good judgments.
- *Hard work is essential.* There's no way to get around it. You must put in all the time. As Woody Allen said: "Ninety percent of existence is showing up." You also must be able to keep trading in perspective.
- *Be confident.* You must possess a repertoire of personal beliefs that constantly reinforces feelings of high self-esteem and confidence in your analysis and execution of trades, whether you win or lose. Needless to say, discipline, patience, personal responsibility, and repeated success make this a lot easier.
- *Cultivate a positive state of mind.* If there is a single variable that guarantees success, it is this one. The top-performing traders have developed an internal terrain that reduces anxiety and promotes excellence. They manage to achieve this end by internally representing external events in such a way that ensures success, adjusting and redefining as they deem appropriate. They do this by employing a belief system that does not allow for the concept of failure, and by possessing a personal focus that concentrates on what is essential to achieving this end. In short, they have mastered the ability to create states of mind and body that are resourceful and ensure whatever it takes to succeed.

PRINCIPLES OF SUCCESSFUL INVESTING REVISITED

- Define your loss.
- Believe in yourself and unlimited market possibilities.

- Have a well-defined money management program.
- Don't take tips.
- Focus on opportunities.
- Consistently apply your investment strategies and rules.
- Be highly motivated and goal-oriented.
- When in doubt, stay out.
- Know how to use your orders.
- Take small losses, big profits.
- Have no bias to either side of the market.
- The crowd is almost always wrong.
- Preserve capital.
- Think in probabilities.
- The market is never wrong.

BOTTOM LINE

Now ask yourself the same question all serious traders and investors must ask: Do I have what it takes?

Investing is a rewarding universe of unlimited possibilities when approached with maturity and well-managed risk. It's intellectually challenging and affords independent-minded individuals the ability to participate in a personally fulfilling and profitable activity.

Remember, it isn't your broker, your brother-in-law, the chairman of the board, the Fed, the fill, the computer, the unemployment report—it is you. It's a simple fact that must be understood in the adoption of any trading strategy. You produce the results. Good or bad, the buck starts—and stops—here. Success in investing!

APPENDIX A

MAJOR STOCKS TRADED: NASDAQ 100 AND S&P 500

NASDAQ 100

Launched in January 1985, the Nasdaq 100 Index represents the largest and most active nonfinancial domestic and international issues listed on The Nasdaq Stock Market® based on market capitalization. As of December 21, 1998, the Nasdaq 100 Index was rebalanced to a modified market capitalization weighted index. Such rebalancing is expected to retain in general the economic attributes of capitalization weighting while providing enhanced diversification. To accomplish this, Nasdaq will review the composition of the Nasdaq 100 Index on a monthly basis and will adjust the weightings of Index components using a proprietary algorithm if certain preestablished weight distribution requirements are not met.

Eligibility criteria for the Nasdaq 100 Index includes a minimum average daily trading volume of 100,000 shares. Generally, companies also must have seasoned on Nasdaq or another major exchange, which means they have been listed for a minimum of two years. If the security is a foreign security, the company must have a world wide market value of at least $10 billion, a U.S. market value of at least $4 billion, and average trading volume of at least 200,000 shares per day. In addition, foreign securities must be eligible for listed-options trading.

Company Name	*Symbol*	*% of Index (Adjusted)*
3Com Corporation	COMS	0.68
Adaptec, Inc.	ADPT	0.21
ADC Telecommunications, Inc.	ADCT	0.76
Adobe Systems Incorporated	ADBE	0.3
Altera Corporation	ALTR	0.83
Amazon.com, Inc.	AMZN	1.26
American Power Conversion Corporation	APCC	0.63
Amgen Inc.	AMGN	1.58
Andrew Corporation	ANDW	0.12
Apollo Group, Inc.	APOL	0.2
Apple Computer, Inc.	AAPL	0.78
Applied Materials, Inc.	AMAT	1.41
Ascend Communications, Inc.	ASND	1.01
Atmel Corporation	ATML	0.13
Autodesk, Inc.	ADSK	0.18
Bed Bath & Beyond Inc.	BBBY	0.61
Biogen, Inc.	BGEN	0.91
Biomet, Inc.	BMET	0.57
BMC Software, Inc.	BMCS	0.83
Cambridge Technology Partners, Inc.	CATP	0.15
CBRL Group Inc.	CBRL	0.11
Centocor, Inc.	CNTO	0.29
Chancellor Media Corporation	AMFM	1.09
Chiron Corporation	CHIR	0.63
Cintas Corporation	CTAS	1
Cisco Systems, Inc.	CSCO	6.34
Citrix Systems, Inc.	CTXS	0.47
Comair Holdings, Inc.	COMR	0.21
Comcast Corporation	CMCSK	1.15
Compuware Corporation	CPWR	0.76
Comverse Technology, Inc.	CMVT	0.4
Concord EFS, Inc.	CEFT	0.39
Corporate Express, Inc.	CEXP	0.04
Costco Companies, Inc.	COST	0.97
Dell Computer Corporation	DELL	5.38
Dollar Tree Stores, Inc.	DLTR	0.22
Electronic Arts Inc.	ERTS	0.27
Electronics for Imaging, Inc.	EFII	0.16
Fastenal Company	FAST	0.11

Company Name	*Symbol*	*% of Index (Adjusted)*
First Health Group Corp.	FHCC	0.06
Fiserv, Inc.	FISV	0.53
Food Lion, Inc.	FDLNB	0.21
FORE Systems, Inc.	FORE	0.16
Genzyme General	GENZ	0.59
Herman Miller, Inc.	MLHR	0.11
Immunex Corporation	IMNX	0.77
Intel Corporation	INTC	8.5
Intuit Inc.	INTU	0.71
Jacor Communications, Inc.	JCOR	0.41
KLA-Tencor Corporation	KLAC	0.67
Level 3 Communications, Inc.	LVLT	1.38
Lincare Holdings Inc.	LNCR	0.19
Linear Technology Corporation	LLTC	1.08
LM Ericsson Telephone Company	ERICY	0.93
Maxim Integrated Products, Inc.	MXIM	0.94
McCormick & Company, Incorporated	MCCRK	0.17
MCI WORLDCOM, Inc.	WCOM	5.75
McLeodUSA Incorporated	MCLD	0.2
Microchip Technology Incorporated	MCHP	0.14
Micron Electronics, Inc.	MUEI	0.12
Microsoft Corporation	MSFT	15.64
Molex Incorporated	MOLX	0.24
Netscape Communications Corporation	NSCP	0.93
Network Associates, Inc.	NETA	0.69
Nextel Communications, Inc.	NXTL	1.22
Nordstrom, Inc.	NOBE	1
Northwest Airlines Corporation	NWAC	0.17
Novell, Inc.	NOVL	0.86
NTL Incorporated	NTLI	0.52
Oracle Corporation	ORCL	2.56
PACCAR Inc.	PCAR	0.43
PacifiCare Health Systems, Inc.	PHSYB	0.21
PanAmSat Corporation	SPOT	0.86
Parametric Technology Corporation	PMTC	0.57
Paychex, Inc.	PAYX	0.77
PeopleSoft, Inc.	PSFT	0.69
QUALCOMM Incorporated	QCOM	0.65
Quantum Corporation	QNTM	0.5

Company Name	Symbol	% of Index (Adjusted)
Quintiles Transnational Corp.	QTRN	0.59
Qwest Communications International Inc.	QWST	1.14
Reuters Group PLC	RTRSY	0.27
Rexall Sundown, Inc.	RXSD	0.06
Ross Stores, Inc.	ROST	0.17
Sanmina Corporation	SANM	0.39
Sigma-Aldrich Corporation	SIAL	0.32
Smurfit-Stone Container Corporation	SSCC	0.41
Staples, Inc.	SPLS	0.97
Starbucks Corporation	SBUX	0.68
Stewart Enterprises, Inc.	STEI	0.14
Sun Microsystems, Inc.	SUNW	1.9
Synopsys, Inc.	SNPS	0.46
Tech Data Corporation	TECD	0.12
Tele-Communications, Inc.	TCOMA	1.64
Tellabs, Inc.	TLAB	0.95
USA Networks, Inc.	USAI	0.59
VERITAS Software Corporation	VRTS	0.42
Vitesse Semiconductor Corporation	VTSS	0.44
Worthington Industries, Inc.	WTHG	0.1
Xilinx, Inc.	XLNX	0.83
Yahoo! Inc.	YHOO	1.66

S&P 500

Symbol	S&P Group	Exchange	Issue Name
$SPX			S&P Stock Index
COMS	Industrial	NASD	3COM CORP
ABT	Industrial	NYSE	ABBOTT LABS
ADBE	Industrial	NASD	ADOBE SYSTEMS
AMD	Industrial	NYSE	ADVANCED MICRO DEVICES
ANV	Industrial	NYSE	AEROQUIP-VICKERS INC
AES	Utilities	NYSE	AES CORP
AET	Financial	NYSE	AETNA INC

Symbol	*S&P Group*	*Exchange*	*Issue Name*
APD	Industrial	NYSE	AIR PRODUCTS & CHEMICALS
ATI	Industrial	NYSE	AIRTOUCH COMMUNICATIONS
ACV	Industrial	NYSE	ALBERTO-CULVER
ABS	Industrial	NYSE	ALBERTSON'S
AL	Industrial	NYSE	ALCAN ALUMINUM LTD
AA	Industrial	NYSE	ALCOA INC
ALT	Industrial	NYSE	ALLEGHENY TELEDYNE INC
AGN	Industrial	NYSE	ALLERGAN INC
ALD	Industrial	NYSE	ALLIEDSIGNAL INC
ALL	Financial	NYSE	ALLSTATE CORP
AT	Industrial	NYSE	ALLTEL CORP DEL
AZA	Industrial	NYSE	ALZA CORP
AHC	Industrial	NYSE	AMERADA HESS CORP
AEE	Utilities	NYSE	AMEREN CORP
AOL	Industrial	NYSE	AMERICA ONLINE
AEP	Utilities	NYSE	AMERICAN ELEC PWR CO INC
AXP	Financial	NYSE	AMERICAN EXPRESS CO
AGC	Financial	NYSE	AMERICAN GENERAL CORP
AM	Industrial	NYSE	AMERICAN GREETINGS CL A
AHP	Industrial	NYSE	AMERICAN HOME PRODS CORP
AIG	Financial	NYSE	AMERICAN INTL GROUP INC
ASC	Industrial	NYSE	AMERICAN STORES CO
AIT	Utilities	NYSE	AMERITECH CORP DE
AMGN	Industrial	NASD	AMGEN INC
AMP	Industrial	NYSE	AMP INC PENNSYLVANIA
AMR	Transportation	NYSE	AMR CORP
APC	Industrial	NYSE	ANADARKO PETROLEUM
ANDW	Industrial	NASD	ANDREW CORP
BUD	Industrial	NYSE	ANHEUSER BUSCH COS INC

Symbol	*S&P Group*	*Exchange*	*Issue Name*
AOC	Financial	NYSE	AON CORP
APA	Industrial	NYSE	APACHE CORP
AAPL	Industrial	NASD	APPLE COMPUTER INC
AMAT	Industrial	NASD	APPLIED MATERIALS INC
ADM	Industrial	NYSE	ARCHER DANIELS MIDLAND CO
ACK	Industrial	NYSE	ARMSTRONG WORLD INDS INC
AR	Industrial	NYSE	ASARCO INC
ASND	Industrial	NASD	ASCEND COMMUNICATIONS
ASH	Industrial	NYSE	ASHLAND INC
AFS	Financial	NYSE	ASSOCIATES FIRST CAPITAL
T	Industrial	NYSE	AT&T CORP
ARC	Industrial	NYSE	ATLANTIC RICHFIELD CO
ADSK	Industrial	NASD	AUTODESK INC
AUD	Industrial	NYSE	AUTOMATIC DATA PROCSG INC
AZO	Industrial	NYSE	AUTOZONE
AVY	Industrial	NYSE	AVERY DENNISON CORP
AVP	Industrial	NYSE	AVON PRODUCTS INC
BHI	Industrial	NYSE	BAKER HUGHES INC
BLL	Industrial	NYSE	BALL CORP
BGE	Utilities	NYSE	BALTIMORE G & E C
BK	Financial	NYSE	BANK OF NEW YORK
ONE	Financial	NYSE	BANK ONE CORP
BAC	Financial	NYSE	BANKAMERICA CORP
BKB	Financial	NYSE	BANKBOSTON CORP
BT	Financial	NYSE	BANKERS TRUST N Y CORP
BCR	Industrial	NYSE	BARD C R INC
ABX	Industrial	NYSE	BARRICK GOLD CORP
BMG	Industrial	NYSE	BATTLE MOUNTAIN GOLD
BOL	Industrial	NYSE	BAUSCH & LOMB INC
BAX	Industrial	NYSE	BAXTER INTERNATIONAL INC

Symbol	*S&P Group*	*Exchange*	*Issue Name*
BBT	Financial	NYSE	BB&T CORP
BSC	Financial	NYSE	BEAR STEARNS COS
BDX	Industrial	NYSE	BECTON DICKINSON & CO
BEL	Utilities	NYSE	BELL ATLANTIC CORP
BLS	Utilities	NYSE	BELLSOUTH CORP
BMS	Industrial	NYSE	BEMIS CO INC
BFO	Industrial	NYSE	BESTFOODS INC
BS	Industrial	NYSE	BETHLEHEM STEEL CORP
BMET	Industrial	NASD	BIOMET INC
BDK	Industrial	NYSE	BLACK & DECKER CORP
HRB	Industrial	NYSE	BLOCK H & R INC
BMCS	Industrial	NASD	BMC SOFTWARE
BA	Industrial	NYSE	BOEING CO
BCC	Industrial	NYSE	BOISE CASCADE CORP
BSX	Industrial	NYSE	BOSTON SCIENTIFIC CORP
BGG	Industrial	NYSE	BRIGGS & STRATTON CORP
BMY	Industrial	NYSE	BRISTOL MYERS SQUIBB CO
BF/B	Industrial	NYSE	BROWN-FORMAN CORP
BFI	Industrial	NYSE	BROWNING FERRIS INDS INC
BC	Industrial	NYSE	BRUNSWICK CORP
BNI	Transportation	NYSE	BURLINGTON NTHRN SANTA FE
BR	Industrial	NYSE	BURLINGTON RESOURCES INC
CS	Industrial	NYSE	CABLETRON SYSTEMS
CPB	Industrial	NYSE	CAMPBELL SOUP CO
COF	Financial	NYSE	CAPITAL ONE FINANCIAL
CAH	Industrial	NYSE	CARDINAL HEALTH, INC
CCL	Industrial	NYSE	CARNIVAL CORP
CPL	Utilities	NYSE	CAROLINA POWER & LIGHT CO
CSE	Industrial	NYSE	CASE CORP
CAT	Industrial	NYSE	CATERPILLAR INC

Symbol	*S&P Group*	*Exchange*	*Issue Name*
CBS	Industrial	NYSE	CBS CORP
CD	Industrial	NYSE	CENDANT CORPORATION
CTX	Industrial	NYSE	CENTEX CORP
CSR	Utilities	NYSE	CENTRAL & SOUTH WEST CORP
CEN	Industrial	NYSE	CERIDIAN CORP
CHA	Industrial	NYSE	CHAMPION INTL CORP
SCH	Financial	NYSE	CHARLES SCHWAB
CMB	Financial	NYSE	CHASE MANHATTAN CORP
CHV	Industrial	NYSE	CHEVRON CORP
CB	Financial	NYSE	CHUBB CORP
CI	Financial	NYSE	CIGNA CORP
CINF	Financial	NASD	CINCINNATI FINANCIAL
CIN	Utilities	NYSE	CINERGY CORP
CC	Industrial	NYSE	CIRCUIT CITY STORES INC
CSCO	Industrial	NASD	CISCO SYSTEMS INC
C	Financial	NYSE	CITIGROUP INC
CCU	Industrial	NYSE	CLEAR CHANNEL COMMUNICATIONS
CLX	Industrial	NYSE	CLOROX CO
CGP	Utilities	NYSE	COASTAL CORP
KO	Industrial	NYSE	COCA COLA CO
CCE	Industrial	NYSE	COCA-COLA ENTERPRISES
CL	Industrial	NYSE	COLGATE PALMOLIVE CO
CG	Utilities	NYSE	COLUMBIA ENERGY GROUP
COL	Industrial	NYSE	COLUMBIA HCA HLTHCRE CORP
CMCSK	Industrial	NASD	COMCAST CORP
CMA	Financial	NYSE	COMERICA INC
CPQ	Industrial	NYSE	COMPAQ COMPUTER CORP
CA	Industrial	NYSE	COMPUTER ASSC INTL INC
CSC	Industrial	NYSE	COMPUTER SCIENCES CORP

Symbol	*S&P Group*	*Exchange*	*Issue Name*
CPWR	Industrial	NASD	COMPUWARE CORP
CAG	Industrial	NYSE	CONAGRA INC
CNC	Financial	NYSE	CONSECO INC
ED	Utilities	NYSE	CONSOLIDATED EDISON CO
CNG	Utilities	NYSE	CONSOLIDATED NAT GAS CO
CNS	Industrial	NYSE	CONSOLIDATED STORES
CBE	Industrial	NYSE	COOPER INDUSTRIES INC
CTB	Industrial	NYSE	COOPER TIRE & RUBBER CO
ACCOB	Industrial	NASD	COORS ADOLPH CO
GLW	Industrial	NYSE	CORNING INC
COST	Industrial	NASD	COSTCO CO
CCR	Financial	NYSE	COUNTRYWIDE CREDIT INDUSTRIES
CR	Industrial	NYSE	CRANE CO
CCK	Industrial	NYSE	CROWN CORK & SEAL INC PA
CSX	Transportation	NYSE	CSX CORP
CUM	Industrial	NYSE	CUMMINS ENGINE CO INC
CVS	Industrial	NYSE	CVS CORP
CYM	Industrial	NYSE	CYPRUS AMAX MINERALS CO
DCN	Industrial	NYSE	DANA CORP
DHR	Industrial	NYSE	DANAHER CORP
DRI	Industrial	NYSE	DARDEN RESTAURANTS
DGN	Industrial	NYSE	DATA GENERAL CORP
DH	Industrial	NYSE	DAYTON HUDSON CORP
DE	Industrial	NYSE	DEERE & CO
DELL	Industrial	NASD	DELL COMPUTER
DAL	Transportation	NYSE	DELTA AIR LINES INC
DLX	Industrial	NYSE	DELUXE CORP
DDS	Industrial	NYSE	DILLARD DEPT STORES CL A
DG	Industrial	NYSE	DOLLAR GENERAL
D	Utilities	NYSE	DOMINION RESOURCES INC VA

Symbol	*S&P Group*	*Exchange*	*Issue Name*
DNY	Industrial	NYSE	DONNELLEY R R & SONS CO
DOV	Industrial	NYSE	DOVER CORP
DOW	Industrial	NYSE	DOW CHEMICAL CO
DJ	Industrial	NYSE	DOW JONES & CO INC
DTE	Utilities	NYSE	DTE ENERGY CO
DD	Industrial	NYSE	DU PONT (E.I.)
DUK	Utilities	NYSE	DUKE ENERGY
DNB	Industrial	NYSE	DUN & BRADSTREET CORP
EGG	Industrial	NYSE	E G & G INC
EFU	Utilities	NYSE	EASTERN ENTERPRISES
EMN	Industrial	NYSE	EASTMAN CHEMICAL CO
EK	Industrial	NYSE	EASTMAN KODAK CO
ETN	Industrial	NYSE	EATON CORP
ECL	Industrial	NYSE	ECOLAB INC
EIX	Utilities	NYSE	EDISON INTERNATIONAL INC
EDS	Industrial	NYSE	ELECTRONIC DATA SYSTEMS
EMC	Industrial	NYSE	EMC CORP
EMR	Industrial	NYSE	EMERSON ELECTRIC CO
EC	Industrial	NYSE	ENGELHARD CORP
ENE	Utilities	NYSE	ENRON CORP
ETR	Utilities	NYSE	ENTERGY CORP
EFX	Financial	NYSE	EQUIFAX INC
XON	Industrial	NYSE	EXXON CORP
FNM	Financial	NYSE	FANNIE MAE
FDX	Transportation	NYSE	FEDERAL EXPRESS CORP
FRE	Financial	NYSE	FEDERAL HOME LOAN MTG
FD	Industrial	NYSE	FEDERATED DEPT STORES DE
FITB	Financial	NASD	FIFTH THIRD BANCORP
FDC	Industrial	NYSE	FIRST DATA CORP
FTU	Financial	NYSE	FIRST UNION CORP
FSR	Financial	NYSE	FIRSTAR CORPORATION
FE	Utilities	NYSE	FIRSTENERGY CORP

Symbol	*S&P Group*	*Exchange*	*Issue Name*
FLT	Financial	NYSE	FLEET FINANCIAL GROUP
FLE	Industrial	NYSE	FLEETWOOD ENTERPRISES INC
FLR	Industrial	NYSE	FLUOR CORP
FMC	Industrial	NYSE	FMC CORP
F	Industrial	NYSE	FORD MOTOR CO
FJ	Industrial	NYSE	FORT JAMES CORP
FO	Industrial	NYSE	FORTUNE BRANDS, INC
FWC	Industrial	NYSE	FOSTER WHEELER CORP
FPL	Utilities	NYSE	FPL GROUP INC
BEN	Financial	NYSE	FRANKLIN RESOURCES INC
FCX	Industrial	NYSE	FREEPORT-MCMORAN COPPER & GOLD
FRO	Utilities	NYSE	FRONTIER CORP
FTL	Industrial	NYSE	FRUIT OF THE LOOM
GCI	Industrial	NYSE	GANNETT CO INC
GPS	Industrial	NYSE	GAP INC
GTW	Industrial	NYSE	GATEWAY 2000 INC
GD	Industrial	NYSE	GENERAL DYNAMICS CORP
GE	Industrial	NYSE	GENERAL ELECTRIC CO
GIC	Industrial	NYSE	GENERAL INSTRUMENT CORP
GIS	Industrial	NYSE	GENERAL MILLS INC
GM	Industrial	NYSE	GENERAL MOTORS CORP
GPC	Industrial	NYSE	GENUINE PARTS CO
GP	Industrial	NYSE	GEORGIA PACIFIC CORP
G	Industrial	NYSE	GILLETTE CO
GDW	Financial	NYSE	GOLDEN WEST FINANCIAL
GR	Industrial	NYSE	GOODRICH B F CO
GT	Industrial	NYSE	GOODYEAR TIRE & RUBBER CO
GPU	Utilities	NYSE	GPU INC
GRA	Industrial	NYSE	GRACE W R & CO HLDG CO
GWW	Industrial	NYSE	GRAINGER W W INC

Symbol	*S&P Group*	*Exchange*	*Issue Name*
GAP	Industrial	NYSE	GREAT ATLANTIC & PAC TEA
GLK	Industrial	NYSE	GREAT LAKES CHEMICAL CORP
GTE	Utilities	NYSE	GTE CORP
GDT	Industrial	NYSE	GUIDANT CORP
HAL	Industrial	NYSE	HALLIBURTON CO
H	Industrial	NYSE	HARCOURT GENERAL INC
HPH	Industrial	NYSE	HARNISCHFEGER INDS INC
HET	Industrial	NYSE	HARRAHS ENT INC
HRS	Industrial	NYSE	HARRIS CORP
HIG	Financial	NYSE	HARTFORD FINANCIAL SVC GP
HAS	Industrial	AMEX	HASBRO INC
HBOC	Industrial	NASD	HBO & COMPANY
HCR	Industrial	NYSE	HCR MANOR CARE
HRC	Industrial	NYSE	HEALTHSOUTH CORP
HNZ	Industrial	NYSE	HEINZ H J CO
HP	Industrial	NYSE	HELMERICH & PAYNE INC
HPC	Industrial	NYSE	HERCULES INC
HSY	Industrial	NYSE	HERSHEY FOODS CORP
HWP	Industrial	NYSE	HEWLETT PACKARD CO
HLT	Industrial	NYSE	HILTON HOTELS CORP
HD	Industrial	NYSE	HOME DEPOT INC
HM	Industrial	NYSE	HOMESTAKE MINING CO
HON	Industrial	NYSE	HONEYWELL INC
HI	Financial	NYSE	HOUSEHOLD INTL INC
HOU	Utilities	NYSE	HOUSTON INDUSTRIES INC
HUM	Industrial	NYSE	HUMANA INC
HBAN	Financial	NASD	HUNTINGTON BANCSHARES
IKN	Industrial	NYSE	IKON OFFICE SOLUTIONS
ITW	Industrial	NYSE	ILLINOIS TOOL WORKS INC
RX	Industrial	NYSE	IMS HEALTH INC

Symbol	*S&P Group*	*Exchange*	*Issue Name*
N	Industrial	NYSE	INCO LTD
IR	Industrial	NYSE	INGERSOLL RAND CO
INTC	Industrial	NASD	INTEL CORP
IBM	Industrial	NYSE	INTERNATIONAL BUSINESS MACHINES
IFF	Industrial	NYSE	INTERNATIONAL FLAV & FRAG
IP	Industrial	NYSE	INTERNATIONAL PAPER CO
IPG	Industrial	NYSE	INTERPUBLIC GROUP COS INC
IIN	Industrial	NYSE	ITT INDUSTRIES INC
JP	Financial	NYSE	JEFFERSON PILOT CORP
JNJ	Industrial	NYSE	JOHNSON & JOHNSON
JCI	Industrial	NYSE	JOHNSON CONTROLS INC
JOS	Industrial	NYSE	JOSTENS INC
KM	Industrial	NYSE	K MART CORP
KBH	Industrial	NYSE	KAUFMAN & BROAD HOME CORP
K	Industrial	NYSE	KELLOGG CO
KMG	Industrial	NYSE	KERR MCGEE CORP
KEY	Financial	NYSE	KEYCORP
KMB	Industrial	NYSE	KIMBERLY CLARK CORP
KWP	Industrial	NYSE	KING WORLD PRODS INC
KLAC	Industrial	NASD	KLA-TENCOR CORP
KRI	Industrial	NYSE	KNIGHT RIDDER INC
KSS	Industrial	NYSE	KOHL'S CORP
KR	Industrial	NYSE	KROGER CO
LDW	Industrial	NYSE	LAIDLAW INC
LEH	Financial	NYSE	LEHMAN BROS HLDGS
LLY	Industrial	NYSE	LILLY ELI & CO
LTD	Industrial	NYSE	LIMITED INC
LNC	Financial	NYSE	LINCOLN NATIONAL CORP
LIZ	Industrial	NYSE	LIZ CLAIBORNE INC
LMT	Industrial	NYSE	LOCKHEED MARTIN CORP
LTR	Financial	NYSE	LOEWS CORP

Symbol	*S&P Group*	*Exchange*	*Issue Name*
LDG	Industrial	NYSE	LONGS DRUG STORES CORP
LPX	Industrial	NYSE	LOUISIANA PACIFIC CORP
LOW	Industrial	NYSE	LOWES COS INC
LSI	Industrial	NYSE	LSI LOGIC CORP
LU	Industrial	NYSE	LUCENT TECHNOLOGIES
MKG	Industrial	NYSE	MALLINCKRODT GROUP INC
MAR	Industrial	NYSE	MARRIOTT INTL INC
MMC	Financial	NYSE	MARSH & MCLENNAN
MAS	Industrial	NYSE	MASCO CORP
MAT	Industrial	NYSE	MATTEL INC
MAY	Industrial	NYSE	MAY DEPT STORES CO
MYG	Industrial	NYSE	MAYTAG CORP
MBI	Financial	NYSE	MBIA INC
KRB	Financial	NYSE	MBNA CORP
MDR	Industrial	NYSE	MCDERMOTT INTL INC
MCD	Industrial	NYSE	MCDONALDS CORP
MHP	Industrial	NYSE	MCGRAW HILL COS INC
WCOM	Industrial	NASD	MCI WORLDCOM
MEA	Industrial	NYSE	MEAD CORP
UMG	Industrial	NYSE	MEDIAONE GROUP INC
MDT	Industrial	NYSE	MEDTRONIC INC
MEL	Financial	NYSE	MELLON BANK CORP
MTL	Financial	NYSE	MERCANTILE BANCORP
MRK	Industrial	NYSE	MERCK & CO INC
MDP	Industrial	NYSE	MEREDITH CORP
MER	Financial	NYSE	MERRILL LYNCH & CO INC
FMY	Industrial	NYSE	MEYER (FRED) INC
MTG	Financial	NYSE	MGIC INVESTMENT
MU	Industrial	NYSE	MICRON TECHNOLOGY INC
MSFT	Industrial	NASD	MICROSOFT CORP
MZ	Industrial	NYSE	MILACRON INC
MIL	Industrial	NYSE	MILLIPORE CORP
MMM	Industrial	NYSE	MINNESOTA MNG & MFG CO

Symbol	*S&P Group*	*Exchange*	*Issue Name*
MIR	Industrial	NYSE	MIRAGE RESORTS
MOB	Industrial	NYSE	MOBIL CORP
MTC	Industrial	NYSE	MONSANTO CO
MCL	Industrial	NYSE	MOORE CORP LTD
JPM	Financial	NYSE	MORGAN J P & CO INC
MWD	Financial	NYSE	MORGAN STANLEY, DEAN WITTER & CO
MII	Industrial	NYSE	MORTON INTL INC IND
MOT	Industrial	NYSE	MOTOROLA INC
NC	Industrial	NYSE	NACCO INDUSTRIES INC
NLC	Industrial	NYSE	NALCO CHEMICAL CO
NCC	Financial	NYSE	NATIONAL CITY CORP
NSM	Industrial	NYSE	NATIONAL SEMI-CONDUCTOR CO
NSI	Industrial	NYSE	NATIONAL SERVICE INDS INC
NAV	Industrial	NYSE	NAVISTAR INTL CORP
NCE	Utilities	NYSE	NEW CENTURY ENERGIES
NYT	Industrial	NYSE	NEW YORK TIMES CL A
NWL	Industrial	NYSE	NEWELL CO
NEM	Industrial	NYSE	NEWMONT MINING CORP
NXTL	Industrial	NASD	NEXTEL COMMUNICATIONS
NMK	Utilities	NYSE	NIAGARA MOHAWK POWER CORP
GAS	Utilities	NYSE	NICOR INC
NKE	Industrial	NYSE	NIKE INC CL B
NOBE	Industrial	NASD	NORDSTROM INC
NSC	Transportation	NYSE	NORFOLK SOUTHERN CORP
NSP	Utilities	NYSE	NORTHERN STES PWR CO MN
NT	Industrial	NYSE	NORTHERN TELECOM LTD
NTRS	Financial	NASD	NORTHERN TRUST CORP
NOC	Industrial	NYSE	NORTHROP GRUMMAN CORP

Symbol	*S&P Group*	*Exchange*	*Issue Name*
NOVL	Industrial	NASD	NOVELL INC
NUE	Industrial	NYSE	NUCOR CORP
OXY	Industrial	NYSE	OCCIDENTAL PETROLEUM CORP
OMC	Industrial	NYSE	OMNICOM GROUP
OKE	Utilities	NYSE	ONEOK INC
ORCL	Industrial	NASD	ORACLE CORP
ORX	Industrial	NYSE	ORYX ENERGY CO
OWC	Industrial	NYSE	OWENS CORNING
OI	Industrial	NYSE	OWENS-ILLINOIS
PCAR	Industrial	NASD	PACCAR INC
PPW	Utilities	NYSE	PACIFICORP
PLL	Industrial	NYSE	PALL CORP
PMTC	Industrial	NASD	PARAMETRIC TECHNOLOGY
PH	Industrial	NYSE	PARKER HANNIFIN CORP
PAYX	Industrial	NASD	PAYCHEX INC
PE	Utilities	NYSE	PECO ENERGY CO
JCP	Industrial	NYSE	PENNEY J C CO INC
PGL	Utilities	NYSE	PEOPLES ENERGY CORP
PSFT	Industrial	NASD	PEOPLESOFT INC
PBY	Industrial	NYSE	PEP BOYS MANNY MOE & JACK
PEP	Industrial	NYSE	PEPSICO INC
PKN	Industrial	NYSE	PERKIN ELMER CORP
PFE	Industrial	NYSE	PFIZER INC
PCG	Utilities	NYSE	PG&E CORP
PNU	Industrial	NYSE	PHARMACIA & UPJOHN INC
PD	Industrial	NYSE	PHELPS DODGE CORP
MO	Industrial	NYSE	PHILIP MORRIS COS INC
P	Industrial	NYSE	PHILLIPS PETROLEUM CO
PHB	Industrial	NYSE	PIONEER HI BRED INTL INC
PBI	Industrial	NYSE	PITNEY BOWES INC
PDG	Industrial	NYSE	PLACER DOME INC
PNC	Financial	NYSE	PNC BANK CORP
PRD	Industrial	NYSE	POLAROID CORP

Symbol	*S&P Group*	*Exchange*	*Issue Name*
PCH	Industrial	NYSE	POTLATCH CORP
PPL	Utilities	NYSE	PP & L RESOURCES INC
PPG	Industrial	NYSE	PPG INDUSTRIES INC
PX	Industrial	NYSE	PRAXAIR INC
PG	Industrial	NYSE	PROCTER & GAMBLE CO
PGR	Financial	NYSE	PROGRESSIVE CORP
PVT	Financial	NYSE	PROVIDENT COMPANIES INC
PVN	Financial	NYSE	PROVIDIAN CORP
PEG	Utilities	NYSE	PUBLIC SERVICE ENTPR GRP
PHM	Industrial	NYSE	PULTE CORP
OAT	Industrial	NYSE	QUAKER OATS CO
RAL	Industrial	NYSE	RALSTON-RALSTN PURINA GRP
RYC	Industrial	NYSE	RAYCHEM CORP
RTN/B	Industrial	NYSE	RAYTHEON CO
RBK	Industrial	NYSE	REEBOK INTL LTD
RGBK	Financial	NASD	REGIONS FINANCIAL CORP
RNB	Financial	NYSE	REPUBLIC NEW YORK
RLM	Industrial	NYSE	REYNOLDS METALS CO
RAD	Industrial	NYSE	RITE AID CORP
RN	Industrial	NYSE	RJR NABISCO HOLDINGS CORP
ROK	Industrial	NYSE	ROCKWELL INTL CORP
ROH	Industrial	NYSE	ROHM & HAAS CO
RDC	Industrial	NYSE	ROWAN COS INC
RD	Industrial	NYSE	ROYAL DUTCH PETROLEUM CO
RBD	Industrial	NYSE	RUBBERMAID INC
RML	Industrial	NYSE	RUSSELL CORP
R	Transportation	NYSE	RYDER SYSTEM INC
SAFC	Financial	NASD	SAFECO CORP
SWY	Industrial	NYSE	SAFEWAY INC
SLE	Industrial	NYSE	SARA LEE CORP
SBC	Utilities	NYSE	SBC COMMUNICATIONS INC

Symbol	*S&P Group*	*Exchange*	*Issue Name*
SGP	Industrial	NYSE	SCHERING-PLOUGH
SLB	Industrial	NYSE	SCHLUMBERGER LTD
SFA	Industrial	NYSE	SCIENTIFIC ATLANTA INC
SEG	Industrial	NYSE	SEAGATE TECHNOLOGY
VO	Industrial	NYSE	SEAGRAM CO LTD
SEE	Industrial	NYSE	SEALED AIR CORP
S	Industrial	NYSE	SEARS ROEBUCK & CO
SRE	Utilities	NYSE	SEMPRA ENERGY
SRV	Industrial	NYSE	SERVICE CORP INTL
SMS	Industrial	NASD	SHARED MEDICAL SYS CORP
SHW	Industrial	NYSE	SHERWIN WILLIAMS CO
SIAL	Industrial	NASD	SIGMA ALDRICH CORP
SGI	Industrial	NYSE	SILICON GRAPHICS INC
SLM	Financial	NYSE	SLM HOLDING CORP
SNA	Industrial	NYSE	SNAP ON INC HOLDING CO
SLR	Industrial	NYSE	SOLECTRON
SNT	Utilities	NYSE	SONAT INC
SO	Utilities	NYSE	SOUTHERN CO
LUV	Transportation	NYSE	SOUTHWEST AIRLINES CO
SMI	Industrial	NYSE	SPRINGS INDUSTRIES INC
FON	Industrial	NYSE	SPRINT CORP FON GROUP
PCS	Industrial	NYSE	SPRINT CORP PCS GROUP
STJ	Industrial	NYSE	ST JUDE MEDICAL INC
SPC	Financial	NYSE	ST PAUL COS INC
SWK	Industrial	NYSE	STANLEY WORKS
SPLS	Industrial	NASD	STAPLES INC
STT	Financial	NYSE	STATE STREET CORP
SUB	Financial	NYSE	SUMMIT BANCORP
SUNW	Industrial	NASD	SUN MICROSYSTEMS INC
SUN	Industrial	NYSE	SUNOCO INC
STI	Financial	NYSE	SUNTRUST BANKS
SVU	Industrial	NYSE	SUPERVALU INC
SNV	Financial	NYSE	SYNOVUS FINANCIAL
SYY	Industrial	NYSE	SYSCO CORP
TAN	Industrial	NYSE	TANDY CORP

Symbol	*S&P Group*	*Exchange*	*Issue Name*
TEK	Industrial	NYSE	TEKTRONIX INC
TCOMA	Industrial	NASD	TELE-COMMUNICATIONS
TLAB	Industrial	NASD	TELLABS INC
TIN	Industrial	NYSE	TEMPLE INLAND INC
THC	Industrial	NYSE	TENET HEALTHCARE CORP
TEN	Industrial	NYSE	TENNECO INC HLDG CO
TX	Industrial	NYSE	TEXACO INC
TXN	Industrial	NYSE	TEXAS INSTRUMENTS INC
TXU	Utilities	NYSE	TEXAS UTILITIES CO
TXT	Industrial	NYSE	TEXTRON INC
TMO	Industrial	NYSE	THERMO ELECTRON
TNB	Industrial	NYSE	THOMAS & BETTS CORP
TWX	Industrial	NYSE	TIME WARNER INC
TMC	Industrial	NYSE	TIMES MIRROR CO
TKR	Industrial	NYSE	TIMKEN CO
TJX	Industrial	NYSE	TJX COMPANIES INC
TMK	Financial	NYSE	TORCHMARK CORP
TOY	Industrial	NYSE	TOYS R US INC
TA	Financial	NYSE	TRANSAMERICA CORP
TRB	Industrial	NYSE	TRIBUNE CO
YUM	Industrial	NYSE	TRICON GLOBAL RESTAURANTS
TRW	Industrial	NYSE	TRW INC
TUP	Industrial	NYSE	TUPPERWARE CORP
TYC	Industrial	NYSE	TYCO INTERNATIONAL LTD
USB	Financial	NYSE	U.S. BANCORP
UCM	Utilities	NYSE	UNICOM CORP HOLDING CO
UN	Industrial	NYSE	UNILEVER N V
UCC	Industrial	NYSE	UNION CAMP CORP
UK	Industrial	NYSE	UNION CARBIDE CORP
UNP	Transportation	NYSE	UNION PACIFIC
UPR	Industrial	NYSE	UNION PACIFIC RESOURCES GROUP
UPC	Financial	NYSE	UNION PLANTERS

Symbol	*S&P Group*	*Exchange*	*Issue Name*
UIS	Industrial	NYSE	UNISYS CORP
UNH	Industrial	NYSE	UNITED HEALTHCARE CORP
UTX	Industrial	NYSE	UNITED TECHNOLOGIES CORP
UCL	Industrial	NYSE	UNOCAL CORP
UNM	Financial	NYSE	UNUM CORP
USW	Utilities	NYSE	US WEST INC
U	Transportation	NYSE	USAIR GROUP INC
UST	Industrial	NYSE	UST INC
MRO	Industrial	NYSE	USX-MARATHON GROUP
X	Industrial	NYSE	USX-U.S. STEEL GROUP
VFC	Industrial	NYSE	V F CORP
VIA/B	Industrial	AMEX	VIACOM INC
WB	Financial	NYSE	WACHOVIA CORP
WMT	Industrial	NYSE	WAL MART STORES INC
WAG	Industrial	NYSE	WALGREEN CO
DIS	Industrial	NYSE	WALT DISNEY CO
WLA	Industrial	NYSE	WARNER LAMBERT CO
WM	Financial	NYSE	WASHINGTON MUTUAL INC
WMI	Industrial	NYSE	WASTE MANAGEMENT
WFC	Financial	NYSE	WELLS FARGO & CO
WEN	Industrial	NYSE	WENDYS INTER-NATIONAL INC
W	Industrial	NYSE	WESTVACO CORP
WY	Industrial	NYSE	WEYERHAEUSER CO
WHR	Industrial	NYSE	WHIRLPOOL CORP
WLL	Industrial	NYSE	WILLAMETTE INDUSTRIES
WMB	Utilities	NYSE	WILLIAMS COS
WIN	Industrial	NYSE	WINN DIXIE STORES INC
WTHG	Industrial	NASD	WORTHINGTON INDS INC
WWY	Industrial	NYSE	WRIGLEY WM JR CO
XRX	Industrial	NYSE	XEROX CORP

APPENDIX B

EXCHANGE AND ASSET CLASS INFORMATION

Exchange Information

Abbreviation	Exchange
CBOT	Chicago Board of Trade
CME	Chicago Mercantile Exchange
CMX	COMEX Division New York Mercantile Exchange
CSCE	Coffee, Sugar, and Cocoa Exchange
CTN	New York Cotton Exchange
FINEX	New York Financial Exchange (CTN)
IMM	International Monetary Market (CME)
KCBT	Kansas City Board of Trade
MCE	Mid-America Commodity Exchange
MGE	Minneapolis Grain Exchange
NYFE	New York Futures Exchange (CTN)
NYM	NYMEX Division New York Mercantile Exchange
WCE	Winnipeg Commodity Exchange

Month Codes

F	January	**J**	April	**N**	July	**V**	October
G	February	**K**	May	**Q**	August	**X**	November
H	March	**M**	June	**U**	September	**Z**	December

Currencies

Sym	Futures Contract	Exch	Delivery Months	Min Tick	Unit Move	MCR Stop
BP	British Pound	IMM	HMUZ	0.02	$625	$2000
CD	Canadian Dollar	IMM	HMUZ	0.01	1000	750
DM	German Mark	IMM	HMUZ	0.01	1250	1000
DX	US Dollar Index	FINEX	HMUZ	0.01	1000	1200
JY	Japanese Yen	IMM	HMUZ	0.01	1250	2000
SF	Swiss Franc	IMM	HMUZ	0.01	1250	2000

Energies

Sym	Futures Contract	Exch	Delivery Months	Min Tick	Unit Move	MCR Stop
CL	Crude Oil	NYM	FGHJKMNQUVXZ	0.01	1000	1250
HO	Heating Oil	NYM	FGHJKMNQUVXZ	0.01	420	2000
HU	Unleaded Gas	NYM	FGHJKMNQUVXZ	0.01	420	1300

Grains & Soy Complex

Sym	Futures Contract	Exch	Delivery Months	Min Tick	Unit Move	MCR Stop
BO	Soybean Oil	CBOT	FHKNQUVZ	0.01	600	1000
C	Corn	CBOT	HKNUZ	1/4	50	1000
KW	Kansas City Wheat	CBOT	HKNUZ	1/4	50	1250
MW	Minneapolis Wheat	CBOT	HKNUZ	1/4	50	1250
O	Oats	CBOT	HKNUZ	1/4	50	1250
S	Soybeans	CBOT	FHKNQUX	1/4	50	1500
SM	Soybean Meal	CBOT	FHKNQUVZ	0.1	100	1500
W	Wheat	CBOT	HKNUZ	1/4	50	1250

Stock Indices

Sym	Futures Contract	Exch	Delivery Months	Min Tick	Unit Move	MCR Stop
KV	Value Line	KCBT	HMUZ	0.05	500	2600
SP	S&P 500	CME	HMUZ	0.05	500	2600
YX	NYSE Composite	NYFE	HMUZ	0.05	500	2000

Interest Rates

Sym	Futures Contract	Exch	Delivery Months	Min Tick	Unit Move	MCR Stop
ED	Eurodollars	IMM	HMUZ	0.005	2500	1250
FV	5-Yr T-Notes	CBOT	HMUZ	1/64	1000	1800
MB	Municipal Bonds	CBOT	HMUZ	1/32	1000	1800
TB	Treasury Bills	IMM	HMUZ	0.01	2500	1250
TY	10-Yr T-Notes	CBOT	HMUZ	1/32	1000	1800
US	30-Yr T-Bonds	CBOT	HMUZ	1/32	1000	2600

Meats

Sym	Futures Contract	Exch	Delivery Months	Min Tick	Unit Move	MCR Stop
FC	Feeder Cattle	CME	FHJKQUVX	0.025	500	1500
LC	Live Cattle	CME	GJMQVZ	0.025	400	1000
LH	Live Hogs	CME	GJMNQVZ	0.025	400	1500
PB	Pork Bellies	CME	GHKNQ	0.025	400	1250

Metals

Sym	Futures Contract	Exch	Delivery Months	Min Tick	Unit Move	MCR Stop
GC	Gold	CMX	GJMQVZ	0.1	100	1250
HG	Copper	CMX	HKNUZ	0.05	250	1500
PL	Platinum	NYM	FJNV	0.1	50	750
SI	Silver	CMX	HKNUZ	0.5	50	3000

Softs & Fibers

Sym	Futures Contract	Exch	Delivery Months	Min Tick	Unit Move	MCR Stop
CC	Cocoa	CSCE	HKNUZ	1	10	1500
CT	Cotton	CTN	HKNVZ	0.01	500	1250
KC	Coffee	CSCE	HKNUZ	0.05	375	1500
LB	Lumber	CME	FHKNUX	0.1	80	1250
JO	Orange Juice	CTN	FNKNUX	0.05	150	1250
SB	Sugar #11	CSCE	HKNV	0.01	1120	1000

GLOSSARY

advance/decline line A measure of market movements composed of the cumulative total of differences between advancing issues (stocks whose prices are up on the day) and declining issues (stocks whose prices are down on the day) of securities prices.

ask The lowest currently stated acceptable price for a specific stock or commodity on the floor of an exchange; also called the offer.

at-the-money An option in which the price of the underlying instrument is exactly the same as the strike price of the option.

bear Anyone who takes a pessimistic view of the forthcoming long-term trend in a market; that is, one who thinks that a market is or soon will be in a long-term downtrend.

bear market A long-term downtrend (a downtrend lasting months to years) in any market, especially in the stock market, characterized by lower intermediate lows interrupted by lower intermediate highs.

bid An indication by an investor, trader, or dealer of the willingness to buy a security or a commodity at a certain price; also, the highest current such indication for a specific stock or commodity at any point in time.

bid and ask The current quote or quotation on the floor of any market exchange for a specific stock or commodity.

block A large amount of specific stock, generally 10,000 or more shares.

blue chip The common stock of an established industry leader whose products or services are widely known that has a solid record of performance in both good and bad economic environments.

book value A measure of the net worth of a share of common stock.

bottom The lowest price within a market movement that occurs before the trend changes and starts moving up.

break A downward price movement that goes below previous important lows and continues to carry downward.

breakout An upward price movement that goes above previous important highs and continues to carry upward.

bull Anyone who takes an optimistic view of the forthcoming long-term trend in a market; that is, one who thinks that a market is or soon will be in a long-term uptrend.

bull market A long-term price movement in any market characterized by a series of higher intermediate highs interrupted by higher consecutive intermediate lows.

butterfly spread An option position involving the simultaneous buying of an at-the-money option, selling of two out-of-the-money options, and buying of one out-of-the-money option.

call option A short- or medium-term contract that allows the purchaser the right, but not the obligation, to go long the underlying investment at the strike price on or before the option expiration date. An option seller receives the premium and assumes the obligation to go long or short the underlying investment at the strike price if the option is exercised.

commission The fee charged to a client by a registered broker for the execution of an order to buy or sell a stock, bond, commodity, option, etc.

correction An intermediate market price movement that moves contrary to the long-term trend.

covered position A combination of an underlying investment and an options transaction that is theoretically less risky than either individual part of the transaction.

Dow Jones Industrial Average (DJIA) The most widely used indicator of market activity, composed of an average of 30 large issues within the industrial sector of the economy.

Dow Jones Transportation Average (TRAN) The most widely reported indicator of stock activity in the transportation sector of the economy, composed of an average of 20 large issues.

Dow Jones Utility Average (UTIL) The most widely reported indicator of stock activity in the utility sector composed of 15 gas, electric, and power company issues.

earnings The net income available for common stock divided by the number of shares outstanding, reported quarterly by most companies; also called earnings per share.

fade Doing the opposite of the immediate market movement.

floor trader A member of an exchange who enters transactions for his or her own account from the floor of the exchange; synonymous with local.

glamour stock A favored, highly traded stock, usually of an established company that has performed well and paid dividends in good times and bad.

growth stock A relatively speculative stock, usually one of a relatively new company that is expected to grow at a fast rate.

high The highest price a security or commodity reaches within a specified time period.

index futures Futures contracts traded on the basis of an underlying cash index or average.

long-term trend Price movements tending to be generally up or generally down, lasting over a period of months to years.

low The lowest price a security or commodity reached during a specific time period.

margin The amount of equity (cash) as a percentage of market value of the underlying market interest held in a margin account.

offer An indication by a trader or investor of the willingness to sell a security or commodity; or, in a quote, the current lowest price anyone is willing to sell a security or commodity.

over the counter (OTC) market A market of stocks traded that are not listed on the major exchanges.

put option An option contract that gives the buyer the right, but not the obligation, to sell the underlying investment at a specific price on or before a specific date.

quote The current bid and offer for a security on the floor of the exchange on which it is traded.

ratio writing A market position using more than one option to hedge an investment position.

resistance Any price level that is deemed as a significant high in trading by the market and offers a place to sell the market.

S&P futures A futures index traded based on the S&P 500 Cash Index.

spread A position that is both long and short in the same investment with different expiration dates or long or short in different but similar investments.

stop order An order given to a broker that becomes a market order when the market price of the underlying instrument reaches or exceeds the specific price stated in the stop order.

straddle An options position consisting of a call and put in the same investment, with the same expiration and strike price.

strangle A position in which one buys (or sells) both an out-of-the-money put and an out-of-the-money call.

support Any price level deemed as a significant low in trading by the market that offers a place to buy the market.

technical analysis A method of market forecasting that relies exclusively on the study of past price and volume behavior to predict future price movements.

volume The number of shares of stocks that change ownership in a given time period.

FOR FURTHER READING

Abell, Howard. *The Day Trader's Advantage: How to Move from One Winning Position to the Next.* Chicago: Dearborn, 1997.

———. *Digital Day Trading: How to Move from One Winning Stock Position to the Next.* Chicago: Dearborn, 1999.

———. *Risk Reward.* Chicago: Dearborn, 1998.

———. *Spread Trading.* Chicago: Dearborn, 1998.

Barach, Roland. *Mindtraps: Mastering the Inner World of Investing.* Burr Ridge, Ill.: Dow Jones-Irwin, 1988.

Baruch, Bernard M. *Baruch: My Own Story.* New York: Holt, Rinehart and Winston, 1957.

Douglas, Mark. *The Disciplined Trader.* New York: New York Institute of Finance, 1990.

Eng, William F. *The Day Trader's Manual: Theory, Art, and Science of Profitable Short-Term Investing.* New York: John Wiley, 1993.

———. *Trading Rules: Strategies for Success.* Chicago: Dearborn, 1990.

Friedfertig, Marc, and George West. *The Electronic Day Trader.* New York: McGraw-Hill, 1998.

Gann, W.D. *How to Make Profits Trading in Commodities.* Pomeroy: Lambert-Gann, 1976.

Houtkin, Harvey, and David Waldman. *Secret of the SOES Bandit.* New York: McGraw-Hill, 1998.

Koppel, Robert. *Bulls, Bears, and Millionaires: War Stories of the Trading Life.* Chicago: Dearborn, 1997.

———. *The Intuitive Trader: Developing Your Inner Market Wisdom.* New York: John Wiley, 1996.

———. *The Tao of Trading.* Chicago: Dearborn, 1997.

Koppel, Robert, and Howard Abell. *The Innergame of Trading: Modeling the Psychology of the Top Traders.* New York: McGraw-Hill, 1993.

———. *The Outer Game of Trading: Modeling the Trading Strategies of Today's Market Wizards.* New York: McGraw-Hill, 1994.

Le Bon, Gustave. *The Crowd: A Study of the Popular Mind.* 2d ed. Atlanta, Ga.: Cherokee, 1982.

Schwager, Jack D. *Market Wizards: Interviews with Top Traders.* New York: New York Institute of Finance, 1989.

———. *The New Market Wizards: Conversations with America's Top Traders.* New York: Harper Business, 1992.

Schwartz, Martin. *Pit Bull: Lessons from Wall Street's Champion Trader.* New York: Harper Business, 1998.

Sperandeo, Victor, with Brown T. Sullivan. *Trader Vic—Methods of a Wall Street Master.* New York: John Wiley and Sons, 1991.

INDEX

T

U–V

W–Z

DISCARD

METUCHEN PUBLIC LIBRARY
480 Middlesex Ave.
Metuchen, NJ 08840